Easy Beauty
with Annuals

The TIME LIFE
Complete Gardener

Easy Beauty
with Annuals

By the Editors of Time-Life Books
ALEXANDRIA, VIRGINIA

The Consultant

Peter Loewer is a prolific garden writer, botanical illustrator, and photographer with many books to his credit. *The Annual Garden* (1988) —now published under the title *Rodale's Annual Garden* (1992)—was cited as one of 50 great garden books by the United States Department of Agriculture Library. *The Wild Gardener* (1991) received three awards from the Garden Writers' Association of America in 1992, and *Gardens by Design* (1986) won the 1987 Philadelphia Book Clinic Award. Other books include *Annuals* (1994), *The New Small Garden* (1994), *The Evening Garden* (1993), and *Tough Plants for Tough Places* (1992), as well as a book on native plants, *Thoreau's Garden* (1996), and a guide to the various seed catalogs and seed exchanges in America and England, *The Book of Seeds* (1996). Loewer is a contributing editor of *Carolina Gardener* magazine and writes a newspaper column, "The Wild Gardener," for New York State's *Sullivan County Democrat*. He was a contributing editor and photographer for *Taylor's Guide to Annuals* (1986) and the editor of *Quill and Trowel*, the newsletter for the Garden Writers' Association of America, from 1988 to 1991. From 1983 to 1986 he hosted *Back to the Garden* on National Public Radio in Asheville, North Carolina. Currently, Loewer is also organizing and conducting garden tours in England as well as Elder Hostel garden and natural history tours for Mars Hill College in North Carolina.

Library of Congress Cataloging-in-Publication Data
Easy beauty with annuals / by the editors of Time-Life Books.
p. cm.—(The Time-Life complete gardener)
Includes bibliographical references (p.) and index.
ISBN 0-7835-4113-9
1. Annuals (Plants) 2. Biennials (Plants) 3. Annuals (Plants)—Pictorial works.
4. Biennials (Plants)—Pictorial works. I. Time-Life Books. II. Series.
SB422.A577 1996   635.9'31—dc20   96-12457   CIP

This volume is one of a series of comprehensive gardening books that cover garden design, choosing plants for the garden, planting and propagating, and planting diagrams.

Time-Life Books is a division of **TIME LIFE INC.**
PRESIDENT and CEO: John M. Fahey Jr.

TIME-LIFE BOOKS

Managing Editor: Roberta Conlan

Director of Design: Michael Hentges
Editorial Production Manager: Ellen Robling
Director of Operations: Eileen Bradley
Director of Photography and Research: John Conrad Weiser
Senior Editors: Russell B. Adams Jr., Janet Cave, Lee Hassig, Robert Somerville, Henry Woodhead
Library: Louise D. Forstall

PRESIDENT: John D. Hall

Vice President, Director of New Product Development: Neil Kagan
Associate Director, New Product Development: Quentin S. McAndrew
Marketing Director: James Gillespie
Vice President, Book Production: Marjann Caldwell
Production Manager: Marlene Zack
Quality Assurance Manager: Miriam Newton

THE TIME-LIFE COMPLETE GARDENER

Editorial Staff for *Easy Beauty with Annuals*

SERIES EDITOR: Janet Cave
Deputy Editors: Sarah Brash, Jane Jordan
Administrative Editor: Roxie France-Nuriddin
Art Director: Alan Pitts
Picture Editor: Jane Jordan
Text Editor: Darcie Conner Johnston
Associate Editors/Research-Writing: Katya Sharpe, Robert Speziale
Technical Art Assistant: Sue Pratt
Senior Copyeditor: Anne Farr
Picture Coordinator: David A. Herod
Editorial Assistant: Donna Fountain
Special Contributors: Jennifer Clark (research); Susan Blair, Meg Dennison, Jocelyn Lindsay, Peter Loewer (research-writing); Rita Pelczar (writing); Marfé Ferguson-Delano (editing); John Drummond (art); Lina B. Burton (index).

Correspondents: Christine Hinze (London), Christina Lieberman (New York).

Cover: *Scarlet and gold Papaver nudicaule (Iceland poppy) and multicolored Viola x wittrockiana (common pansy) thrive in the cool summers of this Colorado mountain garden.* ***End papers:*** *Rowdy masses of annuals—including red and purple spiked salvia, white and rose gomphrena, and crimson zinnias—bloom in Missouri behind a fence draped with purple morning glories.* ***Title page:*** *Hot pink Catharanthus roseus (Madagascar periwinkle), white Begonia x semperflorens-cultorum 'Pizzazz', and the foliage of Coleus x hybridus 'Red Queen' glow like gems in the dappled shade of a Pennsylvania garden.*

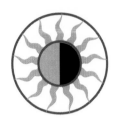

Blooms for Every Garden

To most gardeners, annuals mean dramatic color—and lots of it. From the simplest display in a window box to the most lavish design in a formal garden, these short-lived plants enhance any garden with their exuberance. The California patio garden at right, for example, practically blazes with the red and pink of cosmos and wax begonia blossoms.

Annuals—which in gardening parlance include their short-season cousins, biennials and tender perennials—deserve renown for a number of other virtues as well. They are reliable, easy-care plants and have a tremendous versatility that makes them suitable for any gardening purpose, under almost any condition. However you choose to incorporate annuals in your landscape, this chapter and those that follow will help you pick out the appropriate plants for your site—whether it's sunny or shaded, warm or cool, dry or damp. You'll also learn how to design the myriad beautiful spaces they'll occupy and how to care for them at every stage from seed through flowering.

The key lists each plant type and the number of plants needed to replicate the garden shown. The letters and numbers above refer to the type of plant and the number sited in an area.

A. Begonia x semperflorens-cultorum 'Varsity Pink' (12) **B.** Asparagus densiflorus 'Sprengeri' (1) **C.** Pelargonium peltatum (3) **D.** Dianthus caryophyllus (1) **E.** Echeveria sp. (many) **F.** Cosmos bipinnatus 'Sonata Rose' (6) **G.** Cosmos 'Seashells', 'Candy Stripe', 'Versailles', 'Blush Pink', 'Sonata Pink' (many) **H.** Sedum cv. (many) **I.** Echeveria secunda (5) **J.** Cosmos bipinnatus 'Versailles Red' (many) **K.** Cosmos bipinnatus 'Sensation Pink' (many) **L.** Cosmos bipinnatus 'Sonata White' (many)

Understanding Annuals

Annuals are synonymous with flowers. While perennials and shrubs may produce beautiful blossoms, they last only a few weeks, and thoughtful gardeners choose such plants at least as much for their form and foliage as for any other consideration—including longevity. But for the pure glory of flowers—for a riot of color that lasts from spring through frost—annuals are the way to go.

In the first place, for sheer variety they are unbeatable. Annuals span the rainbow in terms of color, from the bluest blues to the fieriest scarlets. As for plant form, they grow in bushy mounds, creep along the ground, cascade down a wall, climb a fence, or tower from the back of a border. And the size and shape of their flowers and foliage vary enormously. Indeed, the different cultivated varieties that are available number in the thousands, and each year hybridizers produce still more.

Augmenting their remarkable résumé is the fact that annuals are exceedingly easy to care for. With uncomplicated, shallow root systems, they are dependable performers that require little in the way of nutrients, space, and maintenance. And they grow at a rambunctious rate, racing to maturity and flowering in a matter of weeks—and gratifying the most impatient gardener with a prolific and long-lasting display. If they are simply given the right amount of sun, they usually grow readily from seed and are not terribly fussy about soil conditions. Even in less than optimal surroundings, annuals rarely let you down, adapting to many adverse conditions, including drought and extreme heat.

A final virtue is their economy. Of all the flowers your garden can display, annuals give you the biggest return on your investment. You can purchase young annuals from your local garden center at reasonable cost, or you can grow them from seed for next to nothing. As a bonus, many varieties reseed, so you may see them return year after year of their own accord.

What Is an Annual?

Strictly speaking, a true annual is a plant that completes its entire life cycle—from seed germination through flowering, setting seed, and death—in just one season *(opposite)*. Garden petunias, zinnias, and marigolds are just a few popular favorites that are true annuals. From a practical standpoint, however, an annual is any plant that is going to

flower for only a single season or year in your garden, regardless of its potential for greater longevity. The definition of *annual,* then, expands to include biennials and tender perennials.

A typical biennial, left to its own devices, usually requires two growing seasons to complete its life cycle. Sprouting from seed and producing a leafy rosette in the first year, it then flowers in the second, sets seed, and dies. Biennials can be started in the open garden in late spring or seeded in flats and moved to the garden in late summer or early fall for blooms the next spring. By getting seeds started early indoors, though, you can give some biennials enough of a head start that they'll flower late in the first season.

**HARDY ANNUAL
STALWARTS**
The deep carmine-orange hues and open faces of Calendula officinalis (pot marigold) are a perfect foil for the star-shaped blue flowers of Borago officinalis (borage). Borage's blossoms last only a single day but are quickly replaced by new blooms. Both flowers are hardy annuals that can be directly seeded into the ground as soon as it is workable in the spring.

8

Life Cycles of Garden Flowers

FIRST YEAR: *Spring*

FIRST YEAR: *Summer*

FIRST YEAR: *Fall*

Annuals

An annual, such as the impatiens shown here, sprouts from a seed in the spring, sending a few delicate roots below ground and some tender green shoots above (far left). By early summer, the plant has grown fuller and begun to blossom. It blooms with increasing vigor and fullness, reaching its peak in late summer (left, center). With the fall, its roots, stems, and flowers begin to wither (left), and by winter the plant will have died.

FIRST YEAR: *Summer*

SECOND YEAR: *Late Spring*

SECOND YEAR: *Fall*

Biennials

In nature, a typical biennial usually has two distinct growing seasons. The first year the seed will germinate in the spring, then develop roots and foliage, usually in the form of a rosette. During the summer the plant will continue to grow (far left), but won't produce flowers unless it has had an early start indoors. During the fall and winter, it ceases its growth and becomes dormant. Early in the second spring, the plant resumes growing, and flowers appear by late spring (left, center). In midsummer it will set seed and wither; by fall it will have died (left).

FIRST YEAR: *Spring*

FIRST YEAR: *Summer*

FIRST YEAR: *Winter*

SECOND YEAR: *Summer*

Perennials

Unless it is too tender to survive the winter, a perennial goes through a cycle of growth that repeats each year, as illustrated by the daylily shown above. Sprouting from seed in the spring, the plant develops roots and foliage (above, left), and may flower as well during the first summer (above, second from left); by winter the foliage has died back and the roots have gone dormant (above, second from right). The following spring the plant reawakens, and during the summer and into the fall both roots and foliage renew their growth while the plant blossoms (above, right). As subsequent seasons pass, the plant will repeat the process, producing more roots, foliage, and flowers.

Whether a biennial can complete its cycle in one season depends on the variety and your climate. Most foxgloves, for example, take up to 300 days to flower and set seed, and in cooler climates will have to overwinter. If you plant biennial seedlings in their permanent home and plan for blooms the next spring, make sure the variety is hardy enough for your zone *(zone map, page 100).* If it's not, overwinter the young plants in a cold frame for protection.

Tender perennials—which include the popular wax begonias—may live out several seasons in semitropical climates. But these plants don't have hardy roots that can tolerate the winter cold of more northerly zones and so they die with the frost. Since they flower in their first season, tender perennials are treated as annuals in most climates.

Hardy, Half-Hardy, and Tender

When discussing perennials and shrubs, hardiness refers to a plant's ability to survive degrees of winter cold, usually in terms of geographical zones.

When applied to annuals, on the other hand, *hardy* and *tender* instead signify the minimum temperature required for the seeds of a variety to germinate. With annuals, the terms also indicate their frost tolerance once a plant is in the ground.

Hardy annuals are those whose seeds can withstand temperatures below freezing (32° F)—and in fact may even require such frigid conditions to break dormancy and sprout. Moreover, once they germinate, hardy annuals easily weather any number of late-winter and early-spring freezes and thaws. If seeded directly outdoors, they are typically sown as soon as the soil can be worked in the spring or a couple of weeks past the first frost in fall. As mature plants, hardy annuals are able to tolerate hard frosts. Ornamental cabbage, for example, effortlessly stands up to cold temperatures and is a favorite in the winter garden, its colorful foliage offering a sparkling dash of purple or white against the usual backdrop of evergreens.

Tender annuals originate in tropical climates, and to flourish they require equally warm conditions. These annuals can't be sown outdoors—or transplanted—until all danger of frost has passed and the soil has warmed completely. A few

months later, they will usually die at the first indication of a fall frost. The popular New Guinea impatiens, the purple-podded vine *Dolichos lablab* (hyacinth bean), and the heavenly scented *Nicotiana alata* (jasmine tobacco) are examples of tender annuals whose aversion to cold temperatures must be respected if they are to survive, grow vigorously, and flower.

A third group—half-hardy annuals—is a catch-all class composed of annuals that fall anywhere between the two extremes; some tolerate a surprising number of frosts, others just a few. Typically, the half-hardy can be sown or transplanted to the garden after the last spring frost even if the soil has not thoroughly warmed. Half-hardy seedlings willingly accept the extended periods of cold and damp that often accompany mid- to late-spring weather—but they aren't impervious to hard freezes. In semitropical areas of the Deep South and in southern California, where frosts rarely occur, half-hardy annuals can be seeded outdoors in the fall for a late-winter or early-spring flowering season. The encyclopedia at the back of this volume *(pages 102-151)* indicates the hardiness of each plant listed.

Selecting Your Annuals

Each year, hundreds of new flower varieties are introduced as plant breeders and seed companies seek to improve the color, size, drought tolerance, and pest or disease resistance of those already in existence. Seed catalogs offer a wealth for you to choose from, and the selection can change significantly from year to year as new cultivars become available. For this reason, you may not be able to find, for example, the variety of *Ageratum houstonianum* that you loved last year—but rest assured that there's a new one to delight you just as much, if not more.

When choosing the seeds and young plants you'll be putting into your garden, you'll want to take into account your climate and the conditions of the site. Such considerations as sun, shade, and length of growing season—all of which are covered in this chapter—will affect how well your annuals grow and flower. Use the encyclopedia as a guide to finding those plants that you like and that match your environment before venturing to the garden center or placing your catalog order. The encyclopedia is also a handy reference for determining the best way to get them into the ground. You'll find instructions for the various planting methods—sowing seeds indoors and out, and transplanting seedlings—on the following pages.

Getting Annuals into the Garden

Annuals are for every gardener, and if you're a novice, they make for an easy and immediately gratifying introduction to gardening. Starting out can be as simple as sowing seeds directly into the ground and then watching what happens, or pushing aside some soil and setting in young bedding plants purchased from your local nursery or garden center.

If you're an experienced gardener who enjoys devoting more time and effort to a project, you can spend delightful hours poring over catalogs, choosing between the countless beautiful varieties of annuals pictured and described there. You can also get seeds started indoors before spring arrives, then wait for the perfect day to transplant them to the garden. Here and on the next two pages, you'll learn all you need to know about the three techniques for getting your annual garden started—indoor sowing, transplanting, and direct-seeding.

Starting Seeds Indoors

Some annuals have tiny seeds that may be lost if sown outdoors. Others need a long time to grow before they flower. If you want annuals such as zinnias, geraniums, and verbena blooming in your garden as early as possible—and you want to ensure the highest rate of germination for your seeds—get them going in the protected, controlled environment of your home. Seeds can be started indoors in winter so that young plants will be ready to put into the ground in spring.

Purchase a soil mix that has been specifically formulated for starting seeds. Wet the mix completely and let it sit for a few minutes until the water is thoroughly absorbed; then fill seed flats to a depth of about 3 inches. If you don't want to use flats, you can also use individual plastic pots or even small plastic cups or cartons you may find around your house. Simply clean them well first and poke a few drain holes in the bottom.

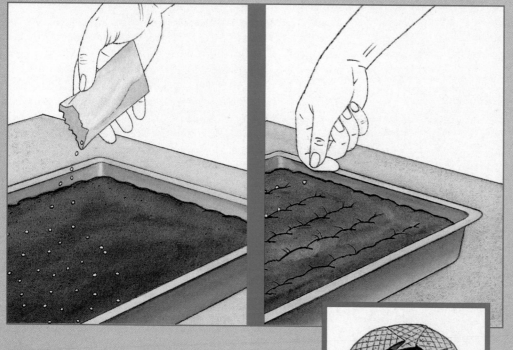

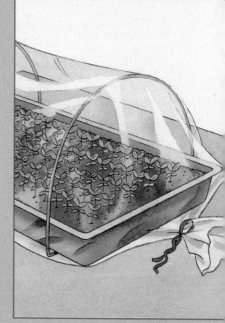

1. Scatter tiny seeds on top of the moistened soil mix (above); place larger seeds one by one in ¼-inch furrows, spaced ½ inch apart (above, right). If the seed-packet directions indicate, cover the seeds with a thin layer of soil. Alternatively, gently press the seeds into a wet peat pot as shown at right. Then set the flats or peat pots under grow lights on a warm, bright but indirectly lit window sill, or in a darkened setting, according to seed-packet instructions. All seedlings should be placed in a well-lit spot once they become visible.

2. Keep the soil mix moist by watering gently and then covering the flat with a clear, thin plastic bag supported by metal hoops (above). You can use clothes hangers for the hoops. Seal the bag with a twist tie to maintain high humidity. After the shoots are plainly visible, remove the plastic covering. Continue watering to keep the soil moist but not soaked; overwatering can cause damping-off, a disease that kills seedlings.

AN INDOOR START FOR EARLY BLOOM
After sprouting in a well-lit greenhouse window, these flats of annual seedlings await transplanting to larger containers. The robust scarlet and yellow potted marigolds were started at an earlier date and are ready to be hardened off and planted in the garden.

Annuals to Start Indoors

Ageratum houstonianum
(flossflower)
***Asclepias* spp.**
(bloodflower)
Browallia speciosa
(browallia)
Cardiospermum halicacabum
(balloon vine)
Coleus* x *hybridus
(coleus)
***Dianthus* spp.**
(pink, sweet William)
Eustoma grandiflorum
(tulip gentian)
***Impatiens* spp.**
(impatiens)
Lagurus ovatus
(hare's-tail grass)
Petunia* x *hybrida
(petunia)
***Salvia* spp.**
(sage)
Torenia fournieri
(wishbone flower)

Note: The abbreviation "spp." stands for the plural of "species"; where used in lists it means that many, but not all, of the species in a genus meet the criterion of the list.

4. Two weeks before transplanting— *which should be done once the danger of frost is past—move your plants to a cold frame to acclimate them to outdoor conditions, a process known as hardening off. Open the frame during the day to maintain proper air circulation and to keep plants from getting too much heat under the glass; close it at night. If you don't have a cold frame, place the seedlings outside a few hours each day, gradually lengthening the exposure time.*

3. After the seedlings produce a second set of leaves (their first true leaves), use a plant marker or similar instrument to separate and lift each one out of the flat (above, left). Hold each seedling by its leaf (it can grow a new leaf, but not a new stem) and place it in a peat pot or other container filled with moist, sterile potting soil. Position the seedling in a hole the size and depth of its tiny root system. Gently tamp the soil without injuring the stem (above, right). Place the pots on a tray to be set under grow lights or near a warm, sunny window. Keep the plants well watered.

13

Transplanting Annuals

Before transplanting seedlings to your garden, take time to ready their new home. If you're preparing a new flower bed, dig in an inch or two of organic matter such as leaf mold or compost before planting. This will improve drainage and supply the young plants with nutrients. If you're adding annuals to an existing bed, use a hand cultivator to loosen the soil and add a slow-release dry fertilizer, using the amount recommended on the package. Transplant your annuals on a cool, cloudy day or in the late afternoon so that the flowers are not stressed by sun and heat.

1. With a trowel, dig a hole slightly larger and deeper than the plant's rootball. *Water the plant thoroughly and allow the excess to drain away. Then gently remove the plant from its cell pack or other container by turning it upside down and easing the plant out. With a cell pack, support the plant with one hand, then gently press your thumb against the bottom of the pack to push the plant out (right).*

2. Use your fingers to gently loosen the roots at the bottom and sides of the plant's rootball (right). *If the plant is extremely root-bound, use a knife to slice partway into the rootball, then fluff the roots apart. For plants in peat pots, gently tear off the lip or the top part of the pot (far right), then set the pot in the ground; this will help the pot's soil retain moisture.*

3. Set the plant into the hole with the base of its stem slightly below the rim. *Return the soil to the hole and firm it around the plant, creating a slight depression around the plant's stem to direct water there. Water thoroughly and mulch with an organic material such as shredded bark, making sure the mulch doesn't touch the stem.*

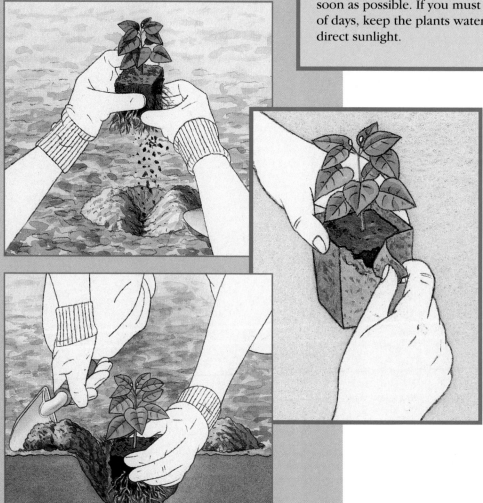

Choosing Bedding Plants

If you want flowers in a jiffy and haven't the time or the inclination to start them from seed, most home and garden centers stock a selection of popular annuals that can immediately go into the ground. These reasonably priced annuals typically come in cell packs that hold anywhere from two to eight plants. Larger specimens are also available but will cost more.

For healthy, long-lasting flowers in your garden, look for compact plants that have many shoots and good bud development but few to no blooms. Leaves should be deep or bright green; avoid plants with blemishes or yellowing leaves. Gently lift or remove annuals from their containers to check that they are not root-bound, and inspect both the soil and the plant for damage from pests and disease. The soil should be dark and moist to the touch, not dry or soaked. Avoid leggy plants.

Healthy annuals will outgrow their containers quickly, so plant your purchases as soon as possible. If you must wait a couple of days, keep the plants watered and out of direct sunlight.

Direct-Seeding

The simplest way to start annuals is by sowing seeds directly into the soil of the garden—and there are, in fact, a number of annuals that prefer to be direct-seeded *(list, right)*. To prepare a seedbed, first clear all vegetation from a patch of ground and amend the soil to a depth of 8 inches with 1 to 2 inches of compost or other organic matter. Break up any soil clumps with a spading fork, and smooth the bed with a tined rake.

You can sow seeds in one of two ways. The easiest is to scatter them on the prepared bed; if planting small seeds, mix some sand in before scattering to prevent them from massing together. The second method, described below and used for a more controlled effect, involves only slightly more effort. With the handle of a rake, draw furrows in the seedbed that are 1 inch deep—or as deep as the seed packet instructs. Follow the packet's recommendation for spacing between furrows, which will vary depending on the species.

1. Sprinkle the seeds out of the packet evenly into the furrows, *sowing about four seeds for every plant you plan for. Cover the seeds with a thin layer of soil, if the seed packet calls for it. To sow very tiny seeds like basil (inset, below), line the furrow with white, unscented toilet paper so that you can easily see their number and distribution. The paper will disintegrate. Lightly tamp the seedbed's surface with a rake to press the seeds gently into the ground; mist or water lightly with an adjustable spray nozzle to dampen the bed, and water daily thereafter so that the ground does not dry out.*

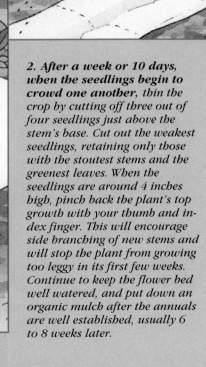

2. After a week or 10 days, when the seedlings begin to crowd one another, *thin the crop by cutting off three out of four seedlings just above the stem's base. Cut out the weakest seedlings, retaining only those with the stoutest stems and the greenest leaves. When the seedlings are around 4 inches high, pinch back the plant's top growth with your thumb and index finger. This will encourage side branching of new stems and will stop the plant from growing too leggy in its first few weeks. Continue to keep the flower bed well watered, and put down an organic mulch after the annuals are well established, usually 6 to 8 weeks later.*

Annuals to Direct-Seed

Adonis aestivalis
(pheasant's-eye)
Agrostemma githago
(corn cockle)
Borago officinalis
(borage)
Callistephus chinensis
(China aster)
Centaurea cyanus
(bachelor's-button)
Cirsium japonicum
(rose thistle)
***Clarkia* spp.**
(clarkia, godetia)
Consolida ambigua
(larkspur)
***Cucurbita* spp.**
(gourd)
Emilia javanica
(tassel flower)
Eschscholzia californica
(California poppy)
Foeniculum vulgare
(fennel)
Gypsophila elegans
(baby's-breath)
Lavatera trimestris
(rose mallow, tree mallow)
***Mentzelia* spp.**
(mentzelia)
Moluccella laevis
(bells of Ireland)
Nigella damascena
(love-in-a-mist)
***Papaver* spp.**
(poppy)
Perilla frutescens
(beefsteak plant)
Phacelia campanularia
(California bluebell)
Phaseolus coccineus
(scarlet runner bean)
Phlox drummondii
(annual phlox)
Reseda odorata
(mignonette)
Sanvitalia procumbens
(sanvitalia, creeping zinnia)
***Silene* spp.**
(campion, catchfly)
Silybum marianum
(blessed thistle)
Tropaeolum majus
(common nasturtium)
***Zinnia* spp.**
(zinnia)

Note: The abbreviation "spp." stands for the plural of "species"; where used in lists it means that many, but not all, of the species in a genus meet the criterion of the list.

Sun: Your Garden's Best Friend

Sunlight is the most important environmental factor affecting the growth and flowering of annuals. Not only is sunlight instrumental in the growth of healthy seedlings, it also provides radiant energy that increases temperature levels, which further encourages flowers to blossom and set seed. Most annuals prefer to sit in a full day of sun, provided it's not scorching hot, and some—including those listed opposite—downright demand it.

To properly assess the suitability of your site for sun-loving annuals, monitor when, where, and how much light reaches the various parts of your garden. In general, look for a place that gets more than 6 hours of sunlight each day. Keep in mind that the conditions may change as the growing season progresses into summer and the surrounding trees leaf out, casting shade where there was none in early spring. If not a single patch of your garden offers this amount of sun throughout the season, you'll need to select annuals that can tolerate shady locations *(pages 20-23)*.

Both the amount and the intensity, or strength, of sunlight affect your garden, and both are determined by your geographic location. In North America, the farther south you live, the greater the sun's intensity and the hotter the temperatures. On the other hand, the farther north you are, the greater the number of daylight hours your garden receives during the summer—and yet temperatures don't rise significantly with these added hours at high latitudes.

In regions of high sun intensity, such as Florida or southern New Mexico, where the afternoon sun can be fiery, you'll need to keep an eye on your garden during the hottest weeks of summer. If your plants begin to fade and wither, provide some shelter or partial shade from noon until 3 p.m.

If you live in a more northerly zone, the longer daylight hours will be a boon. The lengthy days speed up your plants' maturation rate and allow them to blossom in fewer days than they would in more southerly regions. Although the growing season starts later and ends earlier, you'll still have plenty of sun to produce a bounty of blossoms. Hot and cold climates present other issues, which are more fully discussed on pages 24-27.

It's possible to add to the warmth and amount of sunlight in your garden by taking advantage of how light is reflected and absorbed by the various elements there, such as stones and water. Even if your garden gets less than 6 hours of direct sun each day, you may still be able to furnish it with sun-loving annuals.

Most garden areas contain some stone—in the form of foundations, walls, patios, paths, steps, or rocks used as ornament. Stone absorbs and stores most of the warmth it receives from the sun and is an excellent source of radiated heat. Any plants sited on or near pavement or walls can benefit from the radiated warmth long after the sun has passed.

In addition, light-colored stone surfaces reflect a portion of the light they receive, bestowing both additional light and heat on surrounding plants.

Water in pools, ponds, and nearby lakes is another element that both absorbs and radiates heat from the sun and reflects light. The warmed water furnishes nearby plants with warmth—and humidity as well—while light reflected off the water's surface can brighten an area where the sun may not directly shine. This supplemental heat and light may make the difference between a sunny site and a shady one, broadening your choice of plants.

You can increase the intensity of the sun that a spot receives by using light-colored surfaces to reflect added light its way. Whitewash a nearby fence, and the rays will bounce to any nearby plants. Similarly, if your flower beds are nestled in an area between two vertical surfaces, such as a foundation wall and a fence, paint the surfaces a bright white and light will bounce back and forth between them, intensifying the sun's effect even more.

Sunlight in a Border Design

When planting a border, make optimal use of available sunlight by placing taller plants toward the rear—against a backdrop such as a fence or a wall—where they don't block the sun's rays from reaching the shorter plants in front. This design scheme also creates a lush visual effect, in part by hiding the leggy stems of taller flowers at the back.

Planting a lavish line of annuals along a fence can enhance an attractive picket or lath fence—or block an ugly chain-link or other fence from view. When setting out your plants, keep the mature height of your choices in mind. Place the tallest specimens—those that grow 3 or more feet tall—closest to the fence, at the back of the border. Tall varieties that thrive in maximum sunlight include clusters of *Cleome hasslerana* (spider flower), fiery-colored *Tithonia rotundifolia* (Mexican sunflower), and *Zea mays* var. *japonica* (ornamental corn). In front of these plant intermediate-height annuals such as wide-spreading baby's-breath, the cupped flowers of *Moluccella laevis* (bells of Ireland), and the bright foliage of *Kochia scoparia* (burning bush). And along the front place your most petite plants—multicolored candytuft, gazanias, and certain dahlia cultivars work well.

Sun-Loving Annuals

Ageratum houstonianum
(flossflower)
Antirrhinum majus
(snapdragon)
Callistephus chinensis
(China aster)
Celosia cristata
(celosia)
Cleome hasslerana
(spider flower)
Cosmos spp.
(cosmos)
Cuphea spp.
(cigar plant)
Cynara cardunculus
(cardoon)
Dianthus chinensis
(China pink)
Dyssodia tenuiloba
(Dahlberg daisy)
Eschscholzia californica
(California poppy)
Gazania rigens
(gazania)
Gomphrena globosa
(globe amaranth)
Helianthus spp.
(sunflower)
Iberis spp.
(candytuft)
Lathyrus odoratus
(sweet pea)
Linaria maroccana
(Moroccan toadflax)
Nigella damascena
(love-in-a-mist)
Papaver spp.
(poppy)
Pelargonium spp.
(geranium)
Petunia x *hybrida*
(petunia)
Phacelia campanularia
(California bluebell)
Portulaca grandiflora
(portulaca, moss rose)
Rudbeckia hirta
(black-eyed Susan)
Salpiglossis sinuata
(painted tongue)
Salvia splendens
(scarlet sage)
Sanvitalia procumbens
(sanvitalia, creeping zinnia)
Scabiosa spp.
(scabious)
Tagetes spp.
(marigold)
Tithonia rotundifolia
(Mexican sunflower)
Zinnia spp.
(zinnia)
Note: The abbreviation "spp." stands for the plural of "species"; where used in lists it means that many, but not all, of the species in a genus meet the criterion of the list.

Island Beds in the Sun

If you want to take bold advantage of the unimpeded sunlight that falls in the most open areas of your property, try planting an island bed. Set off by itself in the middle of a turf area such as your front or side yard, a garden of colorful annuals can add considerable flair to an otherwise ordinary lawn.

To start a simple island bed, mark the boundaries with stakes and string or, for a curved bed, with a garden hose. Remove the sod in the enclosed area by spading to a depth just below the turf roots, then rolling the sod off. Add new topsoil to bring the surface level of the new bed up to that of the surrounding turf, and check the bed's shape, making any refinements for shape or size. Next, dig several inches of organic matter such as compost or leaf mold into the soil, working to a depth of 8 inches or so. When the bed is ready, plant the flowers with the tallest mature heights first, positioning them in the center of the island; as you make your way out toward the edges of the bed, plant progressively shorter varieties. The final appearance of the bed should give the effect of a gently sloping carpet of color.

When planning your bed and deciding on the plants to fill it, remember to keep proportions in mind. The smaller the bed's overall dimensions, the fewer the number of varieties you should use. Also limit the height of the tallest plants. For example, a low-maintenance yet effective combination for a 4-by-8-foot island bed could include a centerpiece of violet-blooming *Salvia farinacea* 'Victoria' interplanted with drifts of firecracker red *S. splendens* (scarlet sage)—both about 2 feet high—surrounded by a fringe of 8-inch *Dyssodia tenuiloba* (Dahlberg daisy).

Annual Color in Sunny Mixed Borders

Annual plantings are often used as fillers in perennial borders. In this role they both furnish the empty spaces between newly planted perennials that will take 2 to 3 years to mature and also provide seasonal color after many of the perennials have bloomed in late spring and early summer.

If you are adding annuals to your perennial border, take the cultural requirements of all concerned into account, especially as they relate to sun exposure. Many annuals reach their mature height and spread several weeks before frost, so small seedlings and young plants you transplant in late spring will need adequate space in which to grow. You don't want to plant an annual in a spot where a perennial's foliage will eventually block or filter out sunlight and undermine the annual's growth.

One way to avoid plant encroachment is to select annuals whose growth habits differ from those of your perennials. A border filled with ornamental grasses, for example, possesses an upright growth pattern. In this bed you might plant *Tropaeolum majus* (common nasturtium), which has a spreading and trailing habit. Multi-hued nasturtium flowers deliver exciting splashes of color against the subtle tones of the grasses, and their rounded leaf shape creates a pleasing contrast with the linear form of the grasses. Most appealing from the point of view of design, the nasturtiums can spread and wind among the grasses, filling in every available nook and cranny, and giving the border a finished look without robbing any of the other plants of sunlight.

Annuals in the Shade Garden

In the heat of summer, little can be more refreshing than the cool green comfort of a shade garden sparkling with colorful annuals. Although most annuals put on their best display in full sun, partially shaded gardens can make a fine home for some of these plants—and some annuals actually prefer a measure of shade. In addition to the ever popular impatiens, wax begonias, and coleus, for example, multihued tuberous caladiums, the sweetly fragrant white blooms of *Schizopetalon walkeri*, tiny-flowered *Heliotropium arborescens* (heliotrope), and draping blossoms of tuberous begonias thrive in less than the brightest situations.

Shade offers certain benefits that you won't find in sunny sites. For example, many sun lovers such as *Cleome* (spider flower) will grow in partially shaded sites, and although they produce fewer blooms under such conditions, the blooms will last longer. And because plants grow less vigorously with less sun, they require less in the way of maintenance tasks such as watering and cutting back. Finally, in warmer climates where the extreme heat of midsummer can wither annuals that normally prefer full sun, a shady site, with its cooler temperatures, may be the only place where you can reliably cultivate a garden.

What Is Shade?

In the simplest terms, if your garden receives less than 6 hours of direct sunlight per day—with 4 of those hours occurring in the morning—consider the site a shade garden. Shade is created by the living elements on your property—its trees and shrubs—and by physical structures such as walls, fences, and hills or other terrain features. It can even be created, unpredictably, by atmospheric conditions such as cloud cover.

These different sources produce various types of shade. The term *partial shade* refers to the sunniest type, in which your garden gets a full measure of direct morning sun and another hour or two in the afternoon. *Filtered shade* or *dappled shade* is a condition that exists when a light tree cover or lattice creates all-day shifting patterns of sun and shade. In many suburban neighborhoods, filtered-shade settings have developed over a pe-

A SHADE GARDEN IN FULL BLOOM
Glossy white and pink wax begonias, floppy rose-veined caladiums, and bicolored coleus form lush mounds of color in the filtered shade of fully grown deciduous trees in this Ohio summer landscape.

riod of years as young trees have grown to full maturity, fashioning a canopy of foliage that obstructs some of the incoming light. Finally, *full shade* denotes no direct sunlight at all, but a garden in full shade may receive a substantial amount of indirect light or reflected light from other surfaces; the north side of a building or open areas surrounded by structures are usually full-shade sites, for example. You can grow certain annuals successfully in all of these settings; the list at right names many plants that are suitable for shady surroundings. Only deep shade—cast by the densest tree cover—is completely inhospitable to annuals.

Planting Annuals in Shady Spots

Because most seeds need a warm, sunny spot to sprout into healthy seedlings, you'll need to either start seeds indoors for transplant to your shady garden or purchase seedlings at a nursery. Before

A TRIO OF SHADE LOVERS
The emerging leaves of Hosta 'Gold Standard' shelter a pocket of deep violet annual pansies and the cool blue blooms of biennial forget-me-nots. The perennial hosta, a favorite of shade gardens, helps keep the soil in this Washington, D.C., garden cool and moist, even when summer temperatures soar.

you transplant, make sure the soil contains a generous quantity of organic matter. Plants that do well in shade tend to prefer fertile soil. To enrich your soil, work a 2- to 4-inch layer of organic matter, such as leaf mold or compost, into the top 6 to 8 inches of the bed.

To achieve a finished look right off, you may be tempted to group your young plants close together when setting them out—but resist the urge. In shade gardens, correct spacing is more critical to your plants' health than it may be in sunnier areas. Shaded soil tends to remain moist longer, and low-lying branches and canopied ceilings reduce air circulation, two conditions that make such sites vulnerable to fungal diseases.

You can minimize the risk by spacing your plants even farther apart than suggested by catalogs and seed packets.

Moist, shady locations are also prime breeding grounds for snails and slugs. To protect new seedlings—whose tender tissue is loved by these pests—place plant collars around the stem just above the rootball before you plant, or sprinkle diatomaceous earth around each plant after it is in the ground. Alternatively, you can wait a couple of extra weeks for your seedlings to grow larger and tougher before setting them out.

Planting under Trees

A favorite shade spot for annual color is beneath the leafy canopy of a large tree. Before you prepare the soil for planting, be sure you know what kind of tree you have. Some, like the Norway maple, have canopies so dense that they don't allow enough light through to sustain your plantings. If this is the case, prune away or cut back existing tree branches so that more light can work its way through the foliage. Deciduous trees can be pruned and thinned extensively with no ill effects.

Evergreens such as pines are best suited to having their lower limbs removed, which lets in ambient light from all sides. Many of these branches are often dead anyway, so eliminating them not only creates the opportunity for a flower garden but also improves the appearance of the tree itself.

Consider, too, whether your tree is shallow rooted. Elms, sycamores, and sugar and silver maples, for example, have roots that hug the ground's surface, making any planting under the tree difficult. Also, certain trees, particularly black walnuts, produce toxic resins that make the ground harmful to neighboring plant life. In these cases, your best bet may be to plant annuals in large containers (*pages 79-83*) that you can position under the tree. Situate a garden bench next to them for an inviting summer retreat.

Maintaining Annuals in Shade Gardens

Even though the soil in shaded gardens is typically moister and more fertile than that in areas receiving full sun, the plants still need a regular source of water, and they may benefit from an occasional boost of fertilizer as well. If your area doesn't receive regular rainfall, check the top 2 inches of soil every week or so. If it is completely dry to the touch, it's time to water. Be careful not to overwater, however; root rot can set in if the soil is never allowed to dry out. You will also want to avoid overhead watering, especially late in the day when sunlight is on the wane, since water on the foliage and blooms invites fungal diseases. When watering by hand, then, keep the flow low to the ground.

Although your annuals should thrive in the amended soil of your shade bed, you may want to give them occasional nourishment in the form of an all-purpose liquid fertilizer to make sure they're getting all of the nutrients they need— and to get the maximum amount of bloom. Use these commercial formulas at half strength in shade gardens, once a month at the most.

MAJESTIC ACCENTS IN DEEP SHADE
The late-summer blooms of Impatiens wallerana 'Accent Orange' (foreground) gracefully surround an ivy-laden iron-hoop trellis in this mid-Atlantic shade garden. Drawing the eye toward the trees behind them are other varieties of shade-loving impatiens in bright pink and red.

SEASON-LONG COLOR IN THE SHADE
Violet-blooming Salvia farinacea (mealycup sage) contrasts with dense clusters of yellow and red coleus leaves in the dappled shade of a midwestern garden. Spared the intense heat of full afternoon sun, these annuals will maintain their sparkling color for many weeks.

Annuals for Diverse Climates

Although annuals are among the most carefree plants you can grow, different species do have preferences for particular climates. Such features as length of growing season, temperature highs and lows, and precipitation all help determine which varieties will be most successful in your garden. If you know those plants that are best suited to the seasonal changes of your geographic region, you'll be well on your way to cultivating a top-performing garden of flowers.

Warm- and Cool-Season Annuals

In regions where summer afternoons are hot and the temperature never dips below 65° F at night, choose tender annuals and tender perennials for your annual garden. While other plants may languish and even die under such conditions, these warm-season flowers—such as impatiens, Madagascar periwinkles, Dahlberg daisies, and creeping zinnias, to name a few—will flourish.

In addition to atmospheric temperatures, soil temperatures also affect the vigor of warm-season annuals. Rarely will they mature in soils that are cooler than 70° F. Some annuals, such as impatiens, will be stunted if planted too early and will never fulfill their potential. Keep in mind, though, that it is warm temperatures rather than direct sun that prompts these plants to do their best. Impatiens, for example, are happiest in partial shade.

Before installing warm-season annuals, check your soil to make sure it has warmed sufficiently. You can do this with an inexpensive thermometer such as those used in fishtanks. Simply insert the

COOL-SEASON FAVORITES FOR A COOL SUMMER
White-eyed purple lobelia and a frothy swath of pink-tinted Lobularia maritima (sweet alyssum) border this rock-garden path in Montana. Most at home in cool climates and full sun, the low-growing annuals make excellent edging plants.

A RESPITE FROM SOUTHERN HEAT
Purple and scarlet salvia blooms, yellow-orange marigolds, and white Cleome hasslerana endure Georgia's heat and humidity with flair in a shaded enclave between a house and a vine-covered trellis. Around the corner, other annuals, including red cosmos, bloom unfazed by the sun's full force.

thermometer gently into damp but not wet soil to planting depth (about 6 inches) and read the results a minute or so later. You may want to take readings from different parts of your site to be sure the entire area is ready for planting.

If the area where you live experiences not intense heat but comfortable daytime temperatures that stay between 60° and 80° F, cool-season annuals will do well in your garden. These plants, many of which are listed at right, need moderate temperatures if they are to grow and flower to their maximum potential; they will quickly lose their vitality if subjected to the full force of summer heat and humidity.

Pot marigolds, the funnel-shaped blooms of *Nemesia strumosa* (pouch nemesia), and fragrant *Reseda odorata* (mignonette) thrive in regions that experience long, cool growing seasons like that of the coastal Northwest. Alternatively, in areas that follow a fairly traditional change of seasons—including the mid-Atlantic and lower midwestern regions—tough and hardy cool-season plants such as pansies and ornamental cabbage can provide attractive displays that extend into winter and may even last until spring. By definition, biennials such as *Myosotis sylvatica* (forget-me-not) and *Lunaria annua* (honesty) are cool-season plants that do beautifully when planted in the garden in fall. Enjoy their leafy rosettes at the end of the season and, in late spring of the following year, their pretty blooms.

Regional Considerations

In northern and high-elevation areas where winters are long and cold—Nova Scotia and Maine, the northern plains, the Adirondacks, the Rockies, and the Yukon—the growing season is consequently short. To compensate for the shortened growing period, get a step up by starting most of

Cool-Season Annuals

Adonis aestivalis
(pheasant's-eye)
Agrostemma githago
(corn cockle)
Ammi majus
(bishop's flower)
Brachycome iberidifolia
(Swan River daisy)
Brassica oleracea
(ornamental cabbage)
Calendula officinalis
(pot marigold)
Callistephus chinensis
(China aster)
Campanula medium
(Canterbury bells)
Carthamus tinctorius
(safflower)
Centaurea cyanus
(bachelor's-button)
Cheiranthus cheiri
(English wallflower)
***Chrysanthemum* spp.**
(chrysanthemum)
Cirsium japonicum
(rose thistle)
***Clarkia* spp.**
(clarkia, godetia)
Consolida ambigua
(larkspur)
Crepis rubra
(hawksbeard)
Cynoglossum amabile
(hound's-tongue,
Chinese forget-me-not)
Dyssodia tenuiloba
(Dahlberg daisy)
Lathyrus odoratus
(sweet pea)
Linaria maroccana
(Moroccan toadflax)
Nemophila menziesii
(baby-blue-eyes)
Nigella damascena
(love-in-a-mist)
Papaver rhoeas
(corn poppy)
Papaver somniferum
(opium poppy)
Reseda odorata
(mignonette)
Salpiglossis sinuata
(painted tongue)
Schizanthus pinnatus
(butterfly flower)
Silybum marianum
(blessed thistle)
Tropaeolum peregrinum
(canary creeper)
Viola* x *wittrockiana
(common pansy)
Xeranthemum annuum
(everlasting)

Note: The abbreviation "spp." stands for the plural of "species"; where used in lists it means that many, but not all, of the species in a genus meet the criterion of the list.

your flowers indoors at least 6 to 8 weeks before the last frost date. Also important, choose flower varieties that take less than 90 days to reach maturity and bloom, such as snapdragons, Swan River daisies, and *Lupinus texensis* (Texas bluebonnet). To be safe, you might want to use devices such as cold frames or row covers to keep late frosts from killing your new seedlings and transplants. Although the season begins late in the calendar year in the North, your flowers will make up the time by taking advantage of the long hours of daylight during summer. Transplant and direct-seed as soon as conditions will allow.

Another way to jump-start the season is by gardening in raised beds, which warm up faster and maintain their heat more efficiently than in-ground beds. Raised beds for annuals need only be 8 inches deep to accommodate their roots. The easiest are simply unframed mounds of soil imported to a well-chosen sunny site. Or you can construct a frame with bricks, landscaping timbers, or rocks—which can absorb sunlight and ra-

diate even more heat to your plants. Combine 3 parts topsoil with 1 part compost or other organic matter and 1 part garden sand to fill the bed, and allow it to settle for 2 to 3 weeks before planting.

At the other extreme, along the Gulf Coast and in southern California, the climate is semitropical. Freezing temperatures are rare, allowing gardeners to enjoy a full range of annuals all year long. In these areas, you can plant in cycles so that you get several new crops of blooms throughout the year. Just be sure to plant any cool-season annuals during periods of mild winter temperatures and use warm-season flowers at all other times.

In semitropical regions, certain plants, such as fuchsias and New Guinea impatiens, can be treated as perennials. These are tender perennials, which are often short-lived even in mild climates because of their uncomplicated root systems. Nevertheless, they may perform for 2 or 3 years and should be cut back to within 2 to 3 inches of the base of the plant at the end of the growing season to keep them looking full and healthy.

NATIVES IN A DESERT CLIME
The hot days and cool nights of Phoenix, Arizona, are easily tolerated by true blue Phacelia campanularia (California bluebell) and contrasting Lesquerella gordonii (yellow blanket), both Southwest natives.

HOT COLOR IN ARID CONDITIONS
Rudbeckia hirta 'Gloriosa Daisy' blazes in shades of gold and crimson, adding fire to a border planted with cool spikes of Salvia farinacea 'Blue Bedder'. Both are top performers during the occasional summer droughts that visit this Missouri garden.

Hot summers come in two extremes: the humid type of the deep South and the Atlantic seaboard, and the dry kind of the Southwest and the central regions—Nebraska and Idaho, for example. In very hot, humid areas, your flower beds are likely to perform at their best if you site them where they receive only morning sun, since many hours of direct rays can wither even the most ardent sun lovers. If the area you have in mind gets the full day's complement, consider building a fence or trellis to provide shade during the afternoon hours. Finally, but most important, choose annuals that can tolerate heat *(list, right)*.

Because even humid regions sometimes experience periods of drought that can last several weeks, you'll want to protect your soil with an organic mulch. Spread a 2- to 4-inch layer over the bed, keeping the material a couple of inches away from the stems of your seedlings or transplants since mulch on the plant tissue encourages fungal and root diseases. If you seed directly into the ground, wait until your seedlings are at least 3 to 4 inches high before mulching.

To successfully grow annuals in hot climates that are dry, your primary task is topnotch soil preparation. Add extra organic matter to help the soil retain moisture and provide nutrients, incorporating at least 3 inches of compost, leaf mold, or other matter into 8 to 10 inches of unamended topsoil. Then space your annuals closer together than you would in other climates so that the plants' foliage can shade the soil. If you're direct-seeding, do it as early in the season as possible so that your plants can be well established before the stressful hot temperatures arrive.

An organic mulch is extremely important in helping to keep the soil cool and moist. Because annuals have small root systems that can't burrow deep down for water, they'll need careful monitoring with the hose or watering can—especially when they are newly emerging seedlings or recent transplants. Annuals quickly show signs of heat and water stress, particularly those grown in containers. However, you can minimize your watering tasks by selecting annuals that are heat and drought tolerant *(list, right)*.

Heat-Tolerant Annuals

Asclepias fruticosa
(bloodflower)
Catharanthus roseus
(Madagascar periwinkle)
Cleome hasslerana
(spider flower)
Cuphea ignea
(Mexican cigar plant)
Dolichos lablab
(hyacinth bean)
Exacum affine
(German violet)
Gomphrena globosa
(globe amaranth)
Helichrysum bracteatum
(everlasting, strawflower)
Ipomoea spp.
(morning glory)
Mirabilis jalapa
(four-o'clock)
Oenothera spp.
(evening primrose)
Orthocarpus purpurascens
(owl's clover)
*Rhodochiton
atrosanguineum*
(purple bell vine)
Ricinus communis
(castor bean)
Tagetes spp.
(marigold)

Heat- and Drought-Tolerant Annuals

Celosia cristata
(celosia)
Convolvulus tricolor
(dwarf morning glory)
Coreopsis tinctoria
(tickseed, calliopsis)
Cosmos bipinnatus
(cosmos)
Dimorphotheca spp.
(Cape marigold)
Dyssodia tenuiloba
(Dahlberg daisy)
Eschscholzia californica
(California poppy)
Eustoma grandiflorum
(prairie gentian)
Gaillardia pulchella
(blanket-flower)
Helianthus annuus
(sunflower)
Mentzelia lindleyi
(mentzelia)
Onopordum acanthium
(Scotch thistle)
Portulaca grandiflora
(portulaca, moss rose)
Sanvitalia procumbens
(sanvitalia, creeping zinnia)
Tithonia rotundifolia
(Mexican sunflower)
Zinnia angustifolia
(zinnia)
Note: The abbreviation "spp." stands for the plural of "species"; where used in lists it means that many, but not all, of the species in a genus meet the criterion of the list.

CHAPTER TWO

Gardens for Beauty and Fragrance

Annuals provide a feast for the senses. When it comes to spectacular color, they can't be topped, and their flowers can also be depended on to hold their color long after they have been picked, making them perfect for indoor decoration. Even short-lived plants without riotous blooms can mesmerize the eye with foliage that is boldly colored. And in addition to their visual virtues, many annuals are noteworthy for a heady fragrance—another feature that makes them welcome both in the garden and in the home.

Because they are easy to grow and just as easily forgotten the next year, annuals allow you to experiment with aesthetics such as color and scent as no other garden plants can. In the partly shaded Pennsylvania yard at right, for example, the gardener has fashioned stunning circular beds of pink, red, and white 'Elfin Mix' impatiens, partnered with perennial rose pink astilbe—and next year may try something altogether different.

A. *Impatiens wallerana 'Elfin Mix' (many)*
B. *Astilbe x arendsii 'Bressingham Beauty'(many)*
C. *Prunus autumnalis (5)*
D. *Taxus baccata 'Repandens' (many)*

The key lists each plant type and the number of plants needed to replicate the garden shown. The letters and numbers above refer to the type of plant and the number sited in an area.

Artful Combinations with Annuals

Among the many reasons to grow annuals—length of bloom period, ease of care, minimal expense—perhaps the most compelling is that you can choose from an enormous variety of colors. During their short life spans, annuals produce seed so rapidly that hybridizers have been able to tinker with them endlessly, introducing new hues far more quickly than is possible with other types of plants.

The temporary nature of annuals also allows you to experiment with compositions and color schemes that are more daring than any you might be willing to undertake with your more permanent plantings. You can let your imagination loose with the lavish palette that they make available for your garden.

The Mixed Border

Annuals bring a vitality to the mixed border. If your garden is newly planted, their colors and shapes can supply eye-catching contrasts and harmonies during the time it takes for perennials and shrubs to fill out and mature. For example, soft pink *Diascia barberae* and a pale blue cultivar of *Lobelia erinus* contrast soothingly with the large, lustrous dark green leaves of Oregon grape or the simple blue-green to gray-green foliage of *Daphne mezereum*. Tall pink *Cleome hasslerana* can supply height at the back of the border and unify the composition by repeating tints of pink.

If it's bold color you like, try yellow and crim-

CULTIVATED COMPANIONS
'Raspberry Rose' and 'Jolly Joker' pansies and pink and peach 'Oregon Rainbow' Iceland poppies brighten the front of this mixed border in Oregon. Pink and creamy white spires of Digitalis purpurea 'Excelsior' and ruby blooms of 'Red Charm' peony are shaded by a backdrop of white, yellow, and salmon azaleas.

30

Blazing red Salvia splendens 'Hot Shot' sizzles around 'Ultra White Madness' petunias, deep purple Salvia farinacea 'Rhea', and the coarse foliage of rose daphne (upper right), igniting this Pacific Northwest garden with hot color.

son 'Double Madame Butterfly' snapdragons with a smattering of 'Giant Double Mixed' zinnias in red, scarlet, orange, and golden yellow. Low-growing clusters of white *Iberis umbellata* nestled among the fiery hues will help temper them.

Other annuals combine marvelous color with a flower shape so distinctive that they are worthy of the most prominent border. Perfectly at home among showy perennials are the jewel-like red-orange blooms of *Emilia javanica,* which look like miniature paintbrushes atop wiry 2-foot stems; the quill-petaled, urn-shaped rose red flowers of *Cirsium japonicum,* which hover 2 feet above dark green spiny leaves; and the enormous sunburst-shaped pink, lavender, or white flower clusters of cleome, which float on 3- to 4-foot stems. When designing with such striking flowers, plant each species together in large groups, weaving in drifts and ripples of gray-leaved plants such as *Stachys byzantina* (lamb's ears), *Artemisia, Senecio,* and *Santolina* to soften the color scheme.

Some annuals with distinctive blooms have forms that are equally elegant. Consider *Lavatera trimestris* (rose mallow), which grows 3 feet tall and wide. Its densely branching stems, large cup-shaped pink or white flowers, and lower leaves that resemble those of a maple blend in effortlessly with border regulars such as iris, fluffy lady's-mantle, cabbagy bergenia, and old-fashioned shrub roses. In a border with big, downy, early-summer-blooming peonies, rose mallow can carry the flower show from midsummer to early fall.

Annuals that have sparse foliage are at their best when mated with plants that have abundant leaves. Stiff stands of easy-to-grow *Verbena bonariensis,* with its pale lilac-colored flat-topped blooms, pair well with lemon yellow daylilies, whose slender, arching leaves mask the strong but spindly stems of the verbena. The verbena offers summer color long after the perennial's petals have dropped. Simply pull up the stalks of the daylilies once they turn dry and brown, and leave the foliage intact to provide a green backdrop for the verbena.

The Annual Border

Simple borders composed of only a few judiciously chosen floral elements often have the greatest impact. *Cuphea ignea,* an eye-catcher whose

abundant scarlet cigar-shaped flowers have black-and-white tips resembling cigar ash, forms a compact foot-high mat of color; place it before soaring red-blooming cannas with their unfurling, wide-bladed leaves to create a pleasing contrast in form and a harmony of color. An ideal backdrop for this marriage would be a yellow-green hedge of *Philadelphus coronarius* 'Aureus' (mock orange) or tall, woody layers of fast-growing green-leaved *Spiraea prunifolia* (bridal wreath).

For a tall border with a tropical effect, try combining gold, yellow, and apricot cannas with the 5-foot stems of *Abelmoschus manihot* (sunset hibiscus), a Brazilian native whose large, fragile-looking flowers come in shades of pale to buttery yellow with maroon centers. To create a striking border in limited space, pair the red-plumed form of *Celosia cristata* (feather amaranth) with deep yellow marigolds and golden-hued calendulas. In back of the combination plant a fountain of *Miscanthus sinensis* 'Zebrinus', a perennial ornamental grass whose 5- to 6-foot-tall arching, straplike leaves display horizontal bands of creamy yellow and green.

Color Massing

Probably the easiest way to make the most of annual color is to plant a solid mass of a single variety that has especially striking blossoms. Choose an area of your yard that you want to highlight, and plant enough of the annual variety to make a bold statement. Because dramatic shocks of color dominate the area in which they're placed and are difficult to reconcile with more delicate garden scenes, resist the temptation to repeat the planting all around your property—or else the sheer preponderance of the one color will overwhelm the viewer and lose its impact.

No matter how stunning the hue of an individual bloom, however, uncompromising swaths of color tend to tire the eye. They look best in unobtrusive settings seen fleetingly and from a distance. The far corner of your backyard or the side wall of your garage is ideal; a mass of color in such removed, even remote, locations comes as a pleasant surprise when the viewer's eye discovers

MIRROR-IMAGE BEDDING
Four beds filled with pansies—yellow 'Crown Cream', peach, red, and pink 'Imperial Antique Shades', and purple 'Blue Perfection' —square off at the intersection of paths in a Virginia garden. Perennial orange 'Harvest Moon' Oriental poppies rise above the symmetrical arrangement.

AN ALL-STAR HEDGE
Low-growing orange and russet nasturtiums and white candytuft edge an Oregon bed layered with red and pink zinnias and deep gold marigolds and capped by radiant yellow sunflowers. The hedge runs along the periphery of the yard, hiding a busy road from view.

it. And you can extend the pleasure for months by changing the planting as the growing season progresses—replacing an expanse of fading summer-blooming purple petunias, for instance, with the fall flowers of lemon yellow chrysanthemums.

Design Bedding

Compact, profusely blooming annuals are ideal for decorative plantings called design beds, where the creative range is limited only by the gardener's imagination. These plantings can be simple, composed of, say, deep yellow *Rudbeckia hirta* 'Double Gold' blooming behind neat, squat mounds of pink, white, and red 'Prince', 'Princess', and 'Gaiety' *Dianthus chinensis,* all planted in a free-form island in your lawn. Or the beds can be formal, tracing strict geometric lines or neatly defined shapes.

If you prefer the ornate, try fashioning a circle bed divided into precise quadrants of color by flagstone paving. Within the structured bed, plant scarlet geraniums in opposite quadrants and bright

How to Keep Annuals Blooming All Season Long

Once an annual has formed seeds, its life cycle is over and the plant stops producing flowers. For this reason, you'll need to prune off spent flowers before they go to seed if you want your annuals to bloom continuously through the season. In addition, cutting back plants that have become tall and scraggly encourages new, leafy growth. Pruned stems usually form new flower buds within 2 to 3 weeks.

Cut main stems just above a leaf or pair of leaves *(above, left)*. The joint where the leaf or leaves emerge from the stem is the place from which side shoots will grow. Make a clean cut with pruning shears, removing about one-third or more of the stem. This will stimulate branching and the production of new flowers *(above, right)*.

Salvia, zinnias, and most annuals with daisylike blooms take readily to this degree of pruning. Trailing and soft-stemmed annuals such as nasturtiums, petunias, portulaca, and sweet alyssum that have grown shabby looking benefit from a severer treatment that removes all but a few inches of leafy stem. For annuals with decorative seedpods such as love-in-a-mist and those whose seed you plan to collect, stop cutting back at least 2 months before the first fall frost to give them enough time to mature.

blue petunias in the other two; soften them by ringing the perimeter of the bed with the bronzy-leaved 'Early Splendor' cultivar of *Amaranthus tricolor* and by planting an outermost rim of silver *Senecio cineraria* (dusty-miller).

The more stylized the bed, the more formal its appearance. Beds in the shapes of rectangles, circles, and half-moons can be any size that suits your property, but for a large-scale bed, avoid the overused combination of a solid block of one color edged with another color. A mass of blue ageratum skirted with pink wax begonias or yellow marigolds is rescued from the realm of the ordinary when dollops of other varieties that grow or can be trimmed to the same uniform height are interspersed among the rim plantings. Hybrid petunias in violet, blue, and yellow are easy-care annuals that respond well to trimming in such a design.

When planting an edging or a row in a formal design, situate your annuals so that you achieve a lush, unbroken line. Planted single file or on a straight grid, the row will be pocked with unsightly holes. Instead, arrange the plants in a zigzag, or for wider perimeters, position them in slanted, overlapping rows three, four, or five plants deep.

Less formal bedding designs reflect the planting patterns of a border: bands of color interwoven throughout the groupings of plants. A delightful annual bed for a somewhat dry spot in your yard might combine two popular annuals—yellow and white snapdragon and cream and peach-colored common nasturtium—with the lesser-known *Linaria maroccana* (Moroccan toadflax), whose blooms resemble petite snapdragons, and lacy-leaved *Foeniculum vulgare* 'Purpureum' (bronze fennel). Choose white and yellow toadflax and group it near a mass of the snapdragons for a contrast in scale; repeat the pairing as space allows, placing the taller fennel in the middle of the bed and letting the nasturtiums wander throughout.

Multicolored Annuals

Among the most interesting annuals are those that display contrasting colors on a single bloom in zoned, striped, and spotted patterns. Pansies, for example, have been bred to produce symmetrical blotches, with as many as three colors on one flower. Some petunias have bicolored designs in red, purple, blue-violet, or pink with white stripes that look like the spokes of a wheel. The beautiful funnel-shaped flowers of *Salpiglossis sinuata* (painted tongue) carry velvety swatches of purple, red, and brown with overtones of white, yellow, and pink, incised by prominent veining in dark,

contrasting shades. The dianthus tribe, including sweet William and *D. chinensis* (China pink), comprises virtually all types of variegation. In one prevalent type, called picotee, petals sport a thin outer margin in a color that contrasts with the rest of the blossom. Impatiens, wax begonia, and *Nicotiana alata* hybrids are just a few of the many annuals that can have picotee markings.

An ideal plant to blend with multicolored flowers is *Cynoglossum amabile* (Chinese forget-me-not), renowned for its exquisite clear blue color. For early-spring display in Zones 7 through 10, sow Chinese forget-me-nots in late summer and early fall with creamy yellow, dusty pink, and purplish many-toned blooms of 'Imperial Antique Shades' pansies. Add the delicate pastels of the multicolored *Papaver rhoeas* 'Mother of Pearl' (corn poppy); each bloom boasts shades of gray, lilac, peach, and palest pink that blend together like a parfait. For summer bloom in cooler areas, sow Chinese forget-me-nots in early spring with hybrid verbena 'Peaches and Cream' and apricot, peach, lavender, and salmon *Clarkia amoena* (farewell-to-spring), which features speckled and picotee markings.

Annuals with Multicolored Blooms

Abelmoschus spp.
(abelmoschus)
Agrostemma githago
(corn cockle)
Alcea rosea
(hollyhock)
Antirrhinum majus
(snapdragon)
Arctotis stoechadifolia
(African daisy)
Callistephus chinensis
(China aster)
Chrysanthemum carinatum
(chrysanthemum)
Clarkia amoena
(farewell-to-spring)
Cosmos bipinnatus
(cosmos)
Dahlia hybrids
(dahlia)
Dianthus barbatus
(sweet William)
Dianthus chinensis
(China pink)
Digitalis spp.
(foxglove)
Gazania rigens
(treasure flower)
Impatiens spp.
(impatiens)
Layia platyglossa
(tidytips)
Linaria maroccana
(Moroccan toadflax)
Lobelia erinus
(lobelia)
Mimulus x *hybridus*
(monkey flower)
Mirabilis jalapa
(four-o'clock)
Nemesia strumosa
(nemesia)

Nemophila menziesii 'Pennie Black'
(baby-blue-eyes)
Papaver rhoeas
(corn poppy)
Pelargonium spp.
(geranium)
Petunia x *hybrida*
(petunia)
Rudbeckia hirta 'Gloriosa Daisy'
(gloriosa daisy)
Salpiglossis sinuata
(painted tongue)
Tropaeolum spp.
(nasturtium)
Viola spp.
(pansy)

Note: The abbreviation "spp." stands for the plural of "species"; where used in lists it means that many, but not all, of the species in a genus meet the criterion of the list.

Alcea rosea (hollyhock)

The Allure of a Fragrant Garden

From a distance, a garden's impact on the senses is entirely visual, a feast of colors, contours, and patterns. But at close range, the same garden's appeal can increase many times over—when the dimension of fragrance is folded into the sensual mix. Many annuals are treasured for their floral scent, which adds a seductive harmony to a garden composition. Nature often orchestrates flower fragrance with an abandon that defies a gardener's attempt to manage it. And yet, even though scent cannot be arranged with the same precision as other planting considerations, such as flower color and bloom time, its presence enhances even the most pictorially appealing landscape.

Scent and Color

Seldom do flowers possess both rich color and potent fragrance; blooms that are highly scented don't need flashy color to attract pollinators. And fortunately, the odors attractive to bees, butterflies, and hummingbirds are generally pleasant to people as well. *Reseda odorata* (mignonette), for instance, may seem an unlikely candidate for inclusion in your garden because its tiny, unkempt blooms are a dowdy green or brown-yellow. But when planted near your doorstep, its heavenly sweet scent will envelop your entranceway.

Heavy pigment also tends to impede the movement of aromatic oils—a fact that accounts for the scarcity of scent in many flowers bred for fabulous color. The pale lavender Peruvian native *Heliotropium arborescens* (heliotrope), for example, abounds with a spicy almond-vanilla perfume, but the scent of some of heliotrope's deepest purple cultivars, such as 'Dwarf Marine', has been sacrificed in the hybridist's art.

Flower Flavors

Despite the seemingly indescribable and elusive quality of scent, the pleasant-smelling aromas broadcast by garden-worthy flowers fall into four general categories: sweet, spicy or aromatic, citrusy, and earthy. The voluptuous white funnel-shaped blooms of *Datura* species (angel's-trumpet), for example, exude a heavy perfume of such fermented sweetness that it hints of decadence. By contrast, heliotrope, *Matthiola longipetala* (even-

ing stock), and *Nicotiana* species (flowering tobacco) release a fragrance much like cinnamon, cloves, or vanilla. Their spicy redolence is always agreeable, lacking the compounds that occasionally make heavy-scented flowers oppressive.

A handful of flowers possess a fragrance suggesting the zest of a lemon and other citrus fruits. This lively, invigorating scent with just an edge of sharpness is most noticeable in four-o'clocks—*Mirabilis jalapa*—so named because their bright tube-shaped blooms open in the fading light of late afternoon. Earthy aromas, of which there are a wide variety, range from musky to resinous, which are pleasing, to bitter or medicinal, which many find unappealing. For example, the sprawling annual *Proboscidea louisianica* (common devil's-claw), with decorative seedpods that curl and split, produces blooms that give off a smell of camphor.

SATURATED IN SCENT
The vanilla-almond perfume of blue-violet heliotrope engulfs this British Columbia garden. Rose pink wax begonias alternate with the heliotrope to create a soothing color combination, while the deep gold chrysanthemums spilling out of window boxes provide a sunny accent. The rich scent, most intense in the early evenings of late summer, is held captive within the protected confines of the garden.

Growing Sweet Peas

With its rich honey scent and blooms shaped like frilly sunbonnets, *Lathyrus odoratus*—the climbing sweet pea *(left)*—has been a favorite of gardeners in climates with cool nighttime temperatures for more than two centuries. Most fragrant are the old-fashioned purple, blue, crimson, and rose pink strains that haven't been bred for larger blooms. Because sweet peas need a sunny spot but cool, moist soil, these 6-foot tendril-bearing vines do best with the special treatment described below.

Dig a long, narrow trench 1 foot wide and 2 feet deep, keeping the sides vertical. Fill the trench to within 4 inches of the top with a nutrient-rich mixture of 2 parts well-rotted cow manure or compost, 2 parts loam, and 1 part coarse sand, and add a sprinkling of ground limestone (top right). Soak the seeds in water overnight; then, in fall in warm climates and in very early spring in cooler areas, push the seeds ½ inch into the soil, 6 inches apart. When the seedlings are 2 inches tall, add ½ inch of soil around the stems to support the plants (right). Continue backfilling around the stems at the rate of ½ inch of soil for each 2 inches of plant growth until the trench is filled nearly to ground level. Provide support for the climbing plants using, for example, tepees of bamboo canes (bottom). Keep the plants well watered, and re-move spent flowers to ensure continued bloom. Because sweet peas are heavy feeders that take a lion's share of nutrients out of the soil, don't plant them in the same spot 2 years in a row.

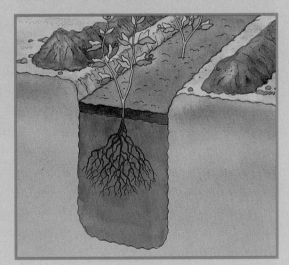

Plant it in nutrient-rich soil in an out-of-the-way nook of your garden; after it flowers you can collect the seedpods for indoor arrangements.

Harnessing Scent

Decide whether you want to plant fragrant annuals throughout your garden or in one particular spot. By sheltering an area from breezes, you can hold the perfume captive, increasing its intensity. Site fragrant annuals beside walkways or beneath a bedroom or dining room window, so the scent wafts in on the air. Floral scent peaks when the air is warm and the humidity is high, especially after a summer shower.

Making scent an integral part of your garden is akin to planning for color harmonies and sequence of bloom. The key is selecting the right plants for your objective. Low-growing, highly aromatic *Exacum affine* (German violet), for instance, makes an ideal edger alongside a well-trodden path. With a treacly perfume and a profusion of bell-shaped blooms in tones of blue, it pays double dividends. For a small border, many of the marigolds offer only a hint of fragrance, but *Tagetes lucida* (sweet-scented marigold) delivers a sassy, lemony aroma from early summer onward. Its yellow three-petaled flowers marry well with bushy mounds of blue or lilac *Nemesia strumosa* in front of a wall of golden yellow snapdragons. An edging of sky blue *Lobelia erinus* 'Cambridge Blue' would complete the cheerful combination.

For the scent of honey in the sunny spots of your garden, depend on 2- to 3-foot-tall *Scabiosa atropurpurea* (sweet scabious), with its cushions of midsummer blooms in pastel lavender, pink, or salmon. Or opt for the thistlelike *Centaurea moschata* (sweet-sultan) in yellow, lilac, or white. Other fragrant sun lovers include the American native *Mentzelia lindleyi* (blazing star) and sweet *Tropaeolum majus* (nasturtium), which thrives in full sun but not in intense heat.

Nocturnal Fragrance

At dusk, when intricate color schemes recede and the graceful outlines of shrubs and trees blend into the shadows, the fragrance of floral beauties that bloom at night plays ever more insistently upon your senses. A suburban deck, a side porch, or a city terrace veiled in scent creates a sanctum of comfort and repose. Many annuals that release their telltale sweetness into the cool evening air have flowers that are white, allowing them to virtually shimmer as night falls. Five-foot-tall *Nicotiana sylvestris*, with clusters of creamy white or pale green-tinged drooping trumpets, is an aristocratic mainstay of the evening garden. It forms a redolent balsamic backdrop for white and pink cosmos. Starry white trumpets of *N. alata* release an equally potent, spicy-sweet aroma. If it is scent you are seeking in this plant, however, avoid hybrids with bright pink, rose, and crimson flowers that stay open all day: They have had their genetic makeup reshuffled to favor color over scent.

Opulently fragrant royal purple trusses of heliotrope harmonize in both scent and color with the gently perfumed, star-shaped pink blooms of 'Domino Mixed' jasmine tobacco and rosy 'Peter Pan' zinnias.

The fragrance of off-white petunias improves after sunset, as do those with pink, lavender, rose, and purple blooms. But be sure to check seed catalogs carefully. Of the hundreds of cultivars available—ruffled, picotee, striped—count on the solid-colored, semiwild strains for delicious scent. Other fragrant night bloomers for your evening garden include angel's-trumpet, evening stock, and *Silene noctiflora* (night-flowering catchfly), with creamy white blooms that last only 3 nights.

The Friendly Toad

Insects abound in the fragrant garden, and wherever they proliferate you're likely to find toads. The native American toad *Bufo americanus,* shown at left, begins feeding at sundown, consuming a remarkable number of insects—over 100 in a 24-hour period—considering its small size of 2 to 3 inches in length. Favorite hunting grounds include damp fields, meadows, and your garden, especially under lights that attract flying insects.

To make your garden appealing to this wholly beneficial amphibian, leave shallow pools of water for breeding. In late spring, you'll discover swarms of coal black tadpoles. Don't worry about mosquitoes breeding in these pools since the tadpoles will eat the mosquito larvae. Within a month, baby toads will have hopped out of the water to commence nightly patrols for food; then you can drain the pools. A word of caution: Welcome homegrown toads in your garden, but don't import exotic species, whose appetites may extend to birds and small animals.

Fragrant Annuals

Centaurea moschata
(sweet-sultan)
Cucumis melo
(pomegranate melon)
Datura spp.
(angel's-trumpet)
Dolichos lablab
(hyacinth bean)
Dyssodia tenuiloba
(Dahlberg daisy)
Exacum affine
(German violet)
Heliotropium arborescens
(cherry pie)
Iberis odorata
(candytuft)
Ipomoea alba
(moonflower vine)
Lathyrus odoratus
(sweet pea)
Lobularia maritima
(sweet alyssum)
Matthiola spp.
(stock)
Mentzelia spp.
(mentzelia)
Mirabilis jalapa
(four-o'clock)
Nicotiana spp.
(flowering tobacco)
Oenothera biennis
(evening primrose)
Reseda odorata
(mignonette)
Scabiosa atropurpurea
(sweet scabious)
Tagetes lucida
(sweet-scented marigold)
Tropaeolum majus
(nasturtium)

Note: The abbreviation "spp." stands for the plural of "species"; where used in lists it means that many, but not all, of the species in a genus meet the criterion of the list.

Fascinating Foliage

MAXIMUM IMPACT
Pairing the huge purplish green palmate leaves and maroon stems of castor bean with the slender-leaved purple stalks and feathery plumes of the tender perennial Pennisetum setaceum 'Rubrum' (red fountain grass) poses a striking contrast in weight and form in this Ohio garden. Castor bean needs abundant water and fertilizer to attain such dimensions.

Distinctive foliage is not just the province of perennials and shrubs. Many in the broad category of plants treated as annuals also possess striking leaves that come in marvelous shapes, sizes, textures, and colors. *Ricinus communis* (castor bean), with deep plum palmate leaves and bronze-red stems, and *Hibiscus acetosella* cultivars, with purple leaves similar in appearance to those of a red maple, are just two whose foliage is the plant's primary attraction. Given ample water, they tend to grow willy-nilly, spreading out in their allotted space and quickly reaching heights of 5 feet for the hibiscus and 8 feet or more for the castor bean. When growing plants in your garden for their foliage appeal, be sure to provide enough room so that their remarkable contours and colors can be admired to their full extent.

Certain foliage plants are imposing specimens, with an architectural bearing that merits them a place of honor in your garden. Many biennials, in particular, produce stunning foliage their first season if left to follow nature's 2-year plan rather than being cultivated to bloom in the first season of growth. *Onopordum acanthium* (Scotch thistle), for example, is a candelabra-like structure whose crinkled foot-long leaves, giant stalk with toothed branches, and spherical flower buds are all accoutered with sharp prickles and cloaked with a ghostly bluish white down. It qualifies as living sculpture, reaching 8 to 10 feet during its second season, and needs plenty of room to grow. Let one or two plants hold sway in the conspicuous sites of your garden—perhaps the front of a border, the edge of a path, or at the garden gate.

Although you can often see the tall biennial *Verbascum* (mullein) species colonizing the poor, dry soil along rural roadsides, these biennials, surprisingly, are desirable for dressing up the more

FANCY FOLIAGE
The massive cream-and-green striated leaves and flashy orange flowers of Canna x generalis 'Stricta' and the bronze-red foliage and apricot blooms of 'Wyoming' impart an aura of tropical splendor to this Connecticut garden, enhanced by orange zinnias (front, right) and a tall stand of orange-red Mexican sunflowers (rear).

Portulaca grandiflora (moss rose) or the American natives yellow *Dyssodia tenuiloba* (Dahlberg daisy) and white, purple, and yellow *Phacelia campanularia* (California bluebell). These, too, grow best in somewhat dry, very well drained soil.

Leaf Textures and Colors

Some annuals possess extremely delicate foliage. Both green- and bronze-leaved *Foeniculum vulgare* (common fennel) produce airy clouds of foliage as tall as 5 feet, topped by round, flattish clusters of flowers resembling those of Queen Anne's lace. Combine the green-leaved fennel with spires of hollyhocks, drifts of summer phlox, and arching nests of ornamental grasses. Slightly shorter *F. vulgare* 'Purpureum', with bronzy featherlike foliage, teams terrifically with the broad, quilted, dusky purple leaves of *Perilla frutescens* (beefsteak plant), another annual grown chiefly for its outstanding foliage. The 'Dark Opal' cultivar of *Ocimum basilicum* (opal basil) also sports purplish black ovate leaves, and the leaf edges of *O. basilicum* 'Fluffy Ruffles' are wavy and serrated. Beefsteak plant and purple basil cultivars look superb commingling with pink cleome and 'Spectra' apricot New Guinea impatiens. Contrast them with the incised silver leaves of *Senecio cineraria* (dusty-miller), which brightens up the scene under overcast skies and at dusk.

One member of the marigold family grown primarily for its foliage is *Tagetes filifolia* (Irish lace). It forms neat little domes of lacy, fernlike foliage beneath tiny, usually white but sometimes yellow, golden, or brownish flowers. This foliage annual shares all the praiseworthy attributes of its clan, including ease of germination, tolerance of harsh conditions and neglectful maintenance, and lush growth. Try Irish lace with orangy red and scarlet salvia and white sweet alyssum.

The foot-long lobed, spiny leaves of *Silybum marianum* (blessed thistle) display an intricate lacework of silver-white veining and spotting. Depending on the climate, it grows as an annual or as a biennial. Group odd-numbered lots of these 3- to 4-foot-high bristles of marbled foliage amid a drift of the annual sunny-faced *Oenothera deltoides* (desert evening primrose) and mounds of *Erigeron karvinskianus* (Santa Barbara daisy). The 2½-inch flowers of the evening primrose open white and turn pale pink with age, and the Santa Barbara daisy is a drought-tolerant tender perennial with a profusion of dainty white daisylike blooms above scraggly foliage.

Two tall annuals—ruddy *Atriplex hortensis*

civilized confines of a garden, provided they have full sun and lean soil with excellent drainage. *Verbascum thapsus* (flannel mullein) flaunts oblong fuzzy gray-green leaves in a floppy rosette spanning 3 feet. From there, a tall unbranched stalk bearing 1-inch yellow flowers with orange anthers arises in the heat of the following summer.

V. bombyciferum (silver mullein) boasts silver-white leaves with a mealy finish that is soft to the touch. Its cup-shaped basal rosette could overflow a bushel basket the first season, and it sends forth a furry gray 6-foot stalk embedded with little sulfur yellow flowers. Into the soil around mulleins, scratch seed of annual scarlet, orange, and yellow

Plants with Noteworthy Foliage

Amaranthus tricolor
(Joseph's-coat)
Atriplex hortensis
(orach)
Canna x generalis
(canna lily)
Coleus x hybridus
(coleus)
Cynara cardunculus
(cardoon)
Foeniculum vulgare
(common fennel)
Hibiscus acetosella
'Red Shield'
(mallow)
Humulus japonicus
(Japanese hopvine)
Kochia scoparia
(burning bush)
Ocimum basilicum
'Dark Opal'
(opal basil)
Onopordum acanthium
(Scotch thistle)
Perilla frutescens
(beefsteak plant)
Ricinus communis
(castor bean)
Silybum marianum
(blessed thistle)
Tagetes filifolia
(Irish lace)
Verbascum spp.
(mullein)

Note: The abbreviation "spp." stands for the plural of "species"; where used in lists it means that many, but not all, of the species in a genus meet the criterion of the list.

'Rubra' (red orach), with arrow-shaped leaves, and *Kochia scoparia* var. *trichophylla* (burning bush), which starts out bright green and turns purple and then scarlet by fall—rapidly reach 4 feet and introduce a shapely vertical component to a border filled with low-growing summer annuals. Both can be conscripted for use as a temporary hedge; trim back the spindlier branches of the orach for a neater appearance. For added personality, the burning bush can be clipped into dignified symmetrical profiles of erect vases, urns, and domes.

Multicolored Foliage

Hybrid coleus is one of the most popular and easiest of annuals to grow. Its foliage comes in virtually every color and combination of colors imaginable—'Molten Lava', for example, is ashen black with carmine edging. Also, leaf shapes range from heart shaped to lancelike; some are deeply lobed, while others have frilly, cut, or toothed edges.

Pinched back during the growing season, coleus forms a neat, shrubby mound rarely more than 3 feet in height, appropriate for both formal and informal gardens. In light shade, pair the brilliant dark oval leaves of 'Red Velvet' with the soft gray pointed fronds and rich burgundy ribs of *Athyrium nipponicum* 'Pictum' (Japanese painted fern). An apron of silvery lamb's ears offers a nest of luxury for deep crimson 'Volcano Red' coleus and gold marigolds. Slender, tapering leaves of yellow and chartreuse coleus—say, 'Wizard Golden'—combine well with the fat, broad leaves of any of the bluish hostas such as 'Halcyon' or 'Hadspen Blue'.

Tender annual *Amaranthus tricolor* hybrids with yellow, red, orange, maroon, and chocolate blotched or spotted leaves such as 'Illumination' and 'Molten Fire' resent sharing the spotlight with partners of equally outrageous coloration. Instead, calm them down with a sober white-flowering *Gomphrena globosa* hybrid from the compact 'Buddy' strain or with the sedate, feathery blooms of *Crepis rubra* 'Snowplume'.

To create an icy effect with annual foliage, try *Euphorbia marginata* (snow-on-the-mountain), with gray-green oval leaves thickly rimmed in clean white. Snow-on-the-mountain reaches its zenith in late summer, when it forms a rangy 3-foot-tall shrub, cooling the feverish yellows, oranges, reds, and scarlets of tall zinnias and celosias.

Coleus x hybridus
'Scarlet Poncho'

A LEAFY COLOSSUS
The formidable size of the woolly gray-green foliage of Verbascum thapsus (flannel mullein) adds stark drama to the corner of a garden path in Santa Fe, New Mexico. When the bristly foliage of perennial red Oriental poppies dies back in midsummer, the mullein's rosette of leaves will mask the bare ground.

Overwintering Biennials

Biennials are by and large a hardy lot that stand up well through the single winter of their life cycle. In cold regions blessed with continuous snow cover in winter, the leafy rosette and root structure remain healthy and dormant until spring with no special care, insulated by the snow. In other areas—or simply for additional protection—apply a 3- to 4-inch blanket of a loose mulch of salt hay, straw, or evergreen boughs once the ground is frozen, arranging the material around the base of the plant without covering it, as shown with the foxglove rosette at left. Avoid matted leaves or other nonporous mulches; they may smother the plants and promote crown rot. Also, make sure the soil in which you grow the plants is porous and well drained. Standing water and thawing ice spell doom for even the most stalwart of biennials.

VYING FOR THE LIMELIGHT
Tall and crinkled, the unearthly gray-green profile of biennial Scotch thistle competes for attention with a majestic blue spruce in this New Jersey border. Silver-leaved perennials such as woolly Artemisia ludoviciana 'Silver King' and narrow-bladed Miscanthus sinensis 'Morning Light' bask in the duo's reflected glory.

Bringing Beauty Indoors

A CASUAL CUTTING GARDEN
This cottage garden in New York supplies an abundance of flowers—mostly annuals—for cutting. Pink and cream snapdragons bloom in the foreground, while yellow everlastings, pink and orange dahlias, and rose thistle populate the rear. Red and pale violet globe amaranth blooms behind a mound of baby's-breath, and the central path is bordered by 'Indigo Spires' salvia and 'Pink Perfection' lilies.

One of the great pleasures of growing annuals is having a steady supply of fresh-cut flowers. Annuals make ideal cut flowers because the more you cut them, the more blooms they produce. If you grow many different varieties you'll have a large collection of colors and fragrances from which to choose, whether you're arranging fresh flowers in a vase or drying the blooms, foliage, and seedpods for year-round bouquets.

Annuals with strong stems and a long vase life—such as those listed on page 47—are ideal for cutting and happen to look magnificent in all manner of beds and borders. For example, the airy, branching stems and delicate starlike blossoms of *Gypsophila elegans* (annual baby's-breath) perform beautifully with early single peonies, creamy white marigold cultivars, and the bright golden spheres of the shrub *Kerria japonica* 'Pleniflora' (globeflower kerria)—both in your garden and in a vase.

Survey your garden and note those places where you can tuck in a half-dozen or more lemon yellow snapdragons and *Eustoma grandiflorum* (prairie gentian), with its sprays of flowers in purple, shell pink, or white. Another combination to brighten up your garden or any room in your house is ethereal blue *Cynoglossum amabile* (Chinese forget-me-not) nestled among cheerful summer blooms of apricot nasturtium, peach-colored calendula, blush pink clarkia, and a creamy verbena. And in a cottage garden just outside your kitchen door, an informal group of pink and white foxglove and blue larkspur towering above clouds of *Nigella damascena* (love-in-a-mist) and *Centaurea cyanus* (bachelor's-button) can supply blooms for dramatic indoor decoration.

A Working Garden

A purely utilitarian garden, where appearance is secondary to the production of flowers for cutting, can be of any size. Allow at least 1 square foot of

Annual Grasses Worth Admiring

When planning flower beds and cutting gardens, don't overlook the charms provided by annual ornamental grasses. Their stunning flowers and seed heads not only add unique interest to sunny beds and borders but also make exquisite dried bouquets. And a few have beautiful foliage as well; *Zea mays* var. *japonica* (variegated corn), with its glorious yellow, white, and pink straplike leaves, is one of the most colorful members of the grass family.

In the backyard of the Oregon property shown here, nodding, oatlike seed heads of *Briza maxima* (quaking grass) have been planted to form a shimmering bed of pale green punctuated by a smattering of deep rose pink poppy mallow; they tremble appealingly both in the garden and in a vase. Another grass, *Coix lacryma-jobi* (Job's-tears), produces hard, oval, pearly white seeds dusted bluish gray or black that for centuries have been used as beads for necklaces and rosaries. This grass may be of only passing interest in the garden but is a true novelty in dried arrangements.

For edging, both *Agrostis nebulosa* (cloud grass), with delicate spikelets floating over short clumps of foliage, and *Lamarckia aurea* (goldentop), whose panicles sport a silver-green patina, spill voluptuously over paths and walkways. Because of their delicate constitutions, they need resowing in midsummer.

If you long for drama in the garden, you can count on the mammoth, bristly plumes of *Pennisetum villosum* (feathertop grass). But beware: They shatter easily when dry. Use them in fresh-cut arrangements, discarding the plumes before they dry to avoid a mess. Also showstopping in the garden are the pendulous seed heads of *Setaria italica* (foxtail millet), whose drooping pods, unlike those of feathertop, seem to last for generations when dried. Shiny and black-seeded, the panicles of robust *Sorghum bicolor* var. *technicum* (black sorghum) quickly spruce up the background of any bed or border. And dense yellow-green stands of *Triticum turgidum* (bearded wheat) and *T. aestivum* (common wheat) shooting skyward add blocks of sculpted simplicity to a contemporary garden and look spectacular crowded into winter bouquets.

space in full sun for each plant—and more for exhibition-size flowers such as 'Cactus Hybrid' dahlias and large sunflower cultivars. Locate the garden near water, and consider placing it near low hedges or walls that don't block the sun to help protect your flowers from damaging wind and rain.

For the greatest number of blooms in the least amount of space, grow your annuals in wide, orderly rows laid out east to west for maximum sun exposure. Position the shortest plants in the southernmost row to prevent their being shaded by taller ones. Wide rows of one type of plant also cut down on weeds and provide neighboring plants with root and stem support. Separate these long rows with wide grassy strips or mulched paths to make the garden convenient for watering, weeding, pruning, and harvesting blooms.

Harvesting Flowers

Select flowers that are halfway to three-quarters open and in perfect condition, and cut them early in the morning after a cool night, when they are plump with moisture. Two exceptions to this rule are marigolds and zinnias, which should be gathered during the warmest part of the day, as their stems draw up water best when warm. Using clean, sharp scissors, cut the stems at a slant, then place them in a bucket of tepid, clean water to which a few drops of chlorine bleach have been added. A water temperature of 100° to 120° F allows most annuals to drink up the maximum amount.

Cut flowers benefit from a period of conditioning before they are displayed indoors. Remove foliage that will be underwater, and sink the stems into a bucket of warm—preferably distilled—water up to the lowest set of remaining leaves. Keep them in a cool, dark place such as a basement for at least 6 hours. Commercial preservative solutions to extend vase life can be added to the water; follow package directions. Or use a homemade solution of 1 tablespoon corn syrup and 10 drops of chlorine bleach to 1 quart of water.

When cut, a few annuals—including poppies, dahlias, and Mexican sunflowers—ooze a milky fluid that fouls water and clogs the cut ends of other flower stems. Before you condition them, sear their stems by placing them in hot, almost boiling water until the sticky sap stops seeping, or hold the cut end of each stem over a candle flame briefly until the flow of sap ceases.

Annuals for Drying

Bouquets and wreaths of dried flowers last almost indefinitely. Not all flowers that make gorgeous fresh bouquets look good dried, however, so it's best to know which ones to work with *(list, right)*. As a rule, dark red or deep purple blossoms tend to turn an unattractive black when dry, and some white flowers turn a dingy brown.

Flowers displaying the brighter hues of the color spectrum generally retain their color the best. For example, 'Pink Tassels' celosia, light green *Moluccella laevis* (bells of Ireland), and golden *Lonas annua* (yellow ageratum) remain pretty and fresh looking when dried properly.

Among the best annuals for drying are those composed of tiny flowers surrounded by leaflike

structures called bracts that arise from the stem and encase the flowerhead. Known as everlastings, these flowers—which include *Helichrysum bracteatum* (strawflower), *Xeranthemum annuum* (immortelle), and *Limonium* (sea lavender)—retain their original form and color when dried.

In addition to flowers, the seed heads of some annuals look splendid in dried displays and wreaths. Most annual grasses dry well, as do the coin-shaped, milky satin seedpods of *Lunaria annua* (honesty), the bronzy round pods of *Scabiosa stellata* (paper moon, sweet scabious), and the split, curling fruits of *Proboscidea louisianica* (common devil's-claw).

Flowers for drying should be cut as they begin to open, on a dry, sunny day after the dew has evaporated. Keep in mind that dry flowers lose half of their original bulk, so gather twice as many for your dry arrangements as for your fresh ones. Sort through the harvest and select unblemished flowers with the most pleasing shapes and colors.

Strip the leaves and bundle the stems without tangling them, fastening the bunches about 1 inch from the stem tips with a rubber band, which will continue to hold the bundle securely together as the stems dry and shrink. Suspend the flowers upside down in a dark, dry, well-ventilated space—perhaps an attic or a garden shed. If you live in a warm, humid climate, make smaller bunches than usual and allow a longer drying time. Your flowers are ready for arranging when the stems are brittle and break with a crisp snap. Depending on the fleshiness of the stems, the size of the bundles, and your humidity level, this should take from several days to 2 weeks.

Annuals for Cutting and Drying

FLOWERS WITH A LONG VASE LIFE
Ammi majus
(bishop's flower)
Antirrhinum majus
(snapdragon)
Calendula officinalis
(pot marigold)
Callistephus chinensis
(China aster)
Centaurea cyanus
(bachelor's-button)
Centaurea moschata
(sweet-sultan)
Consolida ambigua
(rocket larkspur)
Cosmos bipinnatus
(cosmos)
Dahlia hybrids
(dahlia)
Eustoma grandiflorum
(prairie gentian)
Tithonia rotundifolia
(Mexican sunflower)

ANNUALS FOR DRYING
Amaranthus cruentus
(prince's-feather)
Asclepias fruticosa
(gomphocarpus)
Briza maxima
(quaking grass)
Celosia cristata
(celosia)
Gomphrena globosa
(globe amaranth)
Helichrysum bracteatum
(everlasting, strawflower)
Limonium sinuatum
(notchleaf statice)
Lunaria annua
(honesty)
Moluccella laevis
(bells of Ireland)
Scabiosa stellata
(paper moon, sweet scabious)
Xeranthemum annuum
(everlasting, immortelle)

Versatile Beauties

Annuals make obliging summer residents, willingly sharing the garden stage with other types of plants and sometimes stealing the show when spring-flowering bulbs and perennials finish performing. Rapid growers and prolific bloomers, annuals come in a wealth of flower and foliage shapes, colors, sizes, textures, and fragrances to enhance virtually any planting. In the gardens featured here and on the following pages, they are called upon to embellish more permanent plants, to grace the windows of a house, and to provide armloads of cut flowers for indoor decoration. For a list of plants and a planting guide for each of these vibrant gardens, see pages 58-61.

CHILD'S PLAY
Beside a playhouse in a backyard Pennsylvania garden, a raised bed containing pink and white cleome, red and russet strawflower (center), and yellow, white, and red hybrid dianthus is easily cared for by the garden's custodian—a 7-year-old girl.

SMALL GARDEN, LARGE EFFECT
For a bold look and continuous color, the owners of this Virginia garden turned to such annuals as the two massive castor-bean plants near the corner of the walkway. The maroon foliage of hybrid polka-dot plants creates a pool of deep color amid the greenery. Rose pink verbena (foreground) and yellow lantana add textural contrast and continuous bloom.

A DISPLAY DOMINATED BY ANNUALS
Sculpted pines and evergreen shrubbery provide the framework for the planting of annuals in this Portland, Oregon, front yard. Snowy white sweet alyssum edges a bed that includes lemon yellow signet marigolds, pink zonal geraniums, multihued zinnias, and tall, bright yellow African marigolds. These dependable annuals bloom from midsummer to first frost.

WINDOW BOX BEAUTIES

In a compact display of summer blooms, twin window boxes are filled to bursting with pink and violet impatiens and petunias, rose pink zinnias, and the yellow daisylike flowers of Melampodium paludo-sum. Two perennials grown here as annuals—pink-speckled polka-dot plant, which picks up the color of the 19th-century Alexandria, Virginia, townhouse, and variegated ivy, with leaves edged in cream—add foliage interest to the eye-level garden. When individual plants cease blooming or grow beyond their allotted space, the homeowner simply replaces them.

A SIMPLE STATEMENT IN GREEN AND WHITE
*A dense planting of white impatiens seems to float
beside the steps leading up to a terrace in this
north-facing Virginia walled garden. Glowing in
the dappled shade, the creamy flowers help soften
the hard edges of the brickwork, and the cool green-
and-white color scheme calms both eye and spirit.
Pots of ginger with large, lancelike leaves echo the
waxy, fingerlike foliage of the magnolia overhead,
while rounded English boxwood rings the circular
terrace and ivy creeps up the garden's walls.*

A COMPATIBLE DUO FOR DRY SHADE
*Mounds of 'Dwarf Rainbow' coleus alternate with
pink and red 'Shady Lady' hybrid impatiens to create
an ankle-deep wash of color in this Tacoma, Washington, garden. Flourishing beneath a pair of Douglas
firs, where the shaded soil tends to be dry, coleus and
impatiens benefit from being planted close together to
shelter the ground and thereby conserve moisture.*

AN ENCHANTING CUTTING GARDEN
The owner of this delightful backyard garden, which is visible from her kitchen and living room windows, wanted a cutting garden that would still look lush after she collected her bouquets. By densely planting colonies of annuals that thrive in the northern California climate, she was guaranteed blooms from summer until fall. The daisylike blossoms of cosmos, in delicate pink and bold magenta, a planting of fluffy white snow-on-the-mountain, and a few rose pink hybrid cactus dahlias dominate one side of the steppingstone path; on the other side, feathery red-violet celosia, pink cleome, and two perennial salvias—cobalt blue Salvia guaranitica and pale blue S. uliginosa—provide a tangle of tantalizing blooms.

CHILD'S PLAY

pages 48-49

A. *Canna x generalis 'Tillie'* (many)
B. *Polianthes tuberosa* (11)
C. *Tagetes erecta cv.* (3)
D. *Dianthus caryophyllus 'Diane'* (1)
E. *Rosa 'Golden Garden'* (1)
F. *Plumeria rubra f. acutifolia* (3)

G. *Dianthus caryophyllus 'Laced Romeo'* (2)
H. *Rosa 'Sheri Anne'* (1)
I. *D. caryophyllus 'Ballerina'* (2)
J. *D. caryophyllus 'Desmond'* (2)
K. *Rosa 'Beauty Secret'* (1)
L. *D. caryophyllus 'Joy'* (1)

M. *Rosa 'Green Ice'* (1)
N. *Rosa 'Judy Fischer'* (1)
O. *Rosa 'Snow Twinkle'* (1)
P. *Cleome hasslerana* (14)
Q. *Helichrysum bracteatum* (4)
R. *Gardenia jasminoides* (1)
S. *Zinnia elegans cv.* (many)

SMALL GARDEN, LARGE EFFECT

pages 50-51

A. *Ricinus communis* (1)
B. *R. communis 'Carmencita'* (1)
C. *Berberis thunbergii 'Aurea'* (1)
D. *Yucca filamentosa 'Golden Eagle'* (1)
E. *Sedum x 'Autumn Joy'* (4)
F. *Hosta 'Gold Standard'* (1)
G. *Nicotiana alata 'Nikki'* (3)
H. *Tradescantia pallida 'Purple Heart'* (3)
I. *Lantana camara 'Flava'* (2)

J. *Digitalis purpurea 'Shirley Hybrids'* (14)
K. *Iris sibirica 'Flight of Butterflies'* (1)
L. *Verbena 'Sissinghurst'* (2)
M. *Coreopsis verticillata 'Moonbeam'* (6)
N. *Berberis thunbergii 'Crimson Pygmy'* (1)
O. *Ceratostigma plumbaginoides* (3)

P. *Spiraea japonica 'Limemound'* (1)
Q. *Centranthus ruber* (3)
R. *Achillea x 'Moonshine'* (4)
S. *S. japonica 'Little Princess'* (1)
T. *Hemerocallis 'Stella d'Oro'* (3)
U. *Hypoestes phyllostachya* (3)
V. *Rosa 'The Fairy'* (1)
W. *Miscanthus sinensis 'Variegatus'* (1)
X. *Rosa 'Betty Prior'* (1)

A DISPLAY DOMINATED BY ANNUALS

page 51

A. *Acer palmatum* (1)
B. *Rhododendron 'Vulcan'* (1)
C. *Tagetes erecta cv.* (many)
D. *Photinia x fraseri* (many)
E. *Zinnia elegans cv.* (many)
F. *Tagetes erecta 'Lulu'* (many)
G. *Pelargonium x hortorum 'Blues'* (8)
H. *Lobularia maritima* (many)
I. *Pinus mugo var. mugo* (1)
J. *Pseudotsuga menziesii* (1)
K. *Hydrangea macrophylla* (1)
L. *Pinus densiflora 'Umbraculifera'* (2)

WINDOW BOX BEAUTIES

pages 52-53

A. *Hypoestes phyllostachya* (2)
B. *Senecio cineraria cv.* (2)
C. *Impatiens wallerana cv.* (3)
D. *Torenia fournieri* (1)
E. *Melampodium paludosum* (2)

F. *Hedera helix 'Tricolor'* (2)
G. *Petunia x hybrida* (1)
H. *Zinnia cv.* (2)
I. *Salvia farinacea* (1)
J. *Nicotiana alata* (1)

NOTE: *The key lists each plant type and the total quantity needed to replicate the garden shown. The diagram's letters and numbers refer to the type of plant and the number sited in an area.*

**A SIMPLE STATEMENT
IN GREEN AND WHITE**

pages 54-55

A. *Impatiens wallerana cv.* (many)
B. *Hedera helix* (many)
C. *Buxus sempervirens* (7)

D. *Liriope muscari* (many)
E. *Parthenocissus tricuspidata*
(many)

**A COMPATIBLE
DUO FOR
DRY SHADE**

page 55

A. *Pseudotsuga
menziesii* (2)
B. *Coleus x hybridus
'Dwarf Rainbow'* (many)
C. *Impatiens wallerana
'Shady Lady Hybrids'*
(many)

AN ENCHANTING CUTTING GARDEN

pages 56-57

A. *Cleome basslerana 'Lavender Queen', 'Pink Queen', 'Rose Queen'* (6)
B. *Zinnia elegans cv.* (3)
C. *Salvia guaranitica* (1)
D. *Celosia argentea* (2)
E. *Lobularia maritima* (2)
F. *Chrysanthemum x morifolium* (2)
G. *Cosmos bipinnatus 'Sensation Mix'* (6)
H. *Euphorbia marginata* (3)
I. *Tithonia rotundifolia* (1)
J. *Dahlia cv.* (1)
K. *Rosa 'Meidiland Red'* (1)
L. *Salvia uliginosa* (1)

NOTE: The key lists each plant type and the total quantity needed to replicate the garden shown. The diagram's letters and numbers refer to the type of plant and the number sited in an area.

Using Annuals in Your Landscape

No other group of plants can so dramatically change the look of your landscape in so short a time as annuals. Whether your goal is to provide color and interest after bulbs or short-blooming perennials have faded, to fill in the gaps between perennials and shrubs that are still maturing, or to hide an unappealing view or structure, there's an annual for the job. Some even do double duty: In the upstate New York kitchen garden at left, for example, scarlet runner beans and Swiss chard—interplanted with cleome, nicotiana, and petunias—delight both the eye and the palate.

The following pages will show you how to use annuals in a variety of landscape functions, including repairing garden problem spots, dressing up hardscapes, and enhancing naturalized areas. You'll also find advice on bringing favorite annuals indoors for the winter, cleaning up the garden at season's end, and growing annuals in containers.

The key lists each plant type and the total quantity needed to replicate the garden shown. The diagram's letters and numbers refer to the type of plant and the number sited in an area.

A. *Petunia sp. (many)* **B.** *Datura metel (1)* **C.** *Alcea rosea 'Nigra' (1)* **D.** *Iris sibirica (1 clump)* **E.** *Ipomoea batatas 'Blackie' (1)* **F.** *Buxus sempervirens 'Suffruticosa' (1)* **G.** *Beta 'Chioggia' (1)* **H.** *Papaver rhoeas 'Angel Wing' (many)* **I.** *Tagetes tenuifolia 'Lemon Gem' (3)* **J.** *Beta vulgaris 'Charlotte' (1)* **K.** *Beta vulgaris 'Argentata' (5)* **L.** *Papaver rhoeas (many)* **M.** *Tagetes 'Striped Marvel' (2)* **N.** *Chrysanthemum (Tanacetum) parthenium 'Aureum' (1)* **O.** *Artemisia absinthium (2)* **P.** *Nicotiana langsdorffii (2)* **Q.** *Phaseolus coccineus (16)* **R.** *Nicotiana sylvestris (3)* **S.** *Mentha suaveolens 'Variegata' (1)* **T.** *Cleome basslerana (C. spinosa) 'Pink Queen' (3)*

A Practical Eye for Annuals

DEPENDABLE
BLOOMERS
*Thickly planted with
annuals, this vibrant
Oregon garden is pre-
pared for all summer
contingencies. Orange
and yellow mounds
of marigolds and tall
reddish zinnias will
continue to thrive even
during drought, while
lavender petunias
and pink and fuchsia
clouds of nicotiana can
stand up to humidity.*

Fast-growing, colorful annuals virtually have the power of a magic wand to transform your landscape. Plant them in the gaps of a new perennial or shrub bed to give the garden a more finished look while you wait for the fledgling plants to mature. Use them, too, to fill in the bare spots that stand out before a ground cover has grown into a solid blanket. Varieties that reseed readily, such as sweet alyssum, should come up every spring until the ground cover takes over.

If your property has a ramshackle outbuilding or utilitarian fence that is an eyesore, it can easily be masked during the summer with an eye-pleasing cloak of vines such as *Humulus japonicus* (Japanese hopvine). A row of *Ricinus communis* (castor bean) or *Zea mays* (ornamental corn) makes an attractive screen that can shield you from an unsightly road—at least temporarily—while evergreen hedges are maturing. And if you're reserving space for a future building or an addition, you don't have to leave the site bare in the meantime: A lavish display of annuals can dress it up with a minimal outlay of time and expense.

When you're creating a new garden or landscaping a new area of your property, short-lived plants make ideal guinea pigs. Sometimes even the best paper plans can't help you visualize a new layout. A temporary planting of annuals in the proposed space, however, may allow you to determine which arrangements of colors, forms, and sizes look best. And because many annuals grow and bloom adequately in marginal soil, you can sometimes get away with minimal soil preparation as you're experimenting, putting off the work of improving the beds until you're ready to put in a more permanent community of plants.

Annuals as Replacements

Annual flowering and foliage plants make the best understudies when other plant performers lose their luster. They are perfect, for example, for hiding the decline of spring-flowering bulbs such as tulips and daffodils, whose foliage must be allowed to go through an unsightly withering if they are to bloom again the following year. Sow the seeds of hardy annuals among the bulbs in autumn or late winter. After the bulb flowers bloom and fade, the burgeoning annuals will conceal the flat splotches of yellowing leaves. Shallow-rooted

ground huggers such as *Iberis umbellata* (globe candytuft), *Brachycome iberidifolia* (Swan River daisy), pansies, and forget-met-nots can neatly carpet the garden without disturbing the bulbs, as deeper-rooted perennials might.

If you want to sustain color all season in perennial beds that otherwise produce only a short period of bloom, seed annuals among the perenni-

als. It's a good idea to plant extra seeds in flats, following the directions on pages 12-13, in case adverse weather destroys the in-ground seeds or seedlings. If all of your seeds come up in the garden, you can use your standbys as container plants or as replacements later in the season.

Potted seedlings or annuals purchased in cell packs from a nursery or garden center can easily be interplanted among established bulbs or perennials at any time after the last spring frost. Working carefully so as not to harm the roots of the long-term inhabitants, dig small, shallow holes for the annuals, gently remove the young plants from the containers and situate them in the ground, tamp soil around them, and water thoroughly.

If an overwintering virus, a sudden insect invasion, a battering hailstorm, or a destructive pet leaves your perennials ragged, fast-maturing, steady-blooming annuals can repair the view practically overnight. Place species that transplant well directly in the soil after removing them from cell packs or your own containers, as described above. Check the encyclopedia at the back of this volume to identify those plants that don't mind a change of residence. Species that do resent root disturbance—such as *Digitalis* (foxglove) or *Gaillardia* (blanket-flower)—can still be added to your garden: Simply set the pot on the soil surface among the other plants, or sink it into a hole in the soil.

Yet another way that annuals come to the rescue is when drought or a long hot spell sends established perennials into summer dormancy. Indeed, many annuals—including *Rudbeckia hirta* (black-eyed Susan) and *Papaver rhoeas* (corn poppy)—flourish in dry weather. Use these to fill in while your garden regulars recover.

Double-Duty Annuals

More and more, gardeners are discovering that many garden vegetables—the quintessential annuals—can be beautiful as well as delectable. And likewise, some plants that are usually grown as ornamentals, such as marigolds and pansies, are now appearing in the salad bowl. A bed that combines attractive vegetable plants, herbs with interesting or colorful foliage, and edible flowers can both dress up your property and enhance your meals.

Many edible annuals rely on unusual coloration and texture for their visual appeal. Among these are ornamental cabbage and kale—varieties of *Brassica oleracea* that are indispensable in cool-season borders—and rhubarb chard, a *Beta vulgaris* variety whose ruby red stems and glossy green foliage are spectacular in indoor arrangements as well as in the garden. Butterhead lettuce makes a charming early-spring edging at the front of your flower border, while taller edibles, such as burgundy-colored rubine brussels sprouts, add interest in the midborder. For a range of color, plant ornamental peppers *(Capsicum annuum),* whose fruits ripen in shades of red, orange, purple, yellow, and green. At the back of the bed, use annual sunflowers to vary the scale of your flowers; they can also screen an unwanted view and supply next winter's bird feeders to boot.

The sculptured foliage of *Cynara cardunculus* (cardoon) and its relative the purple artichoke *(C. scolymus)* provide dramatically different accents. If you prefer fine detail, plant a minigarden of *Ocimum* (basil), using a range of varieties that includes bright green tiny-leaved mounds of foliage to bushlike plants with leaves of rich purple.

In choosing any part of a plant for the dinner table, always be certain that it's safe to consume. The list at left identifies a number of annuals that are edible, as well as others that must never be ingested; also, check seed packets, catalogs, and other literature, keeping in mind that some species in a genus are edible while others aren't. Even some peppers are too fiery to eat—or even to handle.

Ending the Season

In warm zones, late-blooming annuals die off slowly after exhausting themselves with flowering. In colder areas, autumn frosts abruptly kill many plants that would survive far longer under kinder conditions. This is particularly true of tender perennials. To prolong the pleasures of your garden, bring some of your favorite plants indoors to preserve as houseplants. At least a month before frost is expected, choose a few to put into containers. *Coleus, Begonia, Pelargonium,* and *Impatiens* species are good candidates since they adapt well to the high temperatures and low humidity found in most homes. Select plants that have grown straight, are filled out on all sides, and aren't too large.

Avoid any specimens that have noticeable disease or yellowing or spotty leaves. Also, reject plants showing the webs of red spider mites as well as any with evidence of whiteflies or mealybugs. To be safe, treat them with an insecticidal soap, spraying the soil, stems, and both the tops and the undersides of leaves.

Prevent the spread of undetected pests and diseases—such as soil viruses, which can cause a plant to wilt and die overnight—by quarantining newly potted annuals in a separate room away from other houseplants for at least 2 weeks. If the annuals are still healthy after this time, they can

join the rest of your indoor plant family. Like any transplant, a newly potted annual from the outdoors should be protected from strong sunlight while it adjusts to its new home.

Tidying the Garden

Good garden cleanup at season's end gives you a head start on a healthy, productive garden the following year. Pull up dead annuals, taking care not to disturb nearby perennials or bulbs. Pick up dropped leaves and other organic debris. Plants that look free of pests and diseases can be composted, but those that show signs of trouble should be sealed in a plastic bag and disposed of with the household trash to prevent the problem from spreading.

Now is the perfect time to give your soil a once-over in preparation for the next year. Dig organic matter such as compost or leaf mold into the top

A GARDEN OF EDIBLE DELIGHTS
This southern California garden produces a delightful array of cool-weather annuals that are ready to serve as either decoration or dinner. Displaying their varied forms and foliage as they cluster in harmony are marigolds, carrots, lettuce, rose-toned ornamental kale, organically grown pansies, and purplish stands of red mustard. Regular harvesting of leaves and flower heads ensures a long season of productivity.

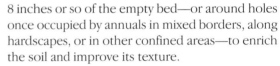

8 inches or so of the empty bed—or around holes once occupied by annuals in mixed borders, along hardscapes, or in other confined areas—to enrich the soil and improve its texture.

Most annuals prefer soil that is slightly acid, measuring between 6 and 7 on the pH scale, where 0 is extremely acid, 7 is neutral, and 14 is extremely alkaline. If your plants performed poorly in one part of the garden, check the soil's pH with a simple hand-held electronic tester available at garden supply centers; for a more extensive analysis, send a sample to a professional lab recommended by your local Cooperative Extension Service. Soils with a pH below 6 can be "sweetened" by adding lime, while an alkaline soil can be made more hospitable with the addition of sulfur, following directions on the package in both cases. Organic matter will also help correct a pH that is too alkaline. Finally, cover the bed with a layer of organic mulch, such as shredded leaves or bark. This will conserve moisture around biennial roots and protect seeds from ground-heaving frosts.

PROLONGING THE PLEASURES
A planter filled with Catharanthus roseus (Madagascar periwinkle) directs the eye to the cheerful pink trumpets of a tropical Mandevilla vine framing the entrance to this Missouri porch, while red and salmon geraniums, marigolds, and ornamental peppers add spots of vivid color. When cold weather comes, the geraniums and peppers will be moved indoors.

Plants to Take the Heat

Annuals are unparalleled helpers when it comes to landscaping around paved driveways, brick paths, stone terraces, concrete walls, and a variety of other hard or rocky surfaces, known collectively as hardscapes. Hardscapes pose special challenges to plants growing close to them. For one thing, they absorb and radiate heat: On a sunny summer day a blacktopped driveway or stuccoed wall can significantly raise the temperature in the immediate area, so anything planted nearby must be reliably heat tolerant. Also, soil that is close to buildings or pavement may contain high levels of minerals deposited by water that has first washed over these surfaces. And driveways are sources of chemical pollution in the form of oily runoff and vehicle exhaust fumes.

Fortunately, there are many heat-loving, poor-soil-tolerant annuals that flourish unfazed in these locales. In addition, the microclimates created by hardscapes can even make it possible for you to grow more kinds of plants than would otherwise be possible under the normal conditions on your property. The warm environment created by a stone patio with a southern exposure, for example, might allow tender annuals to do well in a region where summers are short and cool.

Choosing the Right Plants

When planning any garden, you'll get the best results if you consider the conditions of the site and choose plants that are best suited to them. This is especially so of hardscape locations, which may be dramatically affected by patterns of light and shade, heat, and traffic. Start by noting how many hours of sunlight the site receives. Be aware that the amount may vary widely from one spot to the next because vertical hardscapes such as walls and buildings can block light, forming pools of shade in the midst of sun. Bear in mind, too, that the heat given off by pavement or other hardscape surfaces will cause the surrounding soil to dry out faster than normal, and that walls can keep rainfall from reaching ground adjacent to them. Plan on watering plants in these areas more often, and for added insurance, use annuals that are especially drought resistant. A thick layer of mulch will also help keep the soil cool and moist. For plants that will prefer the conditions around your hardscapes, check the plant selection guide on pages 92-97

A HEAT LOVER FOR A HOT SPOT
Flowering undaunted through a sultry Virginia summer, purple blooms of verbena overflow their raised planter. The dry heat produced by the bricks enclosing the bed is increased by a brick sidewalk beneath. But with regular watering the verbena—descended from plants native to the Americas—is thriving.

A FORMAL HARDSCAPE
Sweet alyssum, purple pansies, silver dusty-miller, and white geraniums fill the beds of this California garden in the spring. The alyssum guards the pansies from contact with heat-retaining gravel and also softens the geometry imposed by the bricks. Pink geraniums make a grand focal point in the stone planter.

and the encyclopedia at the back of this volume.

Last, look at the size and use patterns of walkways and driveways. Broad paths and lightly used hardscapes have the room to accommodate annuals that sprawl over their borders. On the other hand, narrow, heavily trafficked hardscapes—the paths to back or side doors, for instance—are best edged with upright plants that won't spill onto the walkway and get trampled. Varieties of *Tagetes* (marigold), *Begonia* (wax begonia), and *Senecio* (dusty-miller) are just a few candidates for tight situations. The list at right features plants with both neat, vertical habits and more relaxed attitudes.

Dressing Up Your Hardscapes

Unadorned hardscapes beg for the beauty and vitality annuals can bring. Grow them in beds and borders along patios, terraces, and wooden decks. If space is narrow, try planting a mixed-color variety of a bushy annual such as *Salvia splendens* (sage) or *Zinnia elegans* (common zinnia) that will grow 8 to 12 inches tall. If you have room for a wide swath of color, place low-growing, compact specimens such as *Gazania* species and *Ageratum houstonianum* (flossflower) along the edges of the hardscape and larger accent plants—*Zinnia angustifolia* (narrowleaf zinnia) or *Kochia scoparia* (burning bush), for example—behind them.

You need not restrict the beauty to the perimeter of your hardscape. For a weed-inhibiting carpet of blossoms in the midst of a sunny patio where foot traffic is light, plant *Portulaca grandiflora* (moss rose) and *Lobularia maritima* (sweet alyssum) between the pavers. Just remove any grass or weeds, and then fill the spaces with a fast-draining soil that contains 1 part gardener's sand for every 2 parts topsoil. Sow seeds in the soil or set out seedlings, and water lightly. And in your search for hardscape plants, don't overlook herbs. Many, such as basil and sweet marjoram, will like the hot, dry microclimate furnished by sunny hardscapes.

On sloping terrain alongside a flight of stone or concrete steps, plant annuals that are naturally sprawling. They will drape gracefully on the incline, whereas more-upright species will tend to lean uphill or downhill in their efforts to resist gravity. Raised flower beds with sides of brick or other stonework are also pretty when dressed with these trailing plants to soften their edges.

If a wall runs beside your driveway, patio, or walk, with a narrow strip of land separating the two hardscapes, try planting *Cobaea scandens* (cup-and-saucer vine) or *Ipomoea* species (morning glory) along the wall's base. These robust climbers should form a lavish upper growth in a short period of time. (See pages 74-75 for instructions on training vines up a wall or other structure.)

Like other hardscapes, a rock garden creates a special microclimate since its stones absorb heat and block precipitation and wind. Rocks also help maintain moisture in the soil below them by shading it from the sun—and by returning water to the

soil at night as humidity condenses on their cool surfaces and seeps into the ground. For these reasons, well-chosen plants in rock gardens often require little maintenance.

In general, the most appealing rock gardens include a combination of small, mounded plants and sprawlers that can be trained over the edges of the rocks, brightening the surfaces with their flowers and foliage. Petite flowering annuals are well suited to the task because their small roots adapt to the confined spaces between stones and to the shallow soil on rocky outcrops. Also, they are ideal for providing color and interest in the hot season, when many perennials rest.

Spreading *Phlox drummondii* (annual phlox), brightly colored *Brachycome iberidifolia* (Swan River daisy), and dwarf varieties of *Cheiranthus cheiri* (English wallflower) are just a few annuals that thrive in sunny rock gardens. If your site is partially shaded, try snapdragon-like *Collinsia heterophylla* (Chinese houses) or delicate *Exacum affine* (German violet). The lee side of a partially

shaded rock may be moist and chilly enough to let cool-loving *Iberis* species (candytuft) and *Nemophila menziesii* (baby-blue-eyes) bloom all summer long.

If you have a natural rocky area on your property, try planting it with annual wildflowers that are native to your locale or from compatible regions. Natives often self-sow, and they also blend well with the other aspects of the landscape where they evolved. Talk to your local Cooperative Extension Service or check catalogs that sell seeds and young plants specifically for your region to find the right annual wildflowers for your rock garden.

To plant rock-garden annuals, create pockets of well-draining soil, using 2 parts topsoil to 1 part gardener's sand. If the site is partially shaded and you're installing plants that prefer fertile soil, add 1 part compost or leaf mold and 1 part peat moss to the mix as well. Either sow seeds or transplant seedlings into the spaces. Once the seedlings are a few inches high, spread a mulch of shredded bark around them to keep the soil cool and moist.

SOFTENING A STONY SETTING
Heat-loving annuals in this Connecticut garden ease the transition between vertical and horizontal stone surfaces. Red-violet Petunia integrifolia surrounds the base of the center sculpture, while tall white Nicotiana alata, which self-sows from year to year, lightens and brightens throughout.

DROUGHT-TOLERANT DELIGHTS
Petite yellow Dahlberg daisies, open-faced Gaillardia aristata 'Burgundy', spiky Salvia coccinea 'Lady in Red', and orange California poppies flourish through the summer in the rocky Missouri garden at left. The limestone chunks bordering the raised bed prevent rainwater from draining through the soil too quickly.

71

An Assortment of Annual Vines

Annual vines—including tropical perennials grown as annuals—are as functional as they are decorative, performing a variety of roles in your landscape. They can camouflage unsightly fences or walls, accent pleasing architecture, or frame a view, for example, all the while adding color, texture, and height to your garden. You can also press them into service to provide shade or to form a windbreak or privacy screen, and if planted on sloping terrain as a ground cover, they'll help prevent erosion.

The Virtues of Vines

The glory of many annual vines is their spectacular or unusual flowers. The impact of fully open 'Heavenly Blue' morning glories massed on a fence is hard to beat for drama, but there are other vines with intricate and subtle blooms that have a beauty all their own. For example, *Cobaea scandens* produces white or purplish red cup-shaped blossoms with contrasting green calyxes, giving rise to its common name, cup-and-saucer vine.

There is more beauty to annual vines than their flowers, however. Certain climbers are distinguished by exceptional foliage: The leaves of *Ipomoea quamoclit* (cypress vine) split into thin, frondlike segments that flutter in the breeze; the dark purple stems of *Dolichos lablab* (hyacinth bean) are bedecked with purple-tinted heart-shaped foliage; and *Tropaeolum peregrinum* (canary creeper) produces elegant five-lobed leaves reminiscent of the fig plant.

Some vines also offer pretty fruits or useful produce. Varieties of the genus *Cucurbita,* for example, yield edible squash and interestingly shaped ornamental gourds that can be dried for decoration *(page 74).* Though they aren't typically grown as vines, other squashes, melons, and gourds can be coaxed to climb to great effect if the support is strong enough to bear their weight.

For gardeners who welcome the presence of wildlife, vines make a hospitable habitat for all sorts of creatures. Birds appreciate the protected perches they offer, as well as the banquet of insects living among the stems. Hummingbirds, bees, and butterflies are drawn to the nectar and pollen of flowering vines. And squirrels and chipmunks love dense vines for their potential as aerial highways and jungle gyms.

NASTURTIUMS ON THE MOVE
The owner of this Oregon garden planted Tropaeolum majus (common nasturtium) across the front of this border for several purposes: The plants not only provide cheerful red and orange blooms and bold round leaves, they also hide spent bulb foliage and even camouflage an unsightly tree stump.

A FRAGRANT NOCTURNAL DELIGHT
As darkness descends on a September evening in this Virginia garden, the scented white blooms of Ipomoea alba (moonflower) begin to unfurl. Cords attached to the walls of the house support the fast-growing vine, whose bright green heart-shaped leaves endow it with daytime interest as well.

Selecting and Starting Vines

When you're choosing a vining plant, you'll want to consider not only its flowers, foliage, or fruit but also its ultimate height. Depending on the species, annual vines grow from about 6 feet to upward of 30 feet per season. Make sure the species you select has the growth potential to fill the space you have in mind. If you're trying to blanket an old shed, for example, consider 15-foot morning glories or Japanese hopvines, whereas a chain-link fence will require only 6-foot nasturtium vines. The encyclopedia that begins on page 102 can help you choose a suitable species.

Follow seed-packet guidelines on spacing, and plant a sufficient number to ensure that your plants will be close enough together to form a uniform cover yet have enough root room to flourish. Always plant on the windward side of any support, so that prevailing breezes will blow the vines toward the support, not away from it.

For a long season of bloom, most annual vines should be started from seed in late winter and then transplanted outdoors in spring. Some varieties, however, including morning glories, nasturtiums, and sweet peas, should be sown in the ground outdoors after the last frost. Instructions

for growing sweet peas, which require a little extra care, are on page 37. Nearly all annual vines do best where they receive at least half a day's sun. Less than this, and the plants grow grudgingly and may not flower at all.

Vines as Screens

Once they start to grow, your annual vines will take off quickly. Many species grow 20 feet long, leaf out, and come into bud in a matter of weeks. This makes them ideal to plant as screens against sun, wind, or unattractive views. Left to their own devices, vines tend to flower mostly among top growth, leaving several feet of leggy stem exposed at their base. To force better distribution of the blooms, fasten young vine shoots horizontally along supports such as trellises and fences when they begin to grow; this encourages them to form low, lateral shoots that will flower. See pages 74-75 for illustrated instructions on training vines.

Vines can easily transform a small townhouse garden or a narrow side yard by capitalizing on vertical space. Train them up a simple rot-resistant wood post or a freestanding arch or pergola for an added overhead dimension. Vines grown on a wood-framed arbor will provide summer shade

Annual Vines

Cardiospermum balicacabum
(balloon vine)

Cobaea scandens
(cup-and-saucer vine)

Cucumis melo
(pomegranate melon)

Cucurbita ficifolia
(Malabar gourd)

Cucurbita maxima 'Turbaniformis'
(Turk's-cap squash)

Cucurbita pepo **var. ovifera**
(pumpkin gourd)

Dolichos lablab
(hyacinth bean)

Humulus japonicus
(Japanese hopvine)

Ipomoea alba
(moonflower)

Ipomoea purpurea
(common morning glory)

Lagenaria siceraria
(calabash gourd)

Mina lobata
(crimson starglory)

Phaseolus coccineus
(scarlet runner bean)

Rhodochiton atrosanguineum
(purple bell vine)

Thunbergia alata
(black-eyed Susan vine)

Tropaeolum **spp.**
(nasturtium)

Note: The abbreviation "spp." stands for the plural of "species"; where used in lists it means that many, but not all, of the species in a genus meet the criterion of the list.

Growing and Using Gourds

Gourd species, including the *Cucurbita pepo* shown here, are renowned for their useful or decorative fruits. Thanks to their bold foliage, they also make good screening plants when trained up a sturdy trellis—and even do well on overhead arbors.

Because gourds need a long season for their fruit to mature, you should start seeds indoors *(pages 12-13)* a month before your garden soil is warm enough for tender annuals. Plant the seedlings outdoors in full sun, allowing plenty of room for vigorous growth, and fertilize lightly with low-nitrogen compounds. Trimming the main stem to 10 feet will encourage the growth of fruiting lateral stems. When the tendrils beside the stems are brown, cut the fruits off, leaving a short length of stem on the fruit.

Cure gourds on screens or slats in any dry place, turning them weekly until they feel light and their skins are hard. This may take up to 4 months. Dried gourds can be varnished, painted, or even carved for decoration.

over a deck or patio, then die back after frost to admit the rays of the winter sun. To clothe an exterior wall in pretty summer garb, install a trellis of wood or metal tubing about 3 inches away from the wall and plant the climbers along its base to work their way up.

If you're placing a screen across open space, you will need to provide adequate support for the vines. Start with a sturdy, well-built frame of wood or metal and sink the legs of the structure at least 2 feet into the ground—deeper in regions of deep frost so that it won't be heaved up by the freezing and thawing of the ground. Indulge in diagonal or free-form trellis designs, square latticework, or a wide range of other shapes you can find or build. For a swag effect, suspend sturdy chains between posts and train vines up the posts and then along the chains, tying them loosely at 4-inch intervals. Always set your supports in place before you plant the vines; otherwise you may damage the roots or any new growth.

Vines with dense foliage, such as hyacinth bean,

Training Vines

Annual vines use various strategies for climbing, as shown at right, but the planting and maintenance needs for the different types are much the same. First, sow seeds or plant seedlings as close as possible to their support. If you're training them up a solid fence or wall, attach a lath trellis, wires, or other plants such as wisteria or roses that the vines can twine around. Tie the stems loosely to the support to hold them in place *(far right)*, and pinch back the most vigorous stems by several inches to encourage full, bushy growth. For best results with all flowering vines, water deeply and feed them a low-nitrogen fertilizer.

Many vines, including Ipomoea species (morning glory) (above), *climb by twining around another object. If this object has a slippery surface, wind a strip of cloth or string around it to give the vine a place to grip. Guide growing stems to the support and poke them gently around it in the direction they tend to move until they begin to wrap on their own. To cover a trellis, arrange growing tips along the framework, and tie the stems to it as they lengthen.*

are the best choice for totally concealing an unattractive wall or view. *Phaseolus coccineus* (scarlet runner bean) also makes a tough yet beautiful screen, as do common vegetable pole or runner beans, which develop thick, attractive foliage and white flowers—as well as a tasty crop. Species with sparser leaf growth, such as canary creeper, soften a wall or veil a view without covering it completely.

Other Opportunities for Vines

Just as you use annuals in mixed beds and borders to maintain color and interest all through the season, interplant annual vines among your perennial climbers. Morning glories or moonflower vines make good companions for wall-climbing ivy and Virginia creeper. In most zones, annual vines bloom from midsummer to frost; pair them with early-flowering clematis, tall or climbing roses, or spring-flowering bushes and specimen trees so the vines can take over when the other blossoms fade.

To mingle annual climbers with a shrub or tree, sow seeds or transplant seedlings beside the specimen plant and draw the growing vine stems up over their companion as the season progresses. Pull the vines off again at summer's end to display the shrub's autumn color or winter fruits. You can use the same tactic to add color accents to a natural (not clipped) evergreen hedge. Plant scarlet runner beans, cup-and-saucer vines, or *Mina lobata* (crimson starglory) beside forsythia or holly, for example, to cover the dull green summer bushes with flowers.

When planting a vine next to mature perennials, shrubs, or trees, prepare an ample hole for the vine's roots but take care not to disturb those of the other plant. The vine will have to compete with the established plant's root system for nutrients, so feed it with a commercial slow-release formula, taking care not to overfertilize and burn the tender tissue. When choosing a vine for this purpose, be sure to match the scale of the vine to its host: A fine-foliaged host like *Genista hispanica* (broom) offers congenial support to delicate *Thunbergia alata* (black-eyed Susan vine), but it takes a more assertive presence, such as hyacinth bean, to bedeck a bold-foliaged witch hazel.

A number of annual vines make splendid ground covers, particularly trailing types such as *Tropaeolum majus* (common nasturtium), *Cucurbita* species (gourds), and *Pelargonium peltatum* (ivy-leaved geranium). Planted in a dry, sunny spot, nasturtium spreads and sprawls rapidly. Ivy-leaved geranium is noted for its reliable, constant bloom and its vigor in colonizing. You can also set annual vines among established perennial ground covers to increase the area's visual interest.

Special plant features called tendrils hold vines such as Cobaea scandens (cup-and-saucer vine) (above) to their supports. Give these grabbers something slender to climb, since the coiling tendrils can't get around thick poles or slats. Tie the young stems to their supports; as soon as tendrils form the vine will hold itself on. To control the shape of the vine, arrange the stem along the path you want it to follow, and tie it in place until the tendrils secure it.

Sprawling vines such as Tropaeolum species (nasturtium) (above) don't grip their supports as they climb but simply grow long, flexible stems that scramble over neighboring objects. These sprawlers can be woven through the lattice of a trellis or the spaces in a chain-link fence or spread out to ramble across the ground, a low bush, or a rock. When using such vines as ground cover, plant them thickly and trim rampant growth as necessary to keep them in bounds.

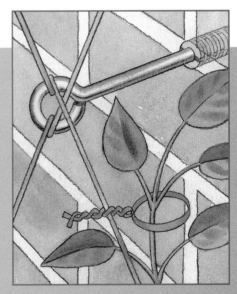

Fasten vine stems to their supports with cloth strips, twist ties from the grocery store, or special plant twine from garden centers. Begin tying the stems when they are still short so that the plant will be held from the bottom up as it grows and will not sag; tie each stem loosely to allow room for it to thicken as the plant matures. Check the ties occasionally during the season; they should be firm enough to hold the vine in place without cutting into the stems.

The Easy Beauty
of Self-Sowing Annuals

Given a hospitable home with the right combination of climate, light, and soil, many annuals will grow and reproduce entirely on their own, a self-sufficiency that makes them attractive to gardeners interested in low-maintenance plants. Many of the most enthusiastic self-sowing species, such as blanket-flower, black-eyed Susan, and annual lupine, are wildflowers that evolved naturally in North America. Other reliable self-sowers, including *Daucus carota* var. *carota* (Queen Anne's lace) and *Mirabilis jalapa* (four-o'clock), are naturalized species—plants that originated on other continents but adapted so well to conditions here that they are now as solidly established as any native.

Unlike native and naturalized species, seed-industry hybrids may be undependable reproducers. Even if they do set seed, the quality of their offspring is unpredictable. Another reason to use well-adapted species over hybrids in any garden where you want self-sowers is that they are more resistant to the diseases and pests of their region.

Selecting Your Plants

When choosing self-sowers for your garden, look for local native and naturalized species, and consider the particular growing conditions of the site. A wetland lover like *Myosotis sylvatica* (forget-me-not), for example, won't flourish on a sunny slope, even in its favored climate. Choose from nursery-propagated specimens or raise your own plants from seed; never collect plants from the wild. Regional wildflower societies, nature centers, and botanical gardens are all good sources of information about native species and where to buy them.

Restricting your plantings of annuals to native and naturalized species need not mean you have little choice. Among the many wildflowers that self-sow throughout most of the Northeast are airy *Gypsophila elegans* (baby's-breath) and upright, branching *Rudbeckia hirta* (black-eyed Susan). Naturalized species include feathery Queen Anne's lace and lancelike *Silene armeria* (sweet William catchfly). In the Southeast, where high heat and humidity prevail, both upright *Gaillardia pulchella* (Indian blanket) and trailing *Nemophila menziesii* (baby-blue-eyes) self-sow, as does the evening-blooming four-o'clock, an import from South America. Across the midwestern and plains states, *Lupinus texensis* (Texas bluebonnet) and *Centaurea cyanus* (bachelor's-button) cast blankets of azure blooms across open land.

In the arid Southwest, *Orthocarpus purpurascens* (owl's clover) forms a thick purple carpet in late winter, succeeded by the bright blooms of *Eschscholzia* species (California poppy). Mountain meadows boast several varieties of *Oenothera* (evening primrose), and black-eyed Susan can be found there too. The Pacific states host natives *Clarkia unguiculata* (clarkia) and California poppy, as well as imported self-sowers like sweet alyssum and *Papaver rhoeas* (corn poppy).

COLORFUL AND WILD
Pink, red, and white cosmos, scarlet-centered golden Indian blanket, and black-eyed Susans dance above the low-growing perennials and grasses of a midsummer Massachusetts meadow. Although these vibrantly colored annuals self-sow in less competitive situations, the splendid show is guaranteed here because the gardener reseeds them yearly.

Supervising Self-Sowers

Where annuals self-sow, they may do so to the extent that they become invasive. Maintenance chores around native and naturalized annuals focus on weeding, thinning out unwanted seedlings, and relocating plants that have seeded themselves where they aren't wanted. Since most weeds themselves are opportunistic annuals, it pays to weed early and often, especially before they set seed.

Thin out seedlings that have sown themselves in tight clumps to permit air to circulate freely. Although most annuals are fairly disease resistant,

A FRONT-YARD MEADOW GARDEN
An exuberant mix of native and naturalized annuals, including California poppy, bachelor's-button, Coreopsis tinctoria, and Linum grandiflorum 'Rubrum', greets those approaching this Santa Fe, New Mexico, home. The meadow was started from a commercial seed mix specifically blended for the Southwest.

mildew and other fast-spreading fungi can be a problem if plants are crowded together. If you want to transplant excess seedlings to another site, pull them out carefully when thinning, handling them by their leaves rather than their fragile stems. You can ease their removal by working when the soil is damp and loosening the tiny roots with a stick. Transplant the seedlings quickly to their new home to keep the roots from drying out.

When removing colonizing annuals from forbidden territory, deal with them as ruthlessly as you would weeds. If an annual regularly self-sows where you don't want it, one low-maintenance option is to replace it completely with a similar-looking but less aggressive variety. Another is to create a barrier of taller plants or fencing between the invasive plant and its target soil, thus blocking the movement of wind-borne seeds.

Establishing a Meadow

A sunny area at the back or side of a large property is an ideal location for the most carefree of gardens: the meadow. In a new meadow, self-sowing annuals can provide color and interest before perennials and grasses—the other constituents of these gardens—mature. To plant in either spring or fall, clear the soil of all vegetation and prepare it for new plantings as you would any other garden. Then simply sow seed by hand, using a seed mix that is 50 percent grasses and the rest a combination of annual and perennial flowers; many mixes are available from regional catalogs. Combine the seeds with an equal volume of gardener's sand to avoid clumping, and sprinkle the mix in furrows 2 inches deep and 18 inches apart. Rake a quarter inch of soil over the seeds and tamp it down. In spring, water lightly every day, but for fall plantings simply leave the seeds in nature's hands.

Even after a meadow has become well established, adding new annuals increases both the amount and the intensity of color in the landscape as no other plants can. To plant new species in an existing meadow, clear vegetation, sod, and roots from a patch about 1 foot square, and loosen the soil to a depth of 1 foot. Plant a hardened-off seedling in the space, and mulch the bare soil around it with salt hay or shredded bark to a depth of 3 inches. Cluster several such foot-square plugs for the most natural look. You can also sow seeds in similar 1-foot patches in early spring or autumn. Although your annuals should return year after year, you may have to replant occasionally where the other plantings are especially dense, since competition can crowd them out.

Buying Wildflower Seed Mixtures

Attractively packaged seed mixtures promise an easy solution to the question of which wildflowers to plant. To obtain the best results with these blends, experts offer gardeners the following advice:

Learn some of the wildflowers that grow in your area so you'll be a knowledgeable shopper. Spiky purple owl's clover *(above),* for instance, is a familiar sight in the Southwest, which makes it a good candidate for mixtures designed for that region. Seed mixtures developed for your immediate locale will produce optimal results; next best are those with a slightly wider purview, labeled, for example, "Pacific U.S." Regional catalogs are one of the best sources for these seed mixes, although a good nursery or garden center may carry one or more.

Buy only mixes that list their contents in detail, including the species names; the percentages of grass, perennial, and annual seed; and the amount of vermiculite filler, if any. Check with local plant organizations or your Cooperative Extension Service to find out what species can be invasive in your area, and don't buy packages that include them. Also, flower-carpet products—seeds embedded in fabric to lay on the soil—are not recommended because they often contain undesirable seed varieties with poor germination rates.

Growing Annuals in Containers

Thanks to their shallow roots, vigorous growth, and bounteous bloom, annuals are perfect for planting in containers. They are an inexpensive way to add a dash of fast color to a dull spot, and indeed, most annuals seem to take on a new character when they're planted in an attractive pot or box and situated where their beauty can be enjoyed up close.

Annuals in containers are extremely versatile. In addition to accenting any corner of your outdoor living space, they are the ideal solution when such space is limited. And since they aren't fixed in the earth, they can live indoors at either end of the gardening season or be moved in temporarily during bad weather to keep them healthy and prolong their display.

Your annuals will thrive in almost any type of container as long as it has a hole at the bottom for drainage. Experienced container gardeners prefer large, deep containers for annuals because they al-low a more diverse planting and don't need to be watered as often.

When choosing your containers, take into consideration where they'll be spending most of their time. Plastic pots hold moisture better than clay ones and, if placed in shadier spots, should be monitored to make sure the soil doesn't stay too wet. Pots and boxes made of clay, which is porous, provide good air circulation and drainage—and for this very reason need to be watered frequently so that the soil doesn't dry out. Use them anywhere, but check the soil daily if they receive full sun. Wooden tubs provide superior protection from both heat and cold and will do well anywhere; they'll need to be replaced eventually, though, because they rot. And if you want to use a copper pot, plant your annuals in another container placed inside the copper one, since most plants find the metal poisonous.

Single containers can add sparkle to any num-

A SHOWCASE ON THE STAIRS
A large clay pot of pink Swan River daisies anchors the many fragrant container plants lining these porch steps in Washington State. The casual yet artful display stars an intriguing array of geraniums—including the cultivars 'Persian Queen', with chartreuse foliage and magenta flowers, 'Wilhelm Langguth', with variegated leaves, and 'Lady Plymouth', a scented variety. The grouping is accented by the white-throated blue flowers of Nolana and the tiny purple blossoms of heliotrope.

A MIX OF HEIGHTS
AND TEXTURES
*Spikes of Pennisetum
setaceum (fountain
grass) arch over low-
growing Setcreasea
pallida (purple-heart)
in this late-summer
container planting in
Maryland (left). A near-
by pot of herbs helps
brighten the gray deck.*

ber of spots around your property. A large, elegant
pot on your front step or a rustic one at the mail-
box will both brighten and distinguish your home.
Even a container placed among your bed or border plantings will add interest and dimension.

A container that isn't itself impressive can be
brought to life with plantings of trailing annuals,
whose flowers and leaves will cover the sides.
Sweet alyssum, baby-blue-eyes, or portulaca, with
their draping foliage, will hide a homely concrete
block, for instance. On the other hand, a pretty pot
might be filled exclusively with an upright variety
to highlight the container as well as its occupants.

Some of the most beautiful arrangements combine different annuals with a variety of habits,
colors, and interest. Mix various flowering
plants—some trailing and some tall and spiked—
with light- and dark-colored foliage such as pale
dusty-miller and purple-toned basil in sunny
spots or multihued coleus and polka-dot plants in
partial shade. Annual grasses, including red or
purple *Pennisetum* (fountain grass), provide a
nice change from commoner flowers and are especially suitable in contemporary settings. Even a
vegetable or two, like a purple eggplant or a red
pepper, can add drama near summer's end.

When choosing your plants, match their size at
maturity with the scale of the pot. An upright plant
shouldn't rise more than about one and a half to

two times the height of the container, or the overall look will be top-heavy. Also, consider your annuals' growth habits: Those that are especially dense and bushy, such as wax begonias and impatiens, are best grown by themselves rather than with other species if your container is small.

For visual impact in large spaces, arrange several containers together. Try juxtaposing contrasting flower colors, placing a tub of golden *Calendula officinalis* (pot marigold) next to deep blue *Centaurea cyanus* (bachelor's-button), for example. Or simply cluster pots blooming with assorted varieties of marigolds or geraniums. Usually, three or four medium-sized containers look better than a large tub surrounded by small pots.

Hanging Baskets

Your container annuals need not be confined to the floor. In fact, nothing shows off a trailing or spreading annual like a basket suspended from above eye level. Hanging plants do need a little more care than those in other containers. Because they are meant to be seen from the bottom as well

as the top, they require more grooming to stay attractive. And because hanging plants are exposed to air on all sides, they dry out faster than other plants. In particular, moss-lined wire baskets *(pages 82-83),* which have no solid sides to hold moisture, need a great deal of water and should be placed in a spot out of the harsh sun.

Planting and Caring for Container Plants

Before you plant your annuals in a container, decide on the arrangement if you're using an array of varieties. The tallest plants should go in the center or the back, the trailers around the rim, and the medium-sized bushy and upright annuals in between. Be sure the plants you've chosen all prefer similar light and soil conditions.

Your pot should be at least 8 inches deep. Place a layer of rocks, gravel, or pottery shards in the bottom to keep the drainage holes clear of soil. Then fill the container to within 2 inches of the top with a potting-soil mix from a gardening center or nursery or with a homemade version. A soil

A CORNER DISPLAY
Annuals and perennials combined create an impression of movement in this Portland, Oregon, container garden. Annuals include yellow Bidens, tall yellow Verbascum, silvery-green-leaved Helichrysum petiolare, and red and fuchsia cosmos. Perennials Astrantia major, with white flowers, and spiky Phormium tenax complete the display.

Tuberous Begonias

Tuberous begonias *(Begonia* x *tuberhybrida)* have an upright or a trailing habit, simple or compound blooms, and come in every color but blue. And although many gardeners treat them as potted annuals, these summer favorites are actually tender bulbs.

Start the tubers indoors in flats several weeks before the last frost date. When the shoots are 3 inches tall, move them to containers filled with a commercial potting-soil mix. Space three or four tubers concave side up in the container, 2 to 3 inches apart, with the top of the tuber at the soil line. For a hanging basket, choose a cascading form. Upright begonias, like the bright red varieties at left, are better suited to pots on the ground.

Tuberous begonias prefer partial to full shade and cool and moist, but not soggy, soil. Keep them well fertilized and watered throughout the season for maximum bloom.

Making a Moss-Lined Basket

A moss-lined hanging basket—fashioned of a simple wire frame and lined with sphagnum moss, both purchased from a garden center—will display lush foliage and colorful blossoms from all sides. Water the container every day to maintain a fresh and vibrant show.

1. Soak the moss in water to make it pliable; squeeze out the excess moisture. Place it in a basket frame (above) and press it into an even 1-inch layer, adding or removing moss as necessary.

2. Cover up any wire showing on the outside of the basket by pressing additional moss around it (above, left). Next, attach the wire hanger, hang the basket, and trim any dangling moss with scissors to achieve a neat but natural appearance (above). In a separate bucket, mix enough commercial potting-soil mix to fill the basket, adding a few handfuls of peat moss to retain moisture. Cover the bottom of the basket with some of the soil mixture.

A BASKET OF BLOSSOMS
Hanging under a leafy arbor, a moss-lined wire basket overflows with hot pink Impatiens wallerana and dangling blooms of tender perennial fuchsia. Both plants prefer the partial shade and humid atmosphere of their Seattle home.

composed of equal parts topsoil, compost, and vermiculite will do nicely.

Plant healthy young annuals that you've purchased or grown from seed. Remove the plants from their cell packs or pots, and gently spread apart the bottom of the rootball. Using a small trowel, dig a hole slightly bigger than the roots and position the annual, distributing its roots evenly in the space. Fill the hole with soil, pressing it firmly in place. Group plants closer together than you would in an outdoor garden. Water the

container, and cover the soil with a bark mulch or sphagnum moss to help hold in moisture.

Sun, wind, and drought can be containers' mortal enemies because they dry them out quickly. Infrequent watering can kill your potted plants outright, and irregular watering will stress them, leaving them vulnerable to disease and insect infestations. To protect outdoor container plants that dry out quickly, water them daily—more often during the height of summer—and when possible move them to sheltered locations during very hot weather. When watering, wet the soil thoroughly and avoid wetting the leaves, which can invite disease.

Although frequent watering is essential, it tends to leach nutrients out of the soil. Keep your plants supplied with vital minerals by feeding them regularly with a commercial liquid fertilizer that contains an equal balance of potassium, phosphorus, and nitrogen. Too much nitrogen will encourage leafy growth at the expense of blooms. If you water several times a week, use the fertilizer at half strength and apply it every 2 weeks or so.

3. Use a pencil to poke a hole through the moss near the bottom of the basket. *Remove a seedling from its cell pack and insert it through the hole (below), firming the moss around it on the outside. Repeat to make a row around the basket, then cover the roots with soil. Continue planting in rows to within 2 inches of the top of the basket. Then plant a few seedlings at the top of the basket (bottom), and water.*

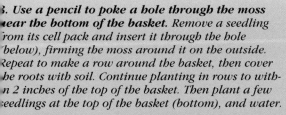

TIPS FROM THE PROS

Waking Up Window Boxes

A window box of annuals pleases the eye from both inside and outside the house. Geraniums are a favorite for window boxes, but you may want to experiment with combinations of unusual varieties of flowers and foliage to enliven a picture that may be growing overly familiar.

In attaching boxes to your windows, keep in mind that they are heavy. Mount them securely with bolts or brackets, and check them yearly to make sure the hardware hasn't weakened by rusting. Also note that if your boxes hang inside the drip line of the house, they may not get much rainfall. This, along with drying winds and the warmth from the house, means they will need diligent watering, although a mulch of shredded bark will help retain some moisture. On the plus side, the extra heat allows early planting in spring and extends the fall blooming season.

A HANDSOME HANGING GARDEN
A wealth of rosy pink petunias flanks this container garden, which hangs from a fence in a seaside Delaware town. Planted in a commercially available "hay basket," the garden also features white African daisies, trailing yellow Bidens, and blue Salvia farinacea 'Victoria'.

Answers to Common Questions

I've always put in beds of annuals that would blossom into a riot of flower color, but now I'd like to try for more variety. Can you suggest some annuals with outstanding foliage or other interesting features besides just flowers?

Many annuals produce unique and colorful leaves. Try *Amaranthus tricolor* (Joseph's-coat), *Euphorbia marginata* (snow-on-the-mountain), *Perilla frutescens* (beefsteak plant), *Ricinus communis* (castor bean), *Silybum marianum* (blessed thistle), and *Zea mays* var. *japonica* (ornamental corn). You can also add variety to your annual beds with plants that grow interesting seedpods. Among the best are *Cleome hasslerana* (spider flower), *Coix lacryma-jobi* (Job's-tears), *Cynara cardunculus* (cardoon), *Diplocyclos palmatus* (marble vine), *Lagenaria siceraria* (calabash gourd), *Lagurus ovatus* (hare's-tail grass), *Papaver rhoeas* 'Hungarian Blue' (corn poppy), *Proboscidea louisianica* (common devil's-claw), and *Scabiosa stellata* 'Drumstick' (paper moon).

One of my great joys is attracting wildlife to my garden. What are the most alluring annuals for butterflies and hummingbirds? Do any annuals produce seed that birds can feed on over the winter?

Of the long list of annuals on the butterfly hit parade, the best are *Cosmos bipinnatus* (garden cosmos), *Gaillardia pulchella* (Indian blanket), *Helianthus* (sunflower), *Heliotropium arborescens* (cherry pie), *Hesperis matronalis* (dame's rocket), *Limonium sinuatum* (notchleaf statice), *Rudbeckia hirta* (black-eyed Susan), *Tithonia rotundifolia* (Mexican sunflower), *Verbena* (vervain), and *Zinnia elegans* (common zinnia). Hummingbirds will flock to *Alcea rosea* (hollyhock), *Antirrhinum majus* (common snapdragon), *Dianthus barbatus* (sweet William), *Digitalis purpurea* (common foxglove), *Ipomopsis aggregata* (scarlet gilia), and *Salvia* (sage). For seed heads that will feed a variety of birds during the cold months, plant *Amaranthus* (amaranth), *Coreopsis* (tickseed), *Cosmos, Gomphrena, Helianthus annuus* (common sunflower), *Rudbeckia hirta,* and *Verbena bonariensis* (Brazilian verbena).

We own a seaside cabin where we spend our summers, and I'd like to put several beds of annuals around it. What plants will do best in the conditions found at the beach?

Even in this trying environment of wind and salt-laden air, a fairly large variety of annuals will succeed. You can choose with confidence from among *Ageratum houstonianum* (flossflower), *Antirrhinum majus* (common snapdragon), *Calendula officinalis* (pot marigold), *Dimorphotheca* (Cape marigold), *Lavatera trimestris* (tree mallow), *Lobelia erinus* (edging lobelia), *Lobularia maritima* (sweet alyssum), *Pelargonium* (geranium), *Phlox drummondii* (annual phlox), *Portulaca grandiflora* (moss rose), *Salvia argentea* (silver sage), *Senecio cineraria* (dusty-miller), *Tagetes patula* (French marigold), and *Verbena* (vervain).

I've seen Canterbury bells (Campanula medium) listed as annual, perennial, and biennial. Which is it?

The genus *Campanula* (bellflower), of which Canterbury bells is a member, is a vast grouping of approximately 300 species of annuals, biennials, and perennials that are used in gardens all over the world. *Campanula medium* is a true biennial.

I'm just crazy about true blue flowers. Are there any true blue annuals?

Although true blue flowers are relatively scarce, a fair number of blue annuals are available, including *Eustoma grandiflorum* 'Blue Lisa', a dwarf form of prairie gentian with brilliant blue bells; *Ipomoea purpurea* 'Heavenly Blue' (common morning glory); *Myosotis sylvatica* (forget-me-not); *Nemophila menziesii* (baby-blue-eyes); *Nigella damascena* 'Miss Jekyll' (love-in-a-mist); *Phacelia campanularia* (California bluebell); and *Salvia patens* (gentian sage), a tender perennial.

Because we almost never can find time to tend our garden except for a bit on weekends, we're looking for flowers that can get along pretty well on their own. Are there any annuals that will bloom nicely from spring to frost without assistance?

Once you make sure of getting them off to a good start in well-prepared soil, you can expect self-sufficient performance from *Begonia* x *semperflorens-cultorum* (wax begonia), *Catharanthus roseus* (Madagascar periwinkle), *Heliotropium arborescens* (cherry pie), *Pentas lanceolata* (Egyptian starcluster), *Petunia* x *hybrida* (common garden petunia), and *Salvia splendens* (scarlet sage).

One side of our patio is quite open to view from several neighbors' yards, and we'd like more privacy. The patio is screened off with shrubs on the other open sides, but I was wondering if there are any annuals that could function as screening?

Annual vines such as *Humulus japonicus* (Japanese hopvine) and *Lagenaria siceraria* (calabash gourd) can be grown on 2-by-3-inch wood poles set in the ground and strung with durable twine or plastic fishline for plant supports. These plants, which can be grown in pots that are set on the edge of the patio, have dense enough foliage to block the view from outside.

GROWING CONDITIONS

There's a patch of ground out near my property line facing the road where the soil is rather infertile, dry, and sandy. I'd like to dress up the area a bit, but without putting in a lot of effort. Are there any annuals that would work in such soil?

Happily, a wide variety of annuals will do well in these unpromising conditions. You can choose from *Arctotis* (African daisy), *Calendula officinalis* (pot marigold), *Callistephus chinensis* (China aster), *Clarkia amoena* (farewell-to-spring), *Coreopsis tinctoria* (tickseed), *Dyssodia tenuiloba* (Dahlberg daisy), *Euphorbia marginata* (snow-on-the-mountain), *Gaillardia pulchella* (Indian blanket), *Kochia scoparia* (burning bush, summer cypress), *Lobularia maritima* (sweet alyssum), *Phlox drummondii* (annual phlox), *Portulaca grandiflora* (moss rose), *Tithonia rotundifolia* (Mexican sunflower), and *Verbena* x *hybrida* (vervain).

I have a little rill running through a corner of my property that I can see from my kitchen window, and I would like to brighten up its banks with annuals. Can you recommend some that will adapt to damp sites?

The versatile clan of annuals includes species that will be right at home in very boggy conditions, including *Limnanthes douglasii* (meadow foam), *Mimulus* x *hybridus* (monkey flower), and *Myosotis sylvatica* (forget-me-not). In soil that is not boggy but is generally moist, you can grow *Caladium* x *hortulanum* (fancy-leaved caladium), *Catharanthus roseus* (Madagascar periwinkle), *Cleome hasslerana* (spider flower), *Coleus* x *hybridus* (coleus), *Exacum affine* (Persian violet), *Impatiens, Torenia fournieri* (bluewings), and *Viola* x *wittrockiana* (garden pansy).

My favorite kind of foundation planting is an annual border, but I know from soil testing that the foundation of my house leaches limestone into the soil, keeping it on the alkaline side of neutral. What annuals are best for alkaline soil?

Within reasonable limits—say, a pH of no more than 8—you can confidently expect the following annuals to adapt comfortably to the soil around your foundation: *Calendula officinalis* (pot marigold), *Catharanthus roseus* (Madagascar periwinkle), *Dianthus barbatus* (sweet William), *Gaillardia pulchella* (Indian blanket), *Gypsophila elegans* (baby's-breath), *Iberis umbellata* (globe candytuft), *Lathyrus odoratus* (sweet pea), *Papaver rhoeas* (corn poppy), *Pelargonium* (geranium), *Phlox drummondii* (annual phlox), *Scabiosa atropurpurea* (pincushion flower), *Senecio cineraria* (dusty-miller), *Tropaeolum majus* (garden nasturtium), *Verbena* x *hybrida* (vervain), and *Zinnia elegans* (common zinnia).

CULTIVATION

I buy annuals at the home store and they look great, but when I plant them, they soon poop out. Am I doing something wrong?

To entice buyers, home centers and roadside stands often display lushly blooming annuals—particularly tender annuals—several weeks before the ground is warm enough to accommodate them. Many of these plants have been forced into early bloom and may also have had extra applications of chemical fertilizers. Plants that have been raised like this are liable to suffer severe transplant shock when set out in the garden, especially if it's done too early in the season. To avoid this kind of frustration, buy plants that are not yet in full bloom and safeguard them under cover or in a cold frame until it is safe to set them out.

What are good dimensions for an annual bed or border?

The answer for borders differs somewhat from that for beds, but in either case you should be careful not to bite off more than you can chew. When planning a border—a planting that backs up to a fence, wall, hedge, or other vertical element—whether of annuals or any other kind of plant, keep it no more than 4 to 5 feet deep so you can reach in to tend to the flowers at the rear. If, however, you build a narrow maintenance path at the back of the border, you can make it twice as deep—the same depth as an island bed—since you'll be able to reach into it from all sides.

What is hardening off, and why is it necessary?

Hardening off is a process of gradually introducing new plants to the rigors of outdoor life by exposing them to it, but in a semiprotected environment such as a cold frame or a temporary bed out of direct sun and wind. Young seedlings that were started indoors while chill winds blew outside have had a pampered life, shielded from the real world. As a result, the surface cells of the leaves and stems are tender and vulnerable to damage. To allow time for these cells to toughen up, the young plants need some protection for the first 4 or 5 days in the garden.

For annuals that I start from seed indoors in early spring, how can I tell when the seedlings are ready for transplanting?

Annuals started indoors usually need to be transplanted twice. The first time is after the seedlings have developed their first set of true leaves *(pages 12-13)*. At this point they are transplanted from seed trays into individual containers. The second transplant occurs when the plants are ready to be set in the ground, which can be any time from 6 to 12 weeks after germination. Hang onto your seed packets for exact information about the best times for putting various species into the garden. If your seedlings don't seem bushy enough or their stems don't stand firmly upright, you may want to give them an extra week or two to become better established before setting them out. Be sure to harden them off before fully exposing them to the elements.

What's the best way to store annual seeds for use in future years? How long will they stay viable if stored properly?

Store seeds in a tightly closed glass jar in the refrigerator—not in the freezer. If that's not practical, find a cool and dry place away from direct sunlight. Most seeds will still grow after 2 or even more years of storage. By contrast, the germination rate for seeds left in the open air will drop from 80 or 90 percent to 20 percent or less. Don't forget to mark the date you purchased each packet of seeds.

Annual bedding plants are fairly inexpensive. Does it make economic sense to start them from seed?

The answer depends on how large an annual garden you are planning and whether or not your interests lie in growing unusual and heirloom varieties. It's true that bedding plants are relatively inexpensive, and for the gardener who has little time to spend on getting a garden started or who got a late start, they make an excellent choice. But for the cost of a single cell pack of four or six plants, you could buy a packet of seeds that will give you 50 or more plants, certainly an important consideration if you are laying out large beds. And if you plan on putting in rare or heirloom annuals, your only option will be to grow them from seed purchased through catalogs and seed exchanges, as garden centers tend to stock only the most popular and easily available plants.

What are the best methods for propping up weak-stemmed annuals?

There are three good approaches to supporting annuals too weak to stay upright on their own. The first is called pea-staking, an English method in which bushy branches with a fairly dense growth of twigs are pruned from trees and set on the ground where seedlings have been planted; the young plants grow up through the twigs and are supported by them. The second is called a cat's cradle; it consists of putting in four short corner stakes and winding green garden twine across and between them. Finally, you can use the bamboo or reed stakes used to support single-stemmed plants like tall dahlias or zinnias.

DESIGN

If I want to plant an annual bed of mixed colors, should I buy mixed-color seed packets or should I buy separate colors and mix the plants myself?

The different colors in packets of premixed seeds are not actually counted out, so once you sow them you can never really be sure what quantities of what colors will come up in your garden. For the most reliable effect, buy good separate colors and mix them according to your own plan.

I understand that there are certain "rules" about how various colors either work well together or clash. How important are these?

The "rules"—generally accepted design principles, in actuality—are only as important as you make them. But some are pretty hard to ignore without creating some jarring vistas. Probably the most broadly useful rule is to make sure adjacent flowers have similar color intensity. If you plant a pale pink next to a vivid orange, the latter will overwhelm the former. For this reason, it's best to group pastel colors together. Another rule is that neither of those two colors will work well against a red brick wall. Yet another practical rule is to keep the use of very dark colors to a minimum, using them only in an accent role, because, from a distance, their colors fade away.

Troubleshooting Guide

Although annuals and biennials seldom suffer serious damage from pests and diseases, problems can arise in even the best-tended garden. It's always better to catch an infestation or infection early, so make it a habit to inspect your plants regularly for warning signs. Remember that lack of nutrients, improper pH levels, and other environmental conditions can cause symptoms like those typical of some diseases. If wilting or yellowing appears on neighboring plants, the source is probably environmental; pest and disease damage is usually more random.

This guide will help you solve the occasional pest and disease problems you may encounter. In general, healthy soil, good drainage, and sufficient air circulation will help prevent infection, and the many beneficial insects that feed on pests should be encouraged. Natural solutions are best, but if you must use chemicals, treat only the affected plant, and try to use insecticidal soaps and botanical insecticides. These products are the least disruptive to beneficial insects and will not destroy the soil balance. If these solutions fail, remove and discard the infected plants.

PESTS

PROBLEM: Leaves curl, are distorted in shape, and may have a black, sooty appearance. A clear, sticky substance often appears on stems and leaves. Buds and flowers are deformed, new growth is stunted, and leaves and flowers may drop.

CAUSE: Aphids are pear shaped, semitransparent, wingless sucking insects about ⅛ inch long and may be green, yellow, red, pink, black, or gray. They suck sap and through feeding may spread viral diseases. Infestations are worst in spring and early summer, when the pests cluster on tender new shoots, the undersides of leaves, and around flower buds. Aphids secrete a sticky substance called honeydew, which fosters the growth of a black fungus called sooty mold.

SOLUTION: Spray plants frequently with a steady stream of water from a garden hose to knock aphids off plants and discourage them from returning. In severe cases, spray with insecticidal soap or kitchen cleanser. As a last resort, remove the plant from the garden and throw it away. Ladybugs, green lacewings, gall midges, and syrphid-fly larvae prey on aphids and may be introduced into the garden.
SUSCEPTIBLE PLANTS: VIRTUALLY ALL, PARTICULARLY THOSE WITH YOUNG OR TENDER FOLIAGE.

PROBLEM: Small, round or irregularly shaped holes are eaten into leaves, leaf edges, and flowers. Leaves may be reduced to skeletons with only veins remaining.

CAUSE: Japanese beetles, iridescent blue-green with bronze wing covers, are the most destructive of a large family of hard-shelled chewing insects ranging in size from ¼ to ¾ inch long. Other genera include flea beetles (1/10 inch long, black, brown, or bronze) and cucumber beetles (up to ½ inch long, yellowish green with black spots or stripes). Japanese and other adult beetles are voracious in the summer. Beetle larvae feed on roots of plants and are present from midsummer through the following spring, when they emerge as adults.

SOLUTION: Handpick, shake, or jar small colonies out of foliage, placing them in a container filled with soapy water. Japanese beetles can be caught in baited traps. Place traps downwind and at least 25 feet away from susceptible plants so as not to attract more beetles to the garden. Larval stages can be controlled with beneficial nematodes and milky spore disease, which can be applied to the whole garden. Neem may be used as a repellent; spray with pyrethrum. Parasitic wasps and tachinid flies may be introduced.
SUSCEPTIBLE PLANTS: MANY ANNUALS, INCLUDING BALSAM, CHINA ASTER, COLEUS, NICOTIANA, PHLOX, AND ZINNIA.

PROBLEM: Stems of emerging seedlings are cut off near the ground, and seedlings may be completely eaten. Leaves of older plants show ragged edges and chewed holes.

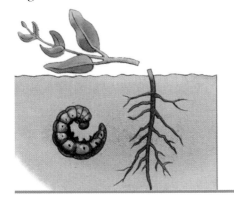

CAUSE: Cutworms, the larvae of various moths, are fat, hairless, and a soft gray-brown in color. These 1- to 2-inch-long night feeders do the most damage during the early growing season in late spring. In the daytime, they curl up into a C-shape, remaining under plant debris or just below the soil surface.

SOLUTION: Place barriers called cutworm collars around the base of a plant. Force cutworms to the surface of the soil either by flooding the area or by turning the soil in late summer, fall, or spring. Once exposed, cutworms can be hand-picked and destroyed. Introduce beneficial nematodes or preying insects such as parasitic braconid wasps and tachinid flies. Spread diatomaceous earth (DE), crushed eggshells, wood ashes, or oak-leaf mulch around plants to discourage cutworms. Keep the garden weeded and free of debris.
SUSCEPTIBLE PLANTS: VIRTUALLY ALL, PARTICULARLY TENDER NEW SEEDLINGS.

PROBLEM: Ragged holes appear on leaves, especially those near the ground. New leaves and entire young seedlings may disappear. Telltale shiny silver streaks appear on leaves and garden paths.

CAUSE: Slugs or snails hide during the day and feed on low-hanging leaves at night or on overcast or rainy days. They prefer damp soil in a shady location and are most damaging in summer, especially in wet regions or during rainy years.

SOLUTION: Keep garden clean to minimize hiding places. Handpick slugs and snails or trap them by placing saucers of beer level with the soil surface near plants. Slugs will also collect under inverted grapefruit halves or melon rinds. Because slugs and snails find it difficult to crawl over rough surfaces, barrier strips of copper, wood ashes, coarse sand, cinders, or diatomaceous earth (DE) placed around plants will deter them. Introduce or encourage rove beetles, which prey on slugs. Turning the soil in spring often destroys dormant slugs and eggs.
SUSCEPTIBLE PLANTS: VIRTUALLY ALL SEEDLINGS AS WELL AS FORGET-ME-NOT, GERANIUM, HIBISCUS, MARIGOLD, NICO-TIANA, PANSY, AND PETUNIA.

PROBLEM: Leaves become stippled and flecked, then discolor, curl, and wither. Spiderlike webbing may appear, particularly on growing tips and on the undersides of leaves.

CAUSE: Mites are pinhead-sized sucking pests that can be reddish, pale green, or yellow. A major problem in hot, dry weather, several generations of mites may occur in a single season. Eggs, and the adults of some species, overwinter in sod and bark, and on weeds and plants that retain foliage.

SOLUTION: Keep plants watered and mulched, especially during hot, dry periods. Regularly spray the undersides of leaves, where mites feed and lay eggs, with a strong stream of water or a diluted insecticidal soap solution, which controls nymphs and adults but not the eggs. Remove and destroy heavily infested leaves, stems, or the entire plant. Introduce predators such as ladybugs and green lacewing larvae. Neem or pyrethrum can also be applied.
SUSCEPTIBLE PLANTS: VIRTUALLY ALL.

PROBLEM: Leaves turn yellow, and plants are stunted. When plants are shaken, a white cloud appears.

CAUSE: Whiteflies, sucking insects 1/16 inch long that look like tiny white moths, generally collect on the undersides of young leaves. Seedlings are especially susceptible. Found year round in warmer climates but only in summer in colder climates, they like warm, still air. Whiteflies are often brought home with greenhouse-raised plants and can carry viruses. They secrete honeydew, a substance that promotes sooty mold.

SOLUTION: Carefully inspect plants, especially the undersides of leaves, before purchasing. Spray plants frequently with a steady stream of water from a garden hose to knock whiteflies off plants and discourage them from returning. Set yellow sticky traps near infected plants. Introduce lacewings and parasitic wasps; apply pyrethrum. Keep the garden well weeded. In severe cases, spray with insecticidal soap or remove the plant from the garden and throw it away. *SUSCEPTIBLE PLANTS: VIRTUALLY ALL, PARTICULARLY CALENDULA AND COLEUS.*

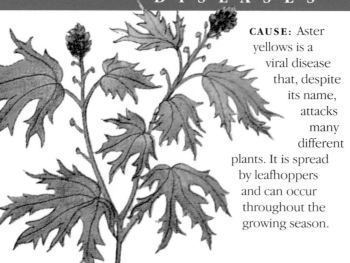

PROBLEM: A slight yellowing along leaf veins occurs on young plants. As the disease progresses, the entire plant yellows. Flowers are small and have a yellow-green color. New root, flower, and leaf growth is distorted, and leaves are stunted. Plants wilt and die.

CAUSE: Aster yellows is a viral disease that, despite its name, attacks many different plants. It is spread by leafhoppers and can occur throughout the growing season.

SOLUTION: Remove and destroy infected plants. Do not plant annuals, especially China asters, in the same spot each year. Keep garden clean; remove perennial weeds in which leafhopper eggs often overwinter. Sterilize heavily infested soil through a process known as solarization: Fix a sheet of clear plastic over the soil and leave it in place 1 to 2 months. *SUSCEPTIBLE PLANTS: PRIMARILY ASTER. COSMOS, GLOBE AMARANTH, KOCHIA, MARIGOLD, PINCUSHION FLOWER, SALPIGLOSSIS, AND ZINNIA ARE ALSO VULNERABLE.*

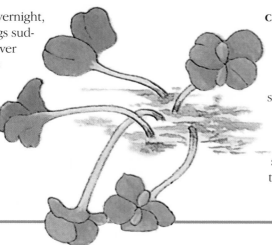

PROBLEM: Overnight, young seedlings suddenly topple over and die. Stems are rotted through at the soil line.

CAUSE: Damping-off is a disease caused by several soil fungi that infect seeds and the roots of seedlings at ground level. The problem often occurs in wet, poorly drained soil with a high nitrogen content.

SOLUTION: Use fresh or treated seeds. Plant in a sterile medium topped with a thin layer of sand or perlite to keep seedlings dry at the stem line. Plants in containers are more susceptible than those growing outdoors. Give them well-drained soil with plenty of light; avoid overcrowding. Do not overwater seed flats or seedbeds. *SUSCEPTIBLE PLANTS: VIRTUALLY ALL SEEDLINGS, PARTICULARLY PHLOX AND SWEET ALYSSUM.*

PROBLEM: Leaves develop small yellow spots that gradually turn brown. Spots are frequently surrounded by a ring of yellow or brownish black tissue and often join to produce large, irregular blotches. The entire leaf may turn yellow, wilt, and drop. Extensive defoliation can occur, weakening the plant. The problem usually starts on lower leaves and moves upward.

CAUSE: Leaf-spot diseases, caused by various fungi, bacteria, and nematodes, are spread by wind and splashing water. Most prevalent from summer into fall, these pathogens thrive when humidity and rainfall are high.

SOLUTION: Remove and destroy infected leaves as they appear; do not leave infected material in the garden over the winter. Water only in the morning. Thin plants out to increase air circulation. Sulfur dust can help control the disease.
SUSCEPTIBLE PLANTS: VIRTUALLY ALL, PARTICULARLY CALENDULA, CELOSIA, CHRYSANTHEMUM, GERANIUM, HELIOTROPE, LOBELIA, MONKEY FLOWER, AND ZINNIA.

PROBLEM: White or pale gray powdery growth appears on upper leaves and is followed by leaf distortion, yellowing, withering, and leaf drop. The powdery growth may also be seen on stems, buds, and shoots.

CAUSE: Powdery mildew, a fungal disease, is especially noticeable in late summer and early fall when cool, humid nights follow warm days. Unlike most fungal diseases, powdery mildew does not spread readily under wet conditions. More unsightly than harmful, it rarely kills the plant.

SOLUTION: Grow mildew-resistant varieties. Place susceptible plants in areas with good air circulation, mist frequently, and spray with baking-soda solution or a fungicide.
SUSCEPTIBLE PLANTS: ANNUAL PHLOX, BELLFLOWER, FUCHSIA, MONKEY FLOWER, SPIDER FLOWER, SWEET PEA, VERBENA, AND ZINNIA.

PROBLEM: Entire plant becomes yellow, wilts, fails to grow, and eventually dies. Symptoms usually appear first on the lower and outer plant parts. A cut across the stem near the base reveals dark streaks or other discoloration on the tissue inside.

CAUSE: Vascular wilt, caused by either fusarium or verticillium fungi in the soil, displays similar symptoms. Fusarium wilt is more prevalent in hot weather, and verticillium wilt in cool weather. In both diseases, the fungus responsible forms strands that penetrate the roots and stems and eventually clog the water-conducting vessels. Both fungi are long-lived, remaining in the soil for years after the host plant has died.

SOLUTION: Destroy infected plants; substitute resistant varieties. Wash hands and disinfect tools. Don't site susceptible plants in an area that has been infected previously. Solarize the soil by fixing a sheet of clear plastic over the ground and leaving it in place 1 to 2 months.
SUSCEPTIBLE PLANTS: CAPE MARIGOLD, CHINA ASTER, CHRYSANTHEMUM, COLEUS, DAHLIA, IMPATIENS, LOBELIA, MARIGOLD, NASTURTIUM, AND PANSY.

Plant Selection Guide

Organized by flower or foliage color, this chart provides information needed to select species and varieties that will thrive in the particular conditions of your garden. For additional information on each plant, refer to the encyclopedia that begins on page 102.

WHITE

	PLANT TYPE			SOIL			LIGHT			HEIGHT				BLOOM SEASON				NOTED FOR				SPECIAL USES			TOLERATES		
	ANNUAL	BIENNIAL	TENDER PERENNIAL	RICH, LOAMY	AVERAGE	POOR	FULL SUN	PARTIAL SHADE	SHADE	UNDER 12 INCHES	1 TO 3 FEET	OVER 3 FEET	VINE OR CREEPER	SPRING	EARLY SUMMER	LATE SUMMER	FALL	FLOWERS	FOLIAGE	FRAGRANCE	FRUIT/SEEDS	CUT FLOWERS	DRIED FLOWERS	CONTAINERS	DROUGHT	HEAT	COASTAL CONDITIONS
AGERATUM HOUSTONIANUM 'SUMMER SNOW'	✓		✓				✓			✓					✓	✓	✓	✓									
AMMI MAJUS	✓		✓				✓	✓			✓				✓	✓		✓				✓	✓				
AMMOBIUM ALATUM			✓	✓			✓				✓				✓	✓		✓	✓			✓	✓				
ANTIRRHINUM MAJUS 'WHITE SONNET'			✓	✓			✓	✓			✓				✓	✓	✓	✓									
ASCLEPIAS FRUTICOSA			✓		✓		✓					✓				✓					✓	✓				✓	
BROWALLIA SPECIOSA 'SILVER BELLS'			✓	✓	✓			✓	✓		✓				✓	✓		✓						✓			
COBAEA SCANDENS 'ALBA'			✓	✓			✓						✓		✓	✓		✓									
COSMOS BIPINNATUS 'SONATA WHITE'	✓		✓				✓	✓			✓				✓	✓		✓				✓					
CREPIS RUBRA 'ALBA'	✓				✓	✓	✓			✓	✓				✓	✓		✓							✓		✓
DATURA METEL	✓		✓				✓	✓			✓				✓	✓		✓		✓							
DAUCUS CAROTA VAR. CAROTA		✓		✓	✓	✓	✓							✓		✓	✓	✓				✓	✓	✓			
DIGITALIS PURPUREA 'ALBA'		✓	✓					✓			✓				✓			✓									
EUPHORBIA MARGINATA	✓			✓			✓				✓					✓	✓		✓			✓					
HELIANTHUS ANNUUS 'ITALIAN WHITE'	✓			✓			✓					✓			✓	✓	✓					✓			✓	✓	
IBERIS AMARA	✓			✓			✓				✓				✓	✓		✓		✓		✓					
IBERIS ODORATA	✓			✓			✓			✓					✓	✓	✓	✓		✓		✓					
IMPATIENS GLANDULIFERA	✓		✓					✓	✓		✓				✓	✓		✓									
IPOMOEA ALBA			✓	✓	✓		✓						✓		✓	✓	✓	✓		✓						✓	
LAGENARIA SICERARIA	✓			✓			✓						✓		✓	✓		✓			✓	✓					
LAGURUS OVATUS 'NANUS'	✓			✓			✓			✓					✓	✓		✓	✓			✓	✓			✓	
LAVATERA TRIMESTRIS 'MONT BLANC'	✓			✓			✓				✓				✓	✓		✓				✓			✓		
LUNARIA ANNUA 'ALBA'		✓		✓	✓	✓		✓			✓			✓							✓		✓		✓		
NICOTIANA SYLVESTRIS	✓		✓				✓	✓				✓			✓	✓	✓	✓		✓							
OMPHALODES LINIFOLIA	✓		✓				✓	✓		✓					✓	✓	✓	✓	✓			✓					
PAPAVER SOMNIFERUM 'WHITE CLOUD'	✓				✓		✓	✓			✓				✓	✓		✓				✓					
RESEDA ODORATA	✓		✓				✓			✓	✓				✓	✓		✓		✓		✓		✓			
SCABIOSA STELLATA 'PING-PONG'	✓			✓			✓				✓				✓	✓		✓				✓	✓				
SENECIO CINERARIA			✓	✓	✓	✓	✓	✓		✓	✓					✓			✓						✓	✓	

	PLANT TYPE			SOIL			LIGHT			HEIGHT				BLOOM SEASON				NOTED FOR				SPECIAL USES			TOLERATES		
	ANNUAL	BIENNIAL	TENDER PERENNIAL	RICH, LOAMY	AVERAGE	POOR	FULL SUN	PARTIAL SHADE	SHADE	UNDER 12 INCHES	1 TO 3 FEET	OVER 3 FEET	VINE OR CREEPER	SPRING	EARLY SUMMER	LATE SUMMER	FALL	FLOWERS	FOLIAGE	FRAGRANCE	FRUIT/SEEDS	CUT FLOWERS	DRIED FLOWERS	CONTAINERS	DROUGHT	HEAT	COASTAL CONDITIONS
YELLOW — CARTHAMUS TINCTORIUS	✔			✔			✔				✔				✔	✔		✔				✔	✔				
CELSIA CRETICA		✔	✔	✔	✔		✔				✔				✔	✔		✔		✔							
DYSSODIA TENUILOBA	✔		✔	✔	✔		✔			✔					✔	✔		✔	✔	✔				✔	✔	✔	✔
ESCHSCHOLZIA CAESPITOSA	✔			✔	✔	✔	✔			✔					✔	✔		✔	✔						✔		
GAZANIA LINEARIS			✔	✔	✔		✔			✔					✔	✔								✔	✔		✔
HELIANTHUS ANNUUS 'TEDDY BEAR'	✔		✔				✔				✔				✔	✔	✔	✔				✔			✔	✔	
HIBISCUS TRIONUM			✔	✔			✔	✔			✔				✔	✔	✔	✔	✔					✔		✔	
LAYIA PLATYGLOSSA	✔			✔			✔				✔			✔	✔			✔				✔			✔		
LONAS ANNUA	✔			✔	✔		✔	✔							✔	✔	✔					✔	✔			✔	
MENTZELIA DECAPETALA		✔		✔	✔		✔				✔				✔	✔	✔			✔					✔	✔	✔
MENTZELIA LAEVICAULIS		✔	✔	✔	✔		✔					✔			✔	✔	✔			✔					✔	✔	✔
OENOTHERA BIENNIS		✔		✔	✔	✔	✔				✔			✔	✔	✔	✔			✔					✔		
OENOTHERA ERYTHROSEPALA 'TINA JAMES'		✔		✔	✔	✔					✔			✔	✔	✔	✔			✔					✔		
RUDBECKIA HIRTA 'DOUBLE GOLD'	✔	✔	✔	✔	✔		✔	✔		✔					✔	✔		✔				✔			✔		
SANVITALIA PROCUMBENS 'GOLD BRAID'	✔			✔	✔		✔			✔					✔	✔	✔							✔	✔	✔	
TAGETES ERECTA 'PRIMROSE LADY'	✔		✔	✔	✔		✔				✔				✔	✔	✔	✔	✔			✔			✔		
TROPAEOLUM PEREGRINUM	✔				✔	✔							✔		✔	✔	✔										
VERBASCUM BOMBYCIFERUM 'SILVER LINING'		✔		✔	✔		✔					✔			✔	✔		✔	✔						✔		
ORANGE — CARTHAMUS TINCTORIUS 'LASTING ORANGE'	✔			✔			✔				✔				✔	✔						✔	✔				
ERYSIMUM PEROFSKIANUM		✔	✔	✔			✔	✔		✔				✔	✔			✔		✔				✔			
ESCHSCHOLZIA CALIFORNICA 'AURANTIACA'		✔		✔	✔		✔			✔				✔	✔	✔	✔	✔							✔		
IPOMOEA QUAMOCLIT	✔			✔	✔		✔						✔		✔	✔	✔	✔								✔	
MINA LOBATA			✔	✔			✔	✔					✔		✔	✔		✔									
SANVITALIA PROCUMBENS 'MANDARIN ORANGE'	✔			✔	✔		✔			✔					✔	✔	✔							✔	✔	✔	
TITHONIA ROTUNDIFOLIA 'GOLDFINGER'	✔			✔	✔		✔				✔				✔	✔		✔				✔			✔	✔	
ZINNIA ANGUSTIFOLIA	✔			✔	✔		✔			✔					✔	✔	✔	✔							✔	✔	
RED — ADONIS AESTIVALIS	✔			✔			✔	✔			✔				✔	✔		✔									✔
AMARANTHUS CAUDATUS	✔			✔	✔		✔					✔			✔	✔	✔	✔				✔	✔				
ASCLEPIAS CURASSAVICA			✔	✔	✔		✔				✔	✔			✔	✔	✔				✔		✔				
ATRIPLEX HORTENSIS 'RUBRA'	✔			✔			✔					✔			✔				✔		✔		✔				✔
CAPSICUM ANNUUM 'HOLIDAY CHEER'			✔	✔						✔					✔	✔					✔			✔			
CLEOME HASSLERANA 'CHERRY QUEEN'	✔			✔	✔		✔	✔			✔				✔	✔	✔	✔		✔						✔	

Color	Plant	ANNUAL	BIENNIAL	TENDER PERENNIAL	RICH, LOAMY	AVERAGE	POOR	FULL SUN	PARTIAL SHADE	SHADE	UNDER 12 INCHES	1 TO 3 FEET	OVER 3 FEET	VINE OR CREEPER	SPRING	EARLY SUMMER	LATE SUMMER	FALL	FLOWERS	FOLIAGE	FRAGRANCE	FRUIT/SEEDS	CUT FLOWERS	DRIED FLOWERS	CONTAINERS	DROUGHT	HEAT	COASTAL CONDITIONS
RED	CUPHEA IGNEA			✓	✓	✓	✓	✓	✓		✓					✓	✓	✓							✓		✓	
	ECHIUM WILDPRETII		✓			✓	✓	✓				✓				✓	✓		✓	✓								
	FOENICULUM VULGARE 'PURPUREUM'			✓	✓	✓	✓	✓				✓				✓			✓	✓					✓			
	HIBISCUS ACETOSELLA 'RED SHIELD'			✓	✓			✓	✓			✓					✓			✓					✓		✓	
	IPOMOEA NIL 'SCARLETT O'HARA'	✓		✓	✓			✓						✓		✓	✓	✓	✓								✓	
	PHASEOLUS COCCINEUS			✓	✓			✓					✓	✓	✓	✓		✓	✓			✓						
	RICINUS COMMUNIS 'CARMENCITA'			✓	✓			✓					✓			✓		✓	✓	✓							✓	
	SALVIA COCCINEA 'LADY IN RED'			✓	✓	✓		✓	✓			✓				✓	✓	✓	✓						✓			
	ZINNIA ELEGANS 'BIG RED'	✓			✓			✓				✓				✓	✓	✓	✓				✓				✓	
PINK	CATHARANTHUS ROSEUS 'TROPICANA'			✓	✓			✓	✓	✓						✓	✓	✓	✓						✓		✓	
	CELOSIA CRISTATA 'PINK TASSELS'	✓			✓			✓				✓				✓	✓	✓					✓	✓		✓	✓	
	CIRSIUM JAPONICUM		✓		✓	✓	✓	✓	✓			✓				✓	✓		✓				✓	✓				
	CLEOME HASSLERANA 'PINK QUEEN'	✓			✓			✓	✓				✓			✓	✓	✓	✓								✓	
	COSMOS BIPINNATUS 'VERSAILLES PINK'	✓			✓			✓	✓			✓				✓	✓	✓	✓				✓					
	CREPIS RUBRA	✓				✓	✓	✓			✓	✓				✓	✓		✓							✓	✓	✓
	DAHLIA HYBRIDS 'AUDACITY'			✓	✓			✓				✓				✓	✓	✓	✓				✓					
	DIASCIA BARBERAE 'PINK QUEEN'	✓			✓			✓			✓					✓	✓	✓	✓									
	DIGITALIS PURPUREA 'GIANT SHIRLEY'		✓		✓				✓			✓				✓			✓									
	LAVATERA TRIMESTRIS 'SILVER CUP'	✓			✓			✓				✓				✓	✓		✓				✓		✓			
	MATTHIOLA BICORNIS	✓			✓			✓	✓			✓				✓	✓		✓		✓		✓	✓				
	PAPAVER SOMNIFERUM 'PINK CHIFFON'	✓			✓			✓	✓				✓			✓	✓		✓				✓					
	PELARGONIUM X HORTORUM 'FRECKLES'			✓	✓			✓			✓				✓	✓	✓		✓	✓					✓			
	PETUNIA X HYBRIDA 'FANTASY PINK MORN'	✓			✓					✓						✓	✓	✓	✓						✓			
	SILENE ARMERIA	✓	✓		✓	✓		✓	✓			✓				✓	✓		✓				✓					
	SILENE PENDULA	✓			✓	✓		✓	✓	✓						✓	✓		✓						✓			
	VERBENA X HYBRIDA 'SILVER ANN'	✓			✓			✓		✓						✓	✓	✓	✓						✓			
PURPLE	ANTIRRHINUM MAJUS 'BLACK PRINCE'			✓	✓			✓	✓			✓			✓	✓	✓	✓	✓				✓					
	CLARKIA CONCINNA	✓				✓	✓	✓	✓			✓			✓	✓			✓									
	COBAEA SCANDENS			✓	✓			✓						✓	✓	✓	✓	✓	✓									
	CYNARA CARDUNCULUS			✓	✓			✓					✓			✓	✓	✓	✓				✓	✓				
	DOLICHOS LABLAB			✓	✓			✓						✓		✓	✓		✓			✓	✓	✓			✓	
	EUSTOMA GRANDIFLORUM		✓	✓	✓			✓				✓				✓			✓				✓		✓	✓	✓	✓

COLOR	NAME	PLANT TYPE			SOIL			LIGHT			HEIGHT				BLOOM SEASON				NOTED FOR				SPECIAL USES			TOLERATES		
		ANNUAL	BIENNIAL	TENDER PERENNIAL	RICH, LOAMY	AVERAGE	POOR	FULL SUN	PARTIAL SHADE	SHADE	UNDER 12 INCHES	1 TO 3 FEET	OVER 3 FEET	VINE OR CREEPER	SPRING	EARLY SUMMER	LATE SUMMER	FALL	FLOWERS	FOLIAGE	FRAGRANCE	FRUIT/SEEDS	CUT FLOWERS	DRIED FLOWERS	CONTAINERS	DROUGHT	HEAT	COASTAL CONDITIONS
PURPLE	HELIOTROPIUM ARBORESCENS			✓	✓			✓	✓		✓					✓	✓		✓		✓		✓		✓			
	OCIMUM BASILICUM 'DARK OPAL'	✓		✓	✓			✓			✓					✓	✓	✓	✓	✓					✓			
	ONOPORDUM ACANTHIUM	✓	✓			✓	✓	✓				✓			✓	✓			✓	✓						✓	✓	
	ORTHOCARPUS PURPURASCENS	✓			✓	✓	✓	✓			✓				✓				✓								✓	
	PENNISETUM SETACEUM 'RUBRUM'			✓	✓			✓				✓				✓	✓	✓		✓			✓	✓				
	PERILLA FRUTESCENS VAR. CRISPA	✓			✓	✓	✓	✓			✓					✓				✓								
	PETUNIA X HYBRIDA 'HEAVENLY LAVENDER'	✓		✓				✓	✓							✓	✓	✓							✓			
	RHODOCHITON ATROSANGUINEUM			✓	✓			✓						✓		✓	✓	✓	✓							✓		
	SALVIA SPLENDENS 'LASER PURPLE'			✓	✓	✓		✓	✓						✓	✓			✓						✓			
	SILYBUM MARIANUM	✓	✓			✓	✓	✓				✓				✓			✓	✓					✓			
	VERBENA BONARIENSIS			✓	✓			✓					✓		✓	✓	✓						✓					
BLUE	AGERATUM HOUSTONIANUM 'BLUE HORIZON'	✓		✓				✓			✓				✓	✓	✓	✓					✓					
	BORAGO OFFICINALIS	✓			✓			✓	✓		✓					✓	✓		✓						✓			
	BROWALLIA SPECIOSA 'BLUE BELLS'			✓	✓	✓			✓	✓	✓	✓				✓	✓		✓						✓			
	CALLISTEPHUS CHINENSIS 'BLUE SKIES'	✓		✓				✓	✓		✓					✓	✓	✓										
	CONSOLIDA AMBIGUA 'IMPERIAL BLUE BELL'	✓		✓				✓	✓				✓			✓	✓						✓					
	CYNOGLOSSUM AMABILE		✓		✓	✓	✓	✓	✓			✓				✓	✓	✓					✓					
	EXACUM AFFINE		✓	✓					✓	✓	✓	✓				✓	✓	✓			✓				✓		✓	
	LOBELIA ERINUS	✓		✓				✓	✓		✓					✓	✓	✓							✓			
	MYOSOTIS SYLVATICA 'VICTORIA BLUE'	✓	✓		✓			✓	✓		✓				✓	✓			✓									
	NEMOPHILA MENZIESII	✓		✓				✓	✓		✓				✓	✓			✓									
	OXYPETALUM CAERULEUM			✓	✓			✓			✓				✓	✓	✓	✓							✓	✓		
	PHACELIA CAMPANULARIA	✓			✓	✓		✓	✓		✓														✓			
	SALVIA FARINACEA 'VICTORIA'			✓	✓	✓		✓	✓		✓					✓	✓	✓	✓						✓			
	SCABIOSA STELLATA	✓		✓				✓			✓					✓	✓						✓	✓				
GREEN	BRIZA MAXIMA	✓			✓			✓				✓			✓	✓			✓	✓			✓	✓				
	CARDIOSPERMUM HALICACABUM			✓	✓			✓						✓	✓	✓				✓		✓				✓	✓	
	FOENICULUM VULGARE			✓	✓	✓	✓	✓				✓					✓		✓	✓					✓			
	HUMULUS JAPONICUS			✓	✓			✓						✓			✓			✓							✓	
	MOLUCELLA LAEVIS	✓		✓				✓				✓				✓	✓	✓					✓	✓				
	NICOTIANA LANGSDORFFII	✓		✓				✓	✓			✓				✓	✓											
	RICINUS COMMUNIS			✓	✓			✓					✓				✓			✓		✓					✓	

	PLANT TYPE			SOIL			LIGHT			HEIGHT				BLOOM SEASON				NOTED FOR				SPECIAL USES			TOLERATES		
	ANNUAL	BIENNIAL	TENDER PERENNIAL	RICH, LOAMY	AVERAGE	POOR	FULL SUN	PARTIAL SHADE	SHADE	UNDER 12 INCHES	1 TO 3 FEET	OVER 3 FEET	VINE OR CREEPER	SPRING	EARLY SUMMER	LATE SUMMER	FALL	FLOWERS	FOLIAGE	FRAGRANCE	FRUIT/SEEDS	CUT FLOWERS	DRIED FLOWERS	CONTAINERS	DROUGHT	HEAT	COASTAL CONDITIONS
MULTI- AND BICOLORED																											
SETARIA ITALICA	✔				✔		✔				✔	✔			✔	✔	✔	✔			✔		✔				
TAGETES FILIFOLIA	✔		✔	✔			✔			✔					✔			✔						✔	✔		
ABELMOSCHUS MANIHOT 'GOLDEN BOWL'			✔	✔			✔	✔			✔				✔		✔	✔								✔	
AMARANTHUS TRICOLOR	✔			✔	✔	✔				✔	✔				✔	✔		✔							✔	✔	
ARCTOTIS STOECHADIFOLIA			✔		✔		✔				✔				✔	✔		✔				✔			✔	✔	✔
BRASSICA OLERACEA 'COLOR UP'		✔		✔			✔			✔	✔								✔					✔			
CHRYSANTHEMUM CARINATUM	✔				✔		✔	✔			✔				✔	✔	✔	✔				✔					
CLARKIA AMOENA	✔				✔	✔	✔	✔			✔				✔	✔		✔									
COLEUS X HYBRIDUS			✔	✔				✔		✔	✔				✔	✔			✔					✔			
COLLINSIA HETEROPHYLLA	✔			✔				✔			✔				✔	✔	✔							✔			
CONVOLVULUS TRICOLOR 'ROYAL ENSIGN'	✔				✔		✔				✔				✔	✔	✔							✔	✔	✔	
CUCUMIS MELO	✔		✔				✔					✔			✔	✔				✔	✔						
CUCURBITA MAXIMA 'TURBANIFORMIS'	✔			✔	✔		✔					✔			✔						✔				✔		
DAHLIA HYBRIDS 'MICKEY'			✔	✔			✔				✔				✔	✔	✔	✔				✔					
DIGITALIS FERRUGINEA		✔						✔			✔				✔	✔		✔									
DIMORPHOTHECA PLUVIALIS	✔				✔	✔	✔				✔			✔	✔	✔	✔	✔							✔	✔	
GAILLARDIA PULCHELLA	✔			✔	✔	✔	✔				✔				✔	✔	✔	✔				✔			✔	✔	✔
GAZANIA RIGENS 'SUNSHINE'			✔	✔	✔	✔	✔			✔					✔	✔		✔						✔	✔		✔
KOCHIA SCOPARIA 'ACAPULCO SILVER'	✔			✔			✔				✔				✔				✔								
LIMONIUM SUWOROWII	✔			✔			✔			✔	✔				✔	✔		✔				✔	✔				✔
LINARIA MAROCCANA 'FAIRY BOUQUET'	✔			✔			✔	✔		✔					✔	✔		✔						✔			
RUDBECKIA HIRTA 'GLORIOSA DAISY'	✔	✔	✔	✔	✔	✔	✔	✔			✔				✔	✔	✔	✔				✔					
SALVIA FARINACEA 'STRATA'			✔	✔			✔	✔			✔				✔	✔	✔	✔				✔					
THUNBERGIA ALATA			✔	✔			✔	✔					✔		✔	✔		✔						✔			
TORENIA FOURNIERI	✔			✔				✔	✔	✔					✔	✔		✔						✔			
VIOLA RAFINESQUII	✔			✔			✔	✔		✔				✔	✔			✔						✔			
VIOLA TRICOLOR	✔			✔			✔	✔		✔				✔	✔			✔		✔				✔			
ZEA MAYS VAR. JAPONICA	✔			✔			✔					✔			✔				✔								
ZINNIA HAAGEANA 'PERSIAN CARPET'	✔				✔		✔				✔				✔	✔	✔	✔				✔				✔	
MIXED																											
AGROSTEMMA GITHAGO	✔			✔	✔	✔	✔				✔				✔	✔		✔				✔		✔			
ALCEA ROSEA 'PINAFORE MIXED'		✔		✔			✔				✔				✔	✔	✔										
BEGONIA 'PIZZAZZ MIXED'			✔	✔				✔	✔	✔					✔	✔	✔	✔	✔	✔				✔			

Table — MIXED (Annuals reference chart)

	PLANT TYPE			SOIL			LIGHT			HEIGHT				BLOOM SEASON				NOTED FOR						SPECIAL USES			TOLERATES
	ANNUAL	BIENNIAL	TENDER PERENNIAL	RICH, LOAMY	AVERAGE	POOR	FULL SUN	PARTIAL SHADE	SHADE	UNDER 12 INCHES	1 TO 3 FEET	OVER 3 FEET	VINE OR CREEPER	SPRING	EARLY SUMMER	LATE SUMMER	FALL	FLOWERS	FOLIAGE	FRAGRANCE	FRUIT/SEEDS	CUT FLOWERS	DRIED FLOWERS	CONTAINERS	DROUGHT	HEAT	COASTAL CONDITIONS
BRACHYCOME IBERIDIFOLIA	✓		✓				✓			✓	✓				✓	✓								✓			
CALENDULA OFFICINALIS 'BON BON'	✓		✓				✓				✓				✓	✓	✓					✓		✓			
CAMPANULA MEDIUM 'CALYCANTHEMA'		✓	✓				✓	✓			✓	✓			✓	✓		✓				✓					
CANNA X GENERALIS			✓	✓			✓				✓	✓			✓	✓	✓	✓						✓			
CENTAUREA CYANUS	✓				✓		✓				✓				✓	✓	✓					✓	✓				
CHEIRANTHUS CHEIRI		✓	✓				✓			✓	✓			✓				✓		✓		✓					✓
COREOPSIS TINCTORIA	✓				✓		✓				✓				✓	✓	✓	✓				✓			✓	✓	
DIANTHUS BARBATUS		✓	✓				✓	✓		✓				✓	✓			✓				✓					
EMILIA JAVANICA	✓			✓	✓		✓				✓				✓	✓						✓	✓		✓	✓	✓
GOMPHRENA GLOBOSA	✓			✓			✓			✓	✓				✓	✓	✓					✓	✓	✓		✓	
GYPSOPHILA ELEGANS	✓			✓			✓				✓			✓	✓	✓	✓					✓	✓				
HELICHRYSUM BRACTEATUM			✓	✓	✓		✓				✓				✓	✓						✓	✓	✓			
IMPATIENS GLANDULIFERA	✓		✓					✓	✓			✓			✓		✓	✓									
IMPATIENS WALLERANA	✓		✓					✓	✓	✓	✓				✓	✓	✓							✓			
LATHYRUS ODORATUS 'BIJOU MIXED'	✓		✓				✓	✓		✓				✓	✓			✓		✓							
LATHYRUS ODORATUS 'ROYAL FAMILY'	✓		✓				✓	✓					✓	✓	✓			✓		✓							
LIMONIUM SINUATUM	✓			✓	✓						✓				✓	✓		✓				✓	✓		✓		✓
LOBULARIA MARITIMA			✓		✓		✓	✓		✓				✓	✓	✓	✓	✓		✓				✓			
MATTHIOLA INCANA		✓	✓				✓	✓			✓				✓	✓		✓		✓		✓		✓			
MIMULUS X HYBRIDUS			✓	✓				✓	✓	✓	✓				✓	✓	✓							✓			
MIRABILIS JALAPA			✓	✓	✓	✓	✓				✓				✓	✓	✓			✓						✓	
NEMESIA STRUMOSA 'CARNIVAL MIXED'	✓		✓				✓	✓		✓					✓	✓	✓							✓			
NICOTIANA ALATA 'NIKKI'	✓		✓				✓	✓			✓			✓	✓	✓		✓		✓							
NIGELLA DAMASCENA	✓				✓		✓				✓				✓	✓		✓			✓	✓			✓		
PELARGONIUM PELTATUM			✓	✓									✓		✓	✓	✓	✓						✓			
PHLOX DRUMMONDII 'TWINKLE' SERIES	✓				✓		✓	✓		✓					✓	✓											
PORTULACA GRANDIFLORA 'SUNDANCE'	✓				✓	✓	✓			✓					✓	✓	✓	✓							✓	✓	✓
PROBOSCIDEA LOUISIANICA	✓				✓	✓	✓				✓				✓			✓			✓		✓				
SALPIGLOSSIS SINUATA 'BOLERO'	✓		✓				✓				✓				✓	✓						✓					
SCHIZANTHUS PINNATUS	✓		✓				✓	✓				✓			✓	✓						✓		✓			
TROPAEOLUM MINUS 'ALASKA MIXED'	✓				✓	✓	✓			✓					✓	✓	✓	✓				✓		✓			
XERANTHEMUM ANNUUM	✓			✓	✓	✓	✓				✓				✓	✓	✓					✓	✓				

Frost Maps of the U.S. and Canada

These maps indicate in general terms the average dates for the last spring frost and the first fall frost in various parts of the U.S. and Canada. The planting dates for most annuals and biennials depend on when these frosts occur; hardy annuals can be safely sown 6 weeks before the last frost, whereas tender annuals should be sown only after all danger of frost is past. Also, while cool-season annuals can withstand some frost, warm-season plants can be grown without protection only in the frost-free period between the last and first frosts. Used together, the maps and the information found in the encyclopedia *(pages 102-151)* will help you select annuals and biennials suited to your area and determine when to plant them. Specific frost dates vary widely within each region, so check with your weather service or extension agent for more precise figures, and keep a record of temperatures in your own garden from year to year. The two larger maps exclude Alaska; Alaska's dates are shown on the two smaller maps.

AVERAGE DATES OF LAST SPRING FROST

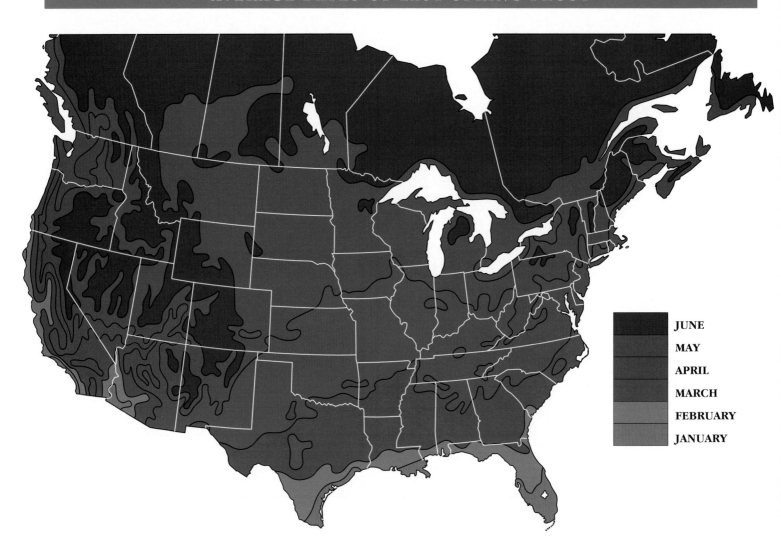

JUNE

MAY

APRIL

MARCH

FEBRUARY

JANUARY

AVERAGE DATES OF FIRST FALL FROST

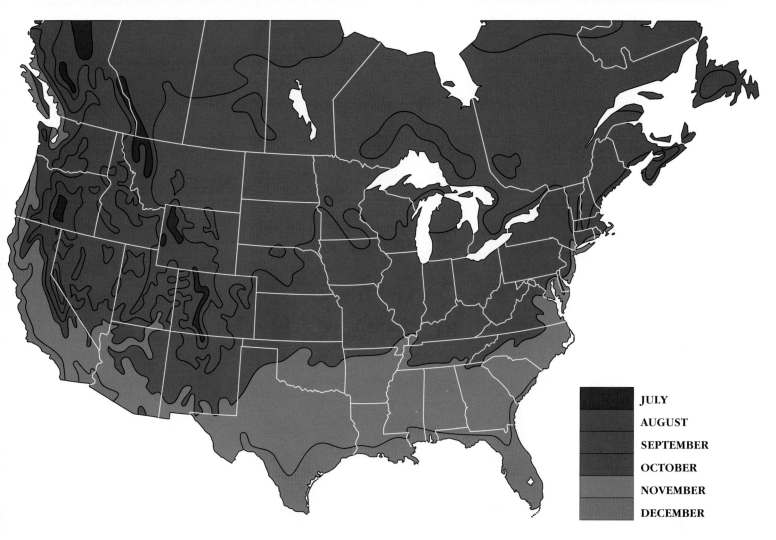

	JULY
	AUGUST
	SEPTEMBER
	OCTOBER
	NOVEMBER
	DECEMBER

AVERAGE DATES OF LAST SPRING FROST

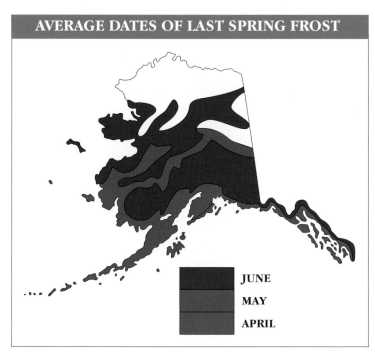

	JUNE
	MAY
	APRIL

AVERAGE DATES OF FIRST FALL FROST

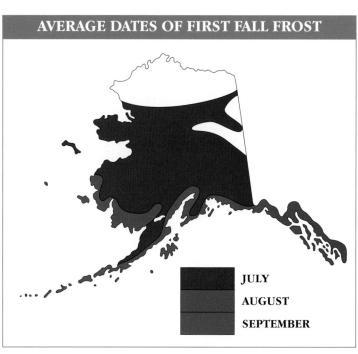

	JULY
	AUGUST
	SEPTEMBER

A Zone Map of the U.S. and Canada

A biennial's winter hardiness is what determines whether it can survive to a second growing season in your garden. The map below divides the U.S. and Canada into 11 climatic zones based on average minimum temperatures, as compiled by the U.S. Department of Agriculture. Find your zone and check the hardiness information in the encyclopedia *(pages 102-151)* if you want to grow biennials for two seasons rather than treat them as annuals.

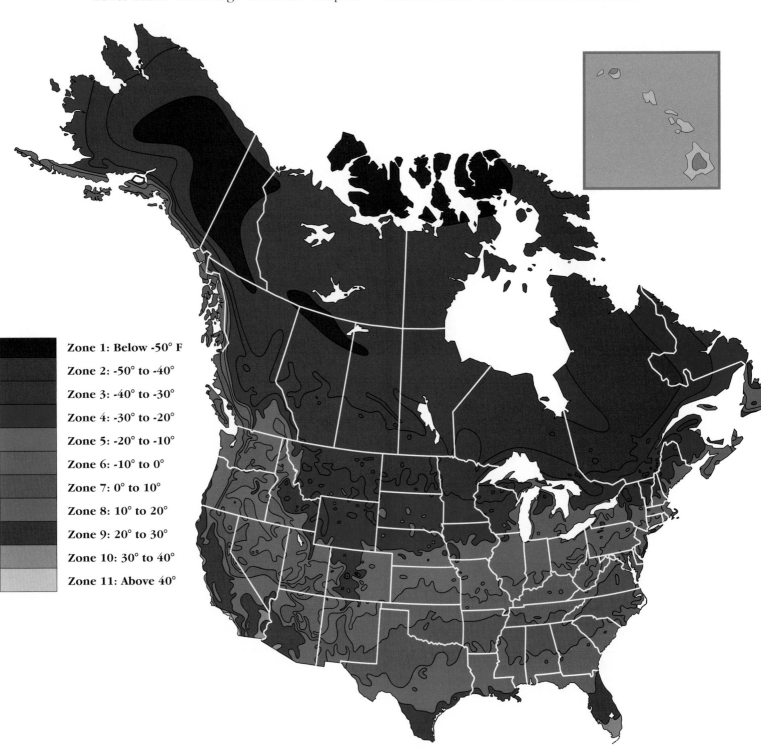

Zone 1: Below -50° F
Zone 2: -50° to -40°
Zone 3: -40° to -30°
Zone 4: -30° to -20°
Zone 5: -20° to -10°
Zone 6: -10° to 0°
Zone 7: 0° to 10°
Zone 8: 10° to 20°
Zone 9: 20° to 30°
Zone 10: 30° to 40°
Zone 11: Above 40°

Cross-Reference Guide to Plant Names

African daisy—*Arctotis*
Ageratum—*Lonas*
Angel's-trumpet—*Datura*
Baby-blue-eyes—*Nemophila*
Baby's-breath—*Gypsophila*
Bachelor's-button—
   Centaurea
Balloon vine—
   Cardiospermum
Balsam—*Impatiens*
Basil—*Ocimum*
Basket flower—*Centaurea*
Bean—*Phaseolus*
Beefsteak plant—*Perilla*
Bellflower—*Campanula*
Bells of Ireland—
   Moluccella
Bishop's flower—*Ammi*
Black-eyed Susan—
   Rudbeckia
Black-eyed Susan vine—
   Thunbergia
Blanket-flower—*Gaillardia*
Blazing star—*Mentzelia*
Bloodflower—*Asclepias*
Blue milkweed—
   Oxypetalum
Bluewings—*Torenia*
Burning bush—*Kochia*
Busy Lizzie—*Impatiens*
Butterfly flower—
   Schizanthus
California bluebell—
   Phacelia
Calliopsis—*Coreopsis*
Campion—*Silene*
Canary creeper—
   Tropaeolum
Candytuft—*Iberis*
Canterbury bells—
   Campanula
Cape marigold—
   Dimorphotheca
Cardoon—*Cynara*
Castor bean—*Ricinus*
Cherry pie—*Heliotropium*
China aster—*Callistephus*
Chinese houses—*Collinsia*
Cigar plant—*Cuphea*
Clock vine—*Thunbergia*
Cockscomb—*Celosia*

Coneflower—*Rudbeckia*
Corn cockle—*Agrostemma*
Cornflower—*Centaurea*
   cyanus
Creeping zinnia—
   Sanvitalia
Crimson starglory—*Mina*
Crown daisy—
   Chrysanthemum
Cup-and-saucer—
   Campanula
Cup-and-saucer vine—
   Cobaea
Cypress vine—*Ipomoea*
Dahlberg daisy—*Dyssodia*
Devil's-claw—*Proboscidea*
Dusty-miller—*Senecio*
Evening primrose—
   Oenothera
Evening star—*Mentzelia*
Everlasting—*Helichrysum*
Everlasting—*Xeranthemum*
False saffron—*Carthamus*
Farewell-to-spring—*Clarkia*
Fennel—*Foeniculum*
Firecracker plant—*Cuphea*
Flossflower—*Ageratum*
Forget-me-not—*Myosotis*
Fountain grass—
   Pennisetum
Four-o'clock—*Mirabilis*
Foxglove—*Digitalis*
Foxtail millet—*Setaria*
Gentian—*Eustoma*
Geranium—*Pelargonium*
Gillyflower—*Matthiola*
   incana
Globe amaranth—
   Gomphrena
Godetia—*Clarkia*
Gourd—*Cucurbita*
Gourd—*Lagenaria*
Groundsel—*Senecio*
Hare's-tail grass—*Lagurus*
Hawksbeard—*Crepis*
Hollyhock—*Alcea*
Honesty—*Lunaria*
Hops—*Humulus*
Hound's-tongue—
   Cynoglossum
Hyacinth bean—*Dolichos*

Immortelle—*Helichrysum*
Immortelle—*Xeranthemum*
Indian blanket—*Gaillardia*
Irish lace—*Tagetes filifolia*
Jimson weed—*Datura*
Johnny-jump-up—*Viola*
Joseph's-coat—*Amaranthus*
Knapweed—*Centaurea*
Larkspur—*Consolida*
Love-in-a-mist—*Nigella*
Love-in-a-puff—
   Cardiospermum
Love-lies-bleeding—
   Amaranthus
Madagascar periwinkle—
   Catharanthus
Mallow—*Hibiscus*
Mallow—*Lavatera*
Marigold—*Tagetes*
Marvel-of-Peru—*Mirabilis*
Mexican sunflower—
   Tithonia
Mignonette—*Reseda*
Milkweed—*Asclepias*
Money plant—*Lunaria*
Monkey flower—*Mimulus*
Moonflower—*Ipomoea alba*
Morning glory—*Ipomoea*
Moss rose—*Portulaca*
Mullein—*Verbascum*
Nasturtium—*Tropaeolum*
Navelwort—*Omphalodes*
Orach—*Atriplex*
Painted tongue—
   Salpiglossis
Pansy—*Viola*
Paper moon—
   Scabiosa stellata
Pepper—*Capsicum*
Pheasant's-eye—*Adonis*
Pink—*Dianthus*
Poppy—*Papaver*
Pot marigold—*Calendula*
Prince's-feather—
   Amaranthus
Purple bell vine—
   Rhodochiton
Quaking grass—*Briza*
Queen Anne's lace—
   Daucus
Rabbit-grass—*Lagurus*

Red-ribbons—*Clarkia*
   concinna
Safflower—*Carthamus*
Sage—*Salvia*
Scorpion weed—*Phacelia*
Silver-dollar—*Lunaria*
Snapdragon—*Antirrhinum*
Snow-on-the-mountain—
   Euphorbia
Southern star—*Oxypetalum*
Spider flower—*Cleome*
Squash—*Cucurbita*
Starflower—*Ipomoea*
   coccinea
Star-glory—*Ipomoea*
   quamoclit
Statice—*Limonium*
Stock—*Matthiola*
Strawflower—*Helichrysum*
Summer cypress—*Kochia*
Sunflower—*Helianthus*
Swan River daisy—
   Brachycome
Sweet alyssum—*Lobularia*
Sweet mace—*Tagetes*
   patula
Sweet pea—*Lathyrus*
Sweet-sultan—*Centaurea*
Sweet William—*Dianthus*
Tassel flower—*Emilia*
Thistle—*Cirsium*
Thistle—*Onopordum*
Thistle—*Silybum*
Tickseed—*Coreopsis*
Tidytips—*Layia*
Toadflax—*Linaria*
Tobacco—*Nicotiana*
Twinspur—*Diascia*
Unicorn plant—
   Proboscidea
Vervain—*Verbena*
Violet—*Browallia*
Viper's bugloss—*Echium*
Wallflower—*Cheiranthus*
Wallflower—*Erysimum*
Wild carrot—*Daucus*
   carota
Winged everlasting—
   Ammobium
Wishbone flower—
   Torenia

Encyclopedia of Plants

Presented here in compact form is information on most of the plants mentioned in this volume. Each genus is listed alphabetically by its Latin botanical name, followed by pronunciation of the Latin and the genus's common name or names. If you know a plant only by its common name, see the cross-reference chart on page 101 or the index.

A botanical name consists of the genus and, usually, a species, both written in italics. Species often have common names of their own, which are given in parentheses in each entry, and many species have one or more cultivars, whose names are set off by single quotation marks. Because new cultivars are constantly being introduced while others become unavailable, these entries concentrate on information regarding the species and identify only a few of the more enduring varieties. Refer to the maps on pages 98-100 to determine which plants will grow most successfully in your region.

Abelmoschus
(a-bel-MOS-kus)
ABELMOSCHUS

Abelmoschus moschatus

Plant type: *tender perennial*

Height: *15 inches to 6 feet*

Interest: *flowers, foliage*

Soil: *moist, well-drained, fertile*

Light: *full sun to partial shade*

Originally from tropical Asia, the hibiscus-like flowers and deeply lobed leaves of abelmoschus add a bold texture and an exotic appearance to borders.

Selected species and varieties: *A. manihot* (sunset hibiscus) grows 5 to 6 feet tall and is a good choice for the back of a border or a fast-growing summer hedge. Its 6-inch flowers appear in late summer; the five overlapping petals are pale yellow to cream with a brown or maroon eye. Dark green leaves are up to a foot long. 'Golden Bowl' bears yellow flowers with maroon centers. *A. moschatus* (musk mallow) grows 15 to 24 inches tall with a mounded habit well suited to the front of a border. From midsummer until frost, showy 3- to 4-inch blooms appear continuously. Colors range from yellow to scarlet with blends of pink and orange; petals fade to white near the center.

Growing conditions and maintenance: Start seed indoors 6 to 8 weeks prior to the last frost. Seed can be sown directly in the garden, but flowering may be delayed. Plants thrive in hot weather, performing well up to Zone 6. Space *A. manihot* 2 to 3 feet apart; *A. moschatus* 12 to 18 inches apart.

Adonis
(a-DOE-nis)
PHEASANT'S-EYE

Adonis aestivalis

Plant type: *annual*

Height: *12 to 18 inches*

Interest: *flowers, foliage*

Soil: *moist, well-drained, rich*

Light: *full sun to partial shade*

Pheasant's-eye produces a large mound of feathery leaves topped with intensely colored blooms in early to midsummer. Plants are most effective planted in drifts in a mixed border.

Selected species and varieties: *A. aestivalis* is a European wildflower with lacy leaves that bend to the ground, forming attractive fernlike mounds. Cup-shaped flowers consist of brilliant crimson petals surrounding black stamens. The prolifically borne flowers are about 1½ inches in diameter.

Growing conditions and maintenance: For earliest flowers, sow seed directly in the garden in late fall, before the ground freezes, thinning plants to stand 6 inches apart after germination. In spring, thin plants to stand 12 inches apart. Seed can also be sown in early spring as soon as the soil can be worked, but flowering will commence somewhat later. This hardy annual performs best in cool coastal or mountainous regions and prefers a soil rich in humus; it does not tolerate extreme heat.

Ageratum
(aj-er-AY-tum)
FLOSSFLOWER

Ageratum houstonianum 'Blue Horizon'

Plant type: *annual*

Height: *6 to 30 inches*

Interest: *flowers, foliage*

Soil: *moist, well-drained*

Light: *full sun*

A profusion of fluffy flowers with thread-like petals crown flossflower's clumps of heart-shaped leaves. With soft colors and a compact mounding habit, dwarf varieties create excellent garden edgings. Taller varieties combine well with other flowers in the middle or back of a border and are good candidates for indoor arrangements.

Selected species and varieties: *A. houstonianum* bears tiny blue or bluish purple flowers in dense, fuzzy clusters from summer through fall; white- and pink-flowered varieties are available; 'Blue Horizon' grows to 30 inches with deep blue flowers that are excellent for cutting; 'Capri' grows to a uniform 12 inches, producing bicolored flowers that are medium blue with white centers, and it is heat tolerant; 'Summer Snow' grows 6 to 8 inches tall with pure white flowers that begin early and continue to frost.

Growing conditions and maintenance: Sow seed indoors 6 to 8 weeks before the last expected frost. Space plants 6 to 12 inches apart. Pinching early growth will promote compactness, and removing spent blooms will encourage continuous production of flowers.

Agrostemma
(ag-roe-STEM-a)
CORN COCKLE

Agrostemma githago

Plant type: *annual or biennial*

Height: *1 to 4 feet*

Interest: *flowers, foliage*

Soil: *poor, well-drained*

Light: *full sun*

Corn cockles are troublefree plants from Europe that have naturalized throughout the eastern United States. They provide a long season of bright blooms for borders. Abundant 1- to 2-inch flowers in shades of pink, lilac, cherry red, or magenta top their stems throughout the summer. Their old-fashioned appearance is effective massed or in combination with other flowers in a cottage garden. Blooms are excellent for cutting.

Selected species and varieties: *A. githago* is a hardy annual with willowy stems up to 4 feet tall and narrow leaves covered with a silvery down; each flower has five petals that sport delicate stripes or spots seeming to radiate from the center; the black seeds are plentiful—and poisonous.

Growing conditions and maintenance: Corn cockle is easy to grow. Sow seed in place in late fall or early spring. Thin plants to stand 6 to 12 inches apart. They tolerate dry conditions and almost any soil. Deadhead to encourage reblooming and prevent excessive self-seeding.

Alcea
(al-SEE-a)
HOLLYHOCK

Alcea rosea

Plant type: *biennial*

Height: *2 to 9 feet*

Interest: *flowers*

Soil: *well-drained, fertile*

Light: *full sun*

The bell-shaped flowers of hollyhock are borne on sturdy, erect stems. The lower flowers open first, and new blossoms appear from midsummer to early fall. It is useful for the back of a border or as a colorful accent against fences or walls.

Selected species and varieties: *A. ficifolia* (Antwerp hollyhock) grows 4 to 7 feet tall with bold foliage and large 3- to 5-inch flowers, usually in shades of yellow or orange; 'Country Garden Mix' is a blend of single-flowered types with a wide color range including mahogany, rose, pink, salmon, and ivory. *A. rosea* grows to 9 feet with 2- to 4-inch flowers; 'Marjorette' bears double flowers in a wide range of colors on plants that are only 24 inches tall; 'Pinafore Mixed' is a blend of single and semidouble flower types in shades of pink, yellow, and white, growing to 3½ feet.

Growing conditions and maintenance: Plant seed indoors in winter for spring transplanting. Some varieties will bloom their first summer. Seed sown outdoors in spring will usually bloom its second year. Space plants 18 to 24 inches apart. Once they become established, hollyhocks will self-seed in Zones 3 to 9.

Amaranthus
(am-a-RAN-thus)
AMARANTH

Amaranthus caudatus

Plant type: *annual*

Height: *18 inches to 6 feet*

Interest: *flowers, foliage*

Soil: *dry to well-drained*

Light: *full sun*

Amaranths are large, brilliantly colored plants that hail from the tropics of the Far East. They add a bold touch to borders with their long-lasting tasseled flowers and colorful leaves. Tall types are effective as accents, while shorter selections are suited to beds or containers. Flowers are suitable for both fresh and dried arrangements.

Selected species and varieties: *A. caudatus* (love-lies-bleeding) grows 3 to 5 feet tall with green or red leaves and huge drooping tassels of red flowers that may reach 2 feet in length; 'Viridis' grows 2 to 3½ feet with greenish yellow flower tassels. *A. cruentus* (purple amaranth, prince's-feather) produces huge 12-inch leaves along erect 6-foot stems, and drooping red or purple flower spikes. *A. tricolor* (Joseph's-coat amaranth, tampala) grows from 1½ to 5 feet tall with variegated leaves up to 6 inches long that sport shades of green, red, and gold.

Growing conditions and maintenance: Seed requires very warm temperatures and can be started indoors 4 to 6 weeks prior to the last frost. In warm areas sow seed directly. Thin to allow 1 to 2 feet between plants. Water sparingly.

Ammi
(AM-mi)
BISHOP'S FLOWER

Ammi majus

Plant type: *annual*

Height: *2 to 3 feet*

Interest: *flowers*

Soil: *moist, fertile*

Light: *full sun to partial shade*

The delicate flower heads of bishop's flower resemble Queen Anne's lace in appearance, but the plant is far more manageable in the garden. Originally from Eurasia, it has naturalized in many parts of North America. It is well suited to flower borders, where it provides fine-textured contrast with coarser and more colorful plants. It can be sprinkled among annuals and perennials or planted in drifts. The flowers are highly valued for indoor arrangements; wear gloves when cutting as sap can irritate skin.

Selected species and varieties: *A. majus* develops thin, well-branched stems up to 3 feet tall with sharply serrated leaves. In summer, stems are topped with 5- to 6-inch umbels, each containing numerous delicate white flowers that tremble with the slightest wind or touch.

Growing conditions and maintenance: Start seed about 6 weeks indoors—or 2 weeks outdoors—before the last frost. Thin or transplant to allow 6 to 12 inches between plants. Plants transplant easily at nearly any stage and, once established, are free flowering. They thrive in cooler regions but may be stressed by high temperatures and humidity.

Ammobium
(a-MOE-bee-um)
WINGED EVERLASTING

Ammobium alatum

Plant type: *tender perennial*

Height: *2 to 3 feet*

Interest: *flowers, foliage, stems*

Soil: *well-drained, sandy*

Light: *full sun*

This Australian native produces its solitary flower heads continuously from early to late summer. The flowers have a papery texture with yellow centers surrounded by silvery white bracts. They are attractive massed in a bed, and are excellent for both fresh and dried arrangements.

Selected species and varieties: *A. alatum* develops a tuft of 6- to 8-inch basal leaves that are covered with fine white woolly hairs. In summer, erect, branched stems rise 3 feet high from the clump. Each stem is topped with a solitary 1- to 2-inch flower head. The common name refers to the unusual wings along the length of the stems.

Growing conditions and maintenance: Start seed indoors 6 to 8 weeks before the last frost, or sow directly in the garden after the last hard frost. In warm regions, seed can be sown in the fall. Thin to allow 8 to 12 inches between plants. Plants self-seed from Zone 7 south and are perennial in Zones 10 and 11. Avoid overwatering. To use in winter arrangements, cut stems before flowers are fully open and hang upside down in an airy room until dry.

Antirrhinum
(an-tir-RYE-num)
SNAPDRAGON

Antirrhinum majus 'White Sonnet'

Plant type: *tender perennial*

Height: *6 inches to 4 feet*

Interest: *flowers*

Soil: *well-drained, fertile*

Light: *full sun to partial shade*

Snapdragons, with their wide range of heights and flower colors and long season of bloom, have been cultivated since ancient times. Short varieties add color to rock gardens and edgings, while taller types are well suited to the middle and rear of mixed borders, where they provide a vertical accent. They are outstanding in fresh arrangements.

Selected species and varieties: *A. majus* bears terminal clusters of flowers that open from the bottom up. Each bloom has five lobes, divided into an upper and a lower lip. Varieties are classified by height: small (6-12 inches), intermediate (12-24 inches), and tall (2-4 feet); 'Black Prince' is 18 inches with deep crimson flowers and bronze foliage; 'Madame Butterfly' grows to 3 feet with flaring blossoms in a range of colors; 'White Sonnet' is 22 inches with white flowers that are superb for cutting.

Growing conditions and maintenance: Start seed indoors in late winter for transplanting in mid- to late spring. Space plants 6 to 18 inches apart. Deadhead to encourage continuous flowering. Taller types may need staking. Perennial in Zones 8 to 11.

Arctotis
(ark-TOE-tis)
AFRICAN DAISY

Arctotis stoechadifolia

Plant type: *tender perennial*

Height: *2 to 3 feet*

Interest: *flowers, foliage*

Soil: *well-drained to dry, sandy*

Light: *full sun*

This native of South Africa produces a steady supply of 3-inch daisy-type flowers from summer until frost. Brightly colored blooms stand out against woolly gray leaves. They are a good choice for beds and borders, and even though flowers close at night, they are cheerful additions to fresh arrangements.

Selected species and varieties: *A. stoechadifolia* has a bushy habit with velvety lobed leaves and slender stems. Flowers petals are typically silvery white with a lavender band at their base where they surround a violet center. The reverse of the petals is lavender. Yellow, orange, red, pink, and bicolored varieties are also available.

Growing conditions and maintenance: For earliest flowers start seed indoors about 8 weeks before the last frost; plant seedlings outside, 8 to 12 inches apart, after all danger of frost has past. In Zones 7 and warmer, seed can also be sown directly in the garden. African daisy tolerates both drought and coastal conditions and is perennial in Zones 9 and 10.

Asclepias
(as-KLEE-pee-as)
MILKWEED

Asclepias curassavica

Plant type: *tender perennial*

Height: *2 to 6 feet*

Interest: *flowers, seedpods*

Soil: *moist to dry*

Light: *full sun*

Often referred to as weeds in South America, *Asclepias* species are suited to the rear of a herbaceous border, where their clusters of flowers put on a fine display from summer until frost. Flowers are followed by attractive seedpods that are useful in dried arrangements.

Selected species and varieties: *A. curassavica* (bloodflower) develops sturdy branched stems 2 to 4 feet tall and narrow 5-inch dark green leaves that clasp the stems in pairs. The 6-inch flower clusters arise from branch tips and axils and are made up of many tiny purplish red and orange flowers. Flowers are followed by 4-inch brown seedpods. *A. fruticosa* (gomphocarpus) grows 3 to 6 feet tall and bears creamy white flowers and spiny silvery green pods.

Growing conditions and maintenance: Start seed indoors in midwinter for transplanting to the garden after all danger of frost has past. Space plants 15 to 18 inches apart and pinch when they reach 4 to 6 inches to promote branching. Plants thrive in warm weather and can be grown as perennials from Zone 8 south.

Atriplex
(AT-ri-plex)
ORACH

Atriplex hortensis

Plant type: *annual*

Height: *3 to 6 feet*

Interest: *foliage*

Soil: *well-drained, fertile*

Light: *full sun*

Orach is grown for its ornamental foliage, which is powdery white when young and green, yellow-green, or purplish red when mature. Native to Asia, this fast-growing annual makes an effective summer hedge or screen, or it can be used as a backdrop for shorter annuals. Stems are often cut for fresh indoor arrangements. Leaves can be eaten as salad greens.

Selected species and varieties: *A. hortensis* (mountain spinach) has an erect habit with somewhat triangular or arrow-shaped leaves. Young leaves are covered with a white bloom. Flowers are insignificant. 'Rubra' (red orach) grows 4 to 5 feet tall with blood red leaves and stems.

Growing conditions and maintenance: Start seed indoors 4 to 6 weeks before the last frost for transplanting to the garden in late spring, or sow directly outdoors after all danger of frost has past. Space or thin plants to stand 12 inches apart. Orach is easy to grow and tolerates wind and coastal conditions.

Begonia
(be-GO-nee-a)
WAX BEGONIA

Begonia 'Cocktail Series'

Plant type: *tender perennial*

Height: *5 to 16 inches*

Interest: *flowers, foliage*

Soil: *moist, fertile*

Light: *partial shade to shade*

Wax begonias add color to the shady garden with both their perpetual clusters of delicate flowers and their glossy rounded leaves. Flowers range from white to pink to red, and leaves may be green, bronze, or variegated green and white. They are useful for edging, massing, and growing in containers both indoors and outside.

Selected species and varieties: *B.* x *semperflorens-cultorum* (bedding begonia) has a mounding habit and produces flowers nonstop from spring until frost. In Zones 9 and 10 they bloom almost year round. Selections vary in both flower and leaf color, flower size, and height; 'Cocktail Series' offers white, pink, rose, salmon, and red flowers on dwarf 5- to 6-inch plants with glossy bronze foliage; 'Pizzazz Mixed' grows to 10 inches with large red, pink, or white flowers and glossy green leaves.

Growing conditions and maintenance: Start seed 4 to 6 months prior to the last frost, or purchase bedding plants in spring. Plants can also be propagated by cuttings. Space 8 to 12 inches apart. Although the ideal site is filtered shade, plants will tolerate full sun if given sufficient water, especially in cooler regions.

Borago
(bor-RAY-go)
BORAGE

Borago officinalis

Plant type: *annual*

Height: *2 to 3 feet*

Interest: *flowers, foliage*

Soil: *well-drained*

Light: *full sun to light shade*

This European native makes an attractive addition to flower or herb gardens, fresh flower arrangements, and summer salads. Both leaves and flowers are edible, with a refreshing cucumber-like flavor, and can be used to garnish salads or fruit cups. It has a somewhat sprawling habit that is best suited to an informal garden, where its soft-textured leaves and sky blue flowers add a cool, gentle touch.

Selected species and varieties: *B. officinalis* (talewort, cool-tankard) is a hardy annual with a rounded, sprawling habit, bristly gray-green foliage, and succulent stems. Flowers are arranged in drooping clusters. Each is ¾ inch across and star shaped, with five petals. Though usually clear blue, they are sometimes light purple. Flower buds are covered with fine hairs.

Growing conditions and maintenance: Sow seed directly in the garden at monthly intervals beginning 2 to 3 weeks prior to the last frost for continuous summer bloom. Once established, plant will self-seed. Allow 12 to 18 inches between plants. Where summers are very hot, afternoon shade is recommended. Borage tolerates drought.

Brachycome
(bra-KIK-o-me)
SWAN RIVER DAISY

Brachycome iberidifolia

Plant type: *annual*

Height: *9 to 14 inches*

Interest: *flowers*

Soil: *moist, well-drained, fertile*

Light: *full sun*

The Swan River daisy is a tender annual from Australia with a neat, mounding habit and colorful daisylike flowers. Although small, the brightly colored flowers are produced in masses, making this plant a good choice for rock gardens, edgings, and containers, including hanging baskets.

Selected species and varieties: *B. iberidifolia* grows to 14 inches tall with a compact habit and a 12-inch spread. The delicate pale green leaves are 3 inches long and are borne on slender stems. Flowers are about 1 inch across and appear for 4 to 6 weeks in the summer, tapering off toward the end of the season. Colors include white, pink, lavender, and blue.

Growing conditions and maintenance: Start seed indoors 5 to 6 weeks prior to the last frost, or sow directly in the garden when the soil has warmed. Successive plantings will lengthen the flowering season. Allow 6 to 12 inches between plants. Water during dry spells.

Brassica
(BRASS-i-ka)
ORNAMENTAL CABBAGE

Brassica oleracea

Plant type: *biennial*

Height: *10 to 15 inches*

Interest: *foliage*

Soil: *moist, well-drained*

Light: *full sun*

This ornamental cousin of the familiar vegetable side dish is highly valued for the splash of color it provides in the fall and winter landscape. A biennial, it is grown as an annual for its brightly colored and intricately curled foliage, which grows in a flowerlike rosette.

Selected species and varieties: *B. oleracea,* Acephala group (ornamental kale) does not form heads but produces an open rosette of leaves that typically spreads 12 inches across. Foliage colors include lavender-blue, white, green, red, purple, pink, and assorted variegations. Color improves in cool weather. Leaves of 'Cherry Sundae' are a blend of carmine and cream; 'Color Up' displays a center of red, pink, cream, white, and green surrounded by green margins; 'Peacock' series has feathery notched and serrated leaves in a variety of colors.

Growing conditions and maintenance: For spring planting, start seed indoors 4 to 6 weeks prior to the last frost. For fall gardens, start seed 6 to 8 weeks prior to the first anticipated frost. Space plants 18 to 24 inches apart. Plants will last all winter in Zones 8 to 10.

Briza
(BRY-za)
QUAKING GRASS

Briza maxima

Plant type: *annual*

Height: *1 to 2 feet*

Interest: *foliage, flowers, seed heads*

Soil: *well-drained*

Light: *full sun*

While they are not appropriate for the formal garden, the arching leaves and nodding seed heads of quaking grass add grace and movement to an informal border or a garden path. They are also a good choice for the cutting garden because their wheatlike spikelets are outstanding for both fresh and dried arrangements. The spikelets dangle from thin stems and tremble when touched, hence the common name.

Selected species and varieties: *B. maxima* produces a tuft of leaves, each leaf 6 inches long and ¼ inch wide. In late spring and early summer, flower heads rise to 2 feet, producing 4-inch nodding panicles on threadlike stems. Flowers start out green and then turn straw colored as they dry.

Growing conditions and maintenance: Plant seed outdoors as soon as soil can be worked in spring. Thin to allow 9 to 12 inches between plants. Provide moisture when plants are young. Once established, plants usually self-seed. For use in winter arrangements, cut the seed heads before seeds ripen.

Browallia
(bro-WALL-ee-a)
BUSH VIOLET

Browallia speciosa

Plant type: *tender perennial*

Height: *8 to 16 inches*

Interest: *flowers*

Soil: *moist, well-drained*

Light: *partial shade to shade*

A good choice for the shady border, bush violet bears clusters of blue, violet, or white flowers from early to late summer. It has a low-growing rounded habit that is well suited for use as an edging, and it's an outstanding choice for window boxes or hanging baskets, where it cascades gracefully over the edge. In fall, plants can be cut back severely and potted to be grown as flowering houseplants through the winter.

Selected species and varieties: *B. speciosa* has a rounded to sprawling habit with 1½- to 2-inch long-throated, star-shaped flowers; 'Blue Bells' bears blue-violet flowers with prominent white centers; 'Jingle Bells' bears flowers in a mixture of colors including shades of blue, white, and lavender; 'Silver Bells' bears large white blooms.

Growing conditions and maintenance: Start seeds indoors about 8 weeks prior to the last frost. Plant in the garden after all danger of frost is past, spacing plants 8 inches apart. Avoid overwatering and overfertilizing.

Calendula
(ka-LEN-dew-la)
POT MARIGOLD

Calendula officinalis

Plant type: *annual*

Height: *12 to 24 inches*

Interest: *flowers*

Soil: *moist, well-drained*

Light: *full sun*

The long-lasting blooms of pot marigolds are daisylike with flattened, wide-spreading rays ranging in color from deep orange to yellow or cream. They are a good choice for mixed beds, containers, or indoor arrangements. Native to the Mediterranean, this hardy annual has long been grown as an ornamental and used as a flavoring for puddings and cakes.

Selected species and varieties: *C. officinalis* has a neat, mounding habit and grows 1 to 2 feet tall with a similar spread. Leaves are 2 to 6 inches long, blue-green, and aromatic. The solitary 2½- to 4½-inch flower heads close at night; 'Bon-Bon' grows 12 inches tall with a compact, early-blooming habit and a mixture of flower colors.

Growing conditions and maintenance: Start seed indoors 6 to 8 weeks prior to the last frost, for transplanting to the garden after the last hard frost. In areas with mild winters it can be sown directly outdoors in fall or early spring. Space plants 12 to 18 inches apart. Deadhead to increase flowering. Calendulas thrive in cool conditions and tolerate poor soils if they have adequate water.

Callistephus
(kal-LIS-tee-fus)
CHINA ASTER

Callistephus chinensis

Plant type: *annual*

Height: *6 to 36 inches*

Interest: *flowers*

Soil: *well-drained, fertile*

Light: *full sun to light shade*

The China aster, as its name implies, is native to Asia. Its flowers display a remarkable range of colors, sizes, and shapes. Dwarf and intermediate-sized selections are good choices for the border, while tall varieties are outstanding for cutting.

Selected species and varieties: *C. chinensis* has an upright, branching habit with 3½-inch irregularly toothed dark green basal leaves and flower heads up to 5 inches across. Flowers may be single, semidouble, or double, and are available in many colors including red, white, pink, blue, purple, and yellow; 'Blue Skies' is a 6-inch dwarf that covers itself with pale lavender-blue double flowers; 'Giant Princess' grows to 2½ feet with large, long-stemmed flowers in many colors.

Growing conditions and maintenance: Start seed indoors in late winter for transplanting into the garden after all danger of frost has passed, or sow directly in the garden. Space plants 12 inches apart. Make successive plantings for continuous flowers. To avoid disease, do not overwater or plant in the same location in successive years.

Campanula
(kam-PAN-yew-la)
BELLFLOWER

Campanula medium

Plant type: *biennial*

Height: *1 to 4 feet*

Interest: *flowers*

Soil: *moist, well-drained*

Light: *full sun to partial shade*

This native of southern Europe is an old-fashioned garden favorite. In late spring and early summer, sturdy flower stalks appear, bearing numerous bell-shaped blossoms, each 2 inches long. Flowers may be blue, violet, white, or pink, and are long-lasting both in a mixed border and in fresh indoor arrangements.

Selected species and varieties: *C. medium* (Canterbury bells) has an erect habit and usually grows 2 to 4 feet tall, although dwarf varieties have a compact habit and reach only 12 inches in height. Leaves are narrow and up to 10 inches long, and bell-shaped flowers are born singly or in pairs along an open raceme; 'Calycanthema' (cup-and-saucer) bears a 3-inch-wide saucerlike, flattened calyx beneath the flower "cup" and is available in blue, white, and rose.

Growing conditions and maintenance: Sow seed outdoors in late spring or summer to bloom the following year. Plants are hardy to Zone 4 but require some winter protection. Some varieties will flower 6 months after seeding and can be started indoors. Transplant in early spring, spacing plants 12 to 18 inches apart. Water during dry periods.

Canna
(CAN-ah)
CANNA

Canna x generalis 'Lerape'

Plant type: *tender perennial*

Height: *18 inches to 6 feet*

Interest: *flowers*

Soil: *moist, well-drained*

Light: *full sun*

Cannas produce 4- to 5-inch flowers with a tousled arrangement of petal-like stamens from summer through frost. Bold leaves provide a dramatic backdrop to the flowers. They are well suited to the back of borders and to massing. Grow dwarf cultivars as edgings or in patio containers.

Selected species and varieties: *C.* x *generalis* (canna lily) is available in standard varieties that grow 4 to 6 feet tall or dwarfs that are less than 3 feet. The flowers are carried on stiff, erect stems; colors include red, orange, salmon, yellow, pink, white, and bicolors. The broad leaves, up to 24 inches long, are usually a deep glossy green but are sometimes bronzy red or striped or veined in white or pink; 'Lerape' bears yellow flowers with bright orange spots; 'Seven Dwarfs Mixed' grows to 18 inches with a wide range of flower colors.

Growing conditions and maintenance: Soak seed prior to planting indoors in midwinter, or start rhizomes indoors 4 weeks before the last frost and move them to the garden when night temperatures reach 60° F. In Zones 9 and 10, plant directly in the garden in spring, spaced 1 to 2 feet apart.

Capsicum
(KAP-si-kum)
PEPPER

Capsicum annuum 'Treasure Red'

Plant type: *tender perennial*

Height: *6 to 20 inches*

Interest: *fruit*

Soil: *moist, well-drained, fertile*

Light: *full sun*

Bushy, rounded pepper plants produce brightly colored fruit that is well displayed against dark green leaves. In its native environment of tropical North and South America, peppers are woody perennials, but in temperate climates they are treated as annuals. Ornamental varieties make tidy and colorful edgings for beds and are superb for containers.

Selected species and varieties: *C. annuum* (ornamental pepper) has a bushy, compact habit with evergreen leaves from 1 to 5 inches long. Flowers are white and small. Fruit ranges from ¾ to 2 inches long and may be red, purple, yellow, green, black, cream, or variegated; 'Holiday Cheer' grows to 8 inches with round 1-inch fruit that turns from cream to red; 'Red Missile' grows to 10 inches with tapered 2-inch fruit; 'Treasure Red' grows 8 inches tall with conical fruit that turns from white to bright red.

Growing conditions and maintenance: Start seed indoors in late winter to transplant to the garden after all danger of frost has past. Space plants to stand 8 to 15 inches apart. Dig and pot plants in the fall to grow as houseplants; perennial in Zones 10 and 11.

Cardiospermum
(kar-dee-o-SPER-mum)
BALLOON VINE

Cardiospermum halicacabum

Plant type: *tender perennial*

Height: *8 to 12 feet*

Interest: *fruit, foliage*

Soil: *light, well-drained*

Light: *full sun*

Native to India, Africa, and tropical America, balloon vine has become naturalized in parts of the southern United States. It produces tiny white summer flowers followed by green balloonlike seedpods that seem to float among the feathery leaves. Climbing by hooklike tendrils, it grows rapidly and is useful for providing a temporary screen or for covering a fence or trellis.

Selected species and varieties: *C. halicacabum* (balloon vine, love-in-a-puff, heart pea, winter cherry) produces attractive doubly compound leaves and ¼-inch white flowers with four petals and four sepals. Pods are green, 1 to 1½ inches across, and contain black pea-like seeds, each with a heart-shaped white spot.

Growing conditions and maintenance: Start seed indoors 6 weeks prior to the last frost; in Zones 8 and warmer plant often reseeds. Transplant outdoors in late spring, allowing 12 to 14 inches between plants. Plants thrive in warm weather and tolerate drought. Provide support for climbing; perennial in Zones 9 to 11.

Carthamus
(KAR-tha-mus)
SAFFLOWER

Carthamus tinctorius

Plant type: *annual*

Height: *1 to 3 feet*

Interest: *flowers*

Soil: *well-drained*

Light: *full sun*

Native to Eurasia and Egypt, where it has been used since ancient times to produce a bright yellow dye, safflower is at home in wildflower and herb gardens, informal borders, and cutting gardens. Its fluffy bright orange flowers are valued for their use in dried arrangements and have been used as a substitute for saffron in flavoring food. Seeds are the source of safflower oil.

Selected species and varieties: *C. tinctorius* (false saffron) has an erect, branched habit with 2½-inch spiny, thistlelike leaves along straight stems. The 1-inch flower heads are surrounded by spiny bracts and are typically orange, but varieties offer a wider range of colors, including yellow, gold, cream, and white; 'Lasting Orange' is an early-blooming selection with 1½-inch clear orange flowers; 'Lasting Yellow' is similar in habit with yellow flowers.

Growing conditions and maintenance: Start seed indoors in late winter in peat pots to minimize transplant shock, or sow directly in garden after danger of frost has past. Space plants 8 to 10 inches apart.

Catharanthus
(kath-ah-RAN-thus)
PERIWINKLE

Catharanthus roseus

Plant type: *tender perennial*

Height: *3 to 18 inches*

Interest: *flowers, foliage*

Soil: *moist, well-drained*

Light: *sun to partial shade*

Periwinkle provides summer-to-fall color for temperate gardens. Its flowers resemble those of *Vinca*, and it is available in both creeping and upright varieties. Use it as a summer ground cover or in mass plantings, annual borders, or containers.

Selected species and varieties: *C. roseus* [sometimes listed as *Vinca rosea*] (Madagascar periwinkle) produces glossy oblong leaves, 1 to 3 inches long. Creeping varieties grow 3 inches tall, spreading 18 to 24 inches across. Erect strains grow 8 to 18 inches tall. Flowers are 1½ inches wide and cover the plant throughout the summer; colors range from shades of pink or mauve to white; 'Parasol' produces large 1½- to 2-inch white flowers with pink eyes on 12- to 18-inch plants; 'Tropicana' grows to 12 inches and produces flowers in several shades of pink from pale blush to deep rose, with contrasting eyes.

Growing conditions and maintenance: Start seed indoors 10 to 12 weeks prior to the last frost for late-spring transplanting to the garden; space 1 to 2 feet apart. Plants can also be started from cuttings. They thrive in warm, humid conditions and are perennial in Zones 9 to 11.

Celosia
(sel-OH-see-a)
CELOSIA

Celosia cristata 'Pink Tassels'

Plant type: *annual*

Height: *6 to 24 inches*

Interest: *flowers, foliage*

Soil: *moist to dry, well-drained*

Light: *full sun*

These vibrant annuals are native to the tropics of Asia. Their crested or plumed flowers are extremely long-lasting, making them ideal for bedding and cutting for both fresh and dried arrangements.

Selected species and varieties: *C. cristata* displays a range of heights and flower types. Leaves may be green, purple, or variegated. Flowers appear from midsummer to fall and are usually deep shades of red, orange, yellow, or gold. The species is divided according to flower type: Childsii group (crested cockscomb) produces crested or convoluted flower heads that resemble lumps of coral. Plumosa group (feather amaranth) bears feathery 6- to 12-inch flower heads. Spicata group bears flowers in slender spikes; 'Pink Tassels' bears long pale pink spikes with bright pink tips.

Growing conditions and maintenance: Start seed indoors 4 to 6 weeks before transplanting to the garden after all danger of frost has passed. In warm areas, sow directly outside. Space plants 6 to 18 inches apart. Celosias thrive in warm weather and tolerate dry soils. For use in winter arrangements, cut flowers at their peak and hang them upside down to dry.

Celsia
(SEL-see-a)
CRETAN CELSIA

Celsia cretica

Plant type: *biennial*

Height: *4 to 6 feet*

Interest: *flowers*

Soil: *well-drained*

Light: *full sun*

This half-hardy biennial is native to the Mediterranean region. It is similar to the more familiar *Verbascum* mulleins, differing mainly in number of stamens: *Celsia* has four, *Verbascum* five. Its yellow flowers are borne on tall, open racemes and appear over a long period in the summer. They are extraordinarily fragrant. The plant's statuesque habit and coarse leaves combine well with other, more delicate flowers in the rear of a mixed border.

Selected species and varieties: *C. cretica* (Cretan mullein) has a stout, erect habit with large, hairy leaves and stems. From the clump of leaves rises a 5- to 6-foot flower stalk bearing yellow flowers. Individual blossoms are 1½ inches across and display purple filaments and two brown or rust-colored spots on their upper petal.

Growing conditions and maintenance: Sow seed directly in the garden. In Zones 6 and south, seed can be sown in fall or early spring; in cooler areas plant in spring. Cover the seed very lightly with soil. Plants tolerate a wide range of soils, provided they are well drained.

Centaurea
(sen-TOR-ee-a)
KNAPWEED

Centaurea cyanus

Plant type: *annual*

Height: *1 to 6 feet*

Interest: *flowers*

Soil: *well-drained*

Light: *full sun*

The tufted blooms of these popular annuals come in shades of pink, blue, lavender, yellow, and white. Sprinkle them liberally in informal borders, wildflower gardens, and the cutting garden. They can be used for both fresh and dried arrangements.

Selected species and varieties: *C. americana* (basket flower) grows up to 6 feet tall with sturdy stems and 4- to 5-inch pink flowers with cream centers and a fringe of thistlelike bracts. *C. cyanus* (bachelor's-button, cornflower) produces gray-green leaves on erect stems to 3 feet; perky 1-inch flowers appear from early summer until frost and are available in many colors. *C. moschata* (sweet-sultan) grows 2 to 3 feet with 2- to 3-inch musk-scented flowers; the hybrid 'Imperialis' grows to 4 feet with pink, purple, or white flowers.

Growing conditions and maintenance: Sow seed in place in late winter or early spring; in areas with mild winters it can also be sown in fall. Space 6 to 12 inches apart. Once established plants often self-seed. For continuous bloom, make successive plantings 2 weeks apart throughout the season.

Cheiranthus
(ky-RAN-thus)
WALLFLOWER

Cheiranthus cheiri 'Bowles' Mauve'

Plant type: *tender perennial*

Height: *6 to 24 inches*

Interest: *flowers*

Soil: *well-drained, fertile*

Light: *full sun*

This Eurasian native bridges the flowering season between early bulbs and bedding plants. Fragrant 1-inch flowers are borne in clusters resembling stock; colors include deep shades of yellow, orange, red, purple, and brown. Dwarf varieties are perfect for rock gardens or growing in gaps of stone walls. Plant taller types in borders.

Selected species and varieties: *C. cheiri* (English wallflower) has a low, erect habit; dwarf varieties grow 6 to 9 inches, while tall varieties may reach 2 feet. Early-flowering strains often bloom their first year from seed, but most varieties are treated as biennials; 'Bowles' Mauve' produces large clusters of deep pink flowers.

Growing conditions and maintenance: Sow seed outdoors in spring or fall for bloom the following season. Provide winter protection in areas with severe winters. Early-flowering varieties can be started indoors in midwinter, hardened in a cold frame, and transplanted to the garden as soon as the soil can be worked in spring. Space plants about 12 inches apart. Wallflowers thrive in cool climates and do well in coastal and mountainous areas such as the Pacific Northwest.

Chrysanthemum
(kri-SAN-the-mum)
CHRYSANTHEMUM

Chrysanthemum coronarium 'Primrose Gem'

Plant type: *annual*

Height: *1 to 3 feet*

Interest: *flowers*

Soil: *well-drained*

Light: *full sun to partial shade*

Annual chrysanthemums, which hail from the Mediterranean region, supply the summer and fall border with a nonstop production of colorful daisylike flowers. They are also cheerful and dependable cut flowers.

Selected species and varieties: *C. carinatum* (tricolor chrysanthemum) grows 2 to 3 feet tall with dark green toothed leaves. It derives its common name from its 2½-inch flower heads that are white with a yellow band surrounding a purple or chocolate brown central disk; 'Court Jesters' produces red, pink, orange, yellow, maroon, and white flowers with red or orange bands. *C. coronarium* (crown daisy, garland chrysanthemum) grows 1 to 2½ feet tall with coarsely cut leaves and yellow and white flowers, 1 to 2 inches across, which may be single, semidouble, or double; 'Primrose Gem' bears semidouble soft yellow blooms with darker yellow centers.

Growing conditions and maintenance: These plants are easily grown from seed planted directly in the garden as soon as soil can be worked in the spring. Thin plants to stand 12 to 18 inches apart. Once established they will self-seed.

Cirsium
(SIR-see-um)
THISTLE

Cirsium japonicum

Plant type: *biennial*

Height: *18 to 30 inches*

Interest: *flowers*

Soil: *light, well-drained*

Light: *full sun to partial shade*

Solitary or small clusters of rose or magenta flower heads top the erect stems of this somewhat coarse Japanese native. The dark green spiny leaves provide a dramatic foil for the intensely colored flowers. This plant adds a bold texture to the mixed border and is excellent for both fresh and dried arrangements.

Selected species and varieties: *C. japonicum* (rose thistle) produces an erect, branched stem with deeply lobed 4-inch leaves. The leaves are deep green with spiny edges and often display silvery veins. Flower heads top each stem in summer. The buds are covered with silvery overlapping scales, and the opened flower heads are 1 to 2 inches across. Each head consists of a mass of tiny tubular flowers.

Growing conditions and maintenance: Sow seed directly in the garden as soon as soil can be worked in spring for late-summer flowers. Once established, plants will self-seed. Space plants 1 to 2 feet apart. They are adaptable to a wide range of soils as long as drainage is good.

Clarkia
(KLAR-kee-a)
GODETIA

Clarkia amoena

Plant type: *annual*

Height: *1 to 3 feet*

Interest: *flowers*

Soil: *dry, sandy*

Light: *full sun to partial shade*

Clarkias are free-flowering annuals from the coastal ranges of the western United States. They are named after the explorer William Clark, who collected their seed during the Lewis and Clark expedition. These species are also listed under the genus *Godetia.*

Selected species and varieties: *C. amoena* (farewell-to-spring, satin-flower) grows 1 to 3 feet tall. Throughout summer, 2- to 4-inch cup-shaped flowers appear in the axils of the upper leaves. Petals number four and are pink to lavender with a bright red or pink splash at the base; the four sepals are red. *C. concinna* (red-ribbons) grows 1 to 2 feet tall and bears rose-purple flowers with deeply cut fan-shaped petals in late spring and early summer. *C. purpurea* grows to 3 feet tall with 1-inch flowers in shades of purple, lavender, red, and pink, often with a dark eye.

Growing conditions and maintenance: Sow seed outdoors in fall where winters are mild, and elsewhere in spring as soon as the soil can be worked. Sow fairly heavily since crowding will encourage flowering. Plants perform best where nights are cool.

Cleome
(klee-O-me)
SPIDER FLOWER

Cleome hasslerana 'Helen Campbell'

Plant type: *annual*

Height: *3 to 4 feet*

Interest: *flowers, seedpods*

Soil: *moist, well-drained*

Light: *full sun to light shade*

Enormous clusters of 1-inch flowers top the stems of cleome continuously from summer until frost. Pink, lavender, or white flower petals surround 2- to 3-inch-long stamens that protrude from the center, creating a spiderlike effect further enhanced by the slender, conspicuous seedpods that follow the flowers. Cleome makes a graceful summer hedge, accent, or border plant.

Selected species and varieties: *C. hasslerana* [also known as *C. spinosa*] has an erect habit with dark green palmately compound leaves and airy, ball-shaped flower heads. While flowers are short-lived, new ones are produced continuously at the top of the stem; 'Cherry Queen' bears rose red flowers; 'Helen Campbell' has white blooms; 'Pink Queen' bears clear pink blossoms; the flowers of 'Violet Queen' are purple, and leaves display a purple tint at their edges.

Growing conditions and maintenance: Start seed indoors 4 to 6 weeks prior to the last frost, or plant directly in the garden in early spring. Plants often self-seed. Space plants about 24 inches apart. Cleome thrives in warm weather and responds well to abundant moisture.

Cobaea
(ko-BEE-a)
CUP-AND-SAUCER VINE

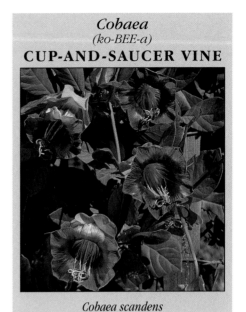

Cobaea scandens

Plant type: *tender perennial*

Height: *10 to 25 feet*

Interest: *flowers*

Soil: *well-drained, sandy*

Light: *full sun*

This extremely vigorous vine is native to Mexico. It derives its common name from showy, velvety blue cup-shaped flowers that are surrounded by a green saucerlike calyx. Technically a tender perennial, it is usually grown as an annual and can reach 25 feet in a single season. It provides a quick, temporary cover for a fence, a wall, an arbor, or a trellis.

Selected species and varieties: *C. scandens,* using branched tendrils, climbs easily on any support. Leaves are divided into two or three pairs of oblong leaflets. Flowers are green at first, turning deep violet or rose-purple as they mature; 'Alba' bears flowers in a pale shade of greenish white.

Growing conditions and maintenance: Start seeds indoors in individual peat pots 6 weeks prior to the last frost, first nicking the hard seed coat, and barely covering the seed. Transplant outdoors in late spring to a warm, sunny site, providing support for growth. Space plants 1 to 2 feet apart, and provide abundant water. In Zones 9 to 11, plant will become a woody vine and grow up to 40 feet.

Coleus
(KO-lee-us)
FLAME NETTLE

Coleus x hybridus

Plant type: *tender perennial*

Height: *8 to 24 inches*

Interest: *foliage*

Soil: *moist, well-drained*

Light: *partial shade*

The exuberantly colored heart-shaped leaves of coleus provide a long season of color to borders and planters in partially shaded sites. Leaves sport attractive patterns, and their colors include chartreuse, green, orange, red, pink, bronze, and white.

Selected species and varieties: *C.* x *hybridus* is available in a very wide range of foliage colors and patterns. Leaves grow opposite each other on square stems, and usually are 3 to 8 inches long with scalloped edges. Plants often grow as wide as they are tall. Dwarf strains grow 8 to 10 inches tall, while taller types may reach 2 feet. Small pale blue flowers bloom on upright spikes but are often removed to encourage leaf growth.

Growing conditions and maintenance: Start seed indoors 8 to 10 weeks prior to the last frost, or grow from leaf-stem cuttings. Transplant outdoors after soil has warmed, allowing 8 to 12 inches between plants. Most varieties grow best in light or partial shade, although some will do fine in full sun if adequate water is supplied. Plants survive as perennials in Zones 10 and 11.

Collinsia
(ko-LIN-see-a)
PAGODA COLLINSIA

Collinsia heterophylla

Plant type: *annual*

Height: *1 to 2 feet*

Interest: *flowers*

Soil: *moist, well-drained*

Light: *partial shade*

Collinsias are native to the western United States. Their clusters of two-toned flowers resemble snapdragons and appear continuously from early summer to early autumn in tiers on stems that reach to 24 inches. They are at home in a shady mixed border, rock garden, or woodland garden, and are also effective in containers.

Selected species and varieties: *C. heterophylla* (Chinese houses) bears bright green leaves in opposite pairs along the stem with loose clusters of flowers. Each flower is two lipped; the upper is pale lilac or white, and the lower is rose-purple or violet. The entire plant is often covered with velvety hairs.

Growing conditions and maintenance: Sow seed outdoors in fall where winters are mild; and in colder climates, in early spring as soon as the ground can be worked. Successive seedings and removal of faded blooms will provide a longer flowering season. Thin seedlings to allow 6 inches between plants. They thrive in filtered sun or dappled shade where night temperatures remain relatively cool.

Consolida
(kon-SO-li-da)
LARKSPUR

Consolida ambigua

Plant type: *annual*

Height: *1 to 4 feet*

Interest: *flowers*

Soil: *well-drained, fertile*

Light: *full sun to light shade*

This native of southern Europe produces dense clusters of flowers upon stately, erect spikes. The flowers are available in shades of blue, lilac, pink, red, purple, and white and are quite long-lasting. Plant tall types toward the rear of a border, where they provide a graceful vertical accent and a fine source of fresh-cut flowers. Shorter varieties can be placed in the mid- or foreground of a mixed border.

Selected species and varieties: *C. ambigua* (rocket larkspur) produces lacy, deeply cut leaves. Spurred flowers in many pastel shades are borne in dense, graceful spikes throughout the summer; 'Imperial Blue Bell' grows to 4 feet with double blue flowers; 'Imperial White King' is similar with double white flowers.

Growing conditions and maintenance: Start seed indoors in peat pots 6 to 8 weeks prior to the last frost. Seed can be sown directly outdoors in fall from Zone 7 south and or in early spring elsewhere. Space plants to stand 8 to 15 inches apart. Tall varieties often require staking. Plants thrive in cool conditions, and where summers are warm will benefit from light shade. Keep soil evenly moist throughout the growing season.

Convolvulus
(kon-VOL-view-lus)
DWARF MORNING GLORY

Convolvulus tricolor

Plant type: *annual*

Height: *6 to 18 inches*

Interest: *flowers*

Soil: *well-drained to dry, sandy*

Light: *full sun*

The dwarf morning glory hails from southern Europe, and unlike the vining morning glory (*Ipomoea* species), has a bushy, spreading habit. Plants grow about a foot tall and 2 feet wide, producing bright flowers in shades of pink, blue, or purple with yellow centers banded by a white stripe. Although each flower lasts but a single day, plants are constantly in bloom from midsummer to early fall and are a good choice for a border edging, window box, or hanging basket.

Selected species and varieties: *C. tricolor* produces small, narrow leaves on well-branched, semitrailing stems. Flowers are funnel shaped and are 1 to 2 inches across; 'Royal Ensign' grows 12 to 18 inches tall and bears 2-inch flowers that are a vivid blue with white throats and yellow centers.

Growing conditions and maintenance: Dwarf morning glories thrive in nearly any well-drained soil. Start seed indoors in individual peat pots 6 weeks before the last frost by first nicking the seed coat and soaking the seed overnight in warm water. Transplant to the garden in late spring, allowing 9 to 15 inches between plants. Plants tolerate heat and dry soils.

Coreopsis
(ko-ree-OP-sis)
TICKSEED

Coreopsis tinctoria

Plant type: *annual*

Height: *2 to 3 feet*

Interest: *flowers*

Soil: *well-drained to dry*

Light: *full sun*

This easy-to-grow annual is native to the eastern United States and is a common component of wildflower mixtures. Daisylike flower heads are borne on wiry stems and appear throughout the summer to early fall. Colors include yellow, orange, red, mahogany, and bicolors. Plant them in mixed borders and wildflower gardens, and cut them for fresh indoor arrangements.

Selected species and varieties: *C. tinctoria* (calliopsis) produces wiry, multiply branched stems with opposite-lobed or dissected leaves. Flower heads may be solitary or appear in branched clusters. Ray flowers are notched and often banded, surrounding a dark red or purple center. Double-flowered and dwarf varieties are available.

Growing conditions and maintenance: Start seed indoors 6 to 8 weeks before the last frost or sow directly in the garden in early spring. Space plants 6 to 8 inches apart. Make a second sowing in midsummer for fall flowers. Deadhead to prolong flowering. Plants tolerate hot weather and drought.

Cosmos
(KOS-mos)
COSMOS

Daisylike flowers crown the wiry stems of this tropical American native. Its showy, delicate blossoms appear singly or in long-stalked loose clusters from midsummer until frost. Cosmos makes a graceful addition to mixed borders, where it will attract numerous butterflies, and is an excellent source of long-lasting cut flowers.

Selected species and varieties: *C. bipinnatus* grows to 6 feet with delicate, finely cut leaves and flowers in shades of red, pink, and white; 'Candy Stripe' grows 30 inches tall with white flowers with crimson markings; 'Seashells Mixture' grows 3 to 3½ feet with fluted petals of white, pink, or crimson surrounding a yellow center; 'Sonata White' grows 24 inches tall with snowy white blooms; 'Versailles Pink' develops strong, tall stems and pink flowers and is recommended for cutting. *C. sulphureus* grows to 6 feet—and cultivars to 18 to 36 inches—with yellow, orange, or scarlet flowers.

Growing conditions and maintenance: Sow seed directly in the garden after the last frost in spring. Thin to allow 12 to 18 inches between plants. Do not fertilize. Taller types are subject to lodging and may need staking. Plants often self-seed.

Cosmos bipinnatus 'Sonata White'

Plant type: *annual*

Height: *10 inches to 6 feet*

Interest: *flowers*

Soil: *well-drained to dry*

Light: *full sun to light shade*

Crepis
(KREEP-is)
HAWKSBEARD

Crepis rubra

Plant type: *annual*

Height: *8 to 18 inches*

Interest: *flowers*

Soil: *well-drained to dry, sandy*

Light: *full sun*

This late-summer and fall bloomer produces fluffy flower heads that look like pink dandelions. It is native to eastern Europe and is very easy to grow. It makes an effective edging for a border and is a good rock-garden specimen.

Selected species and varieties: *C. rubra* produces a clump of slender pale green basal leaves. Beginning in late summer, flower stems rise about 12 inches above the leaves. Each stem is topped by a feathery pink flower head, often with a darker pink or red center. Because the flowers close in the afternoon, they are not good for cutting. 'Alba' produces white flowers.

Growing conditions and maintenance: Sow seed directly in the garden in fall or spring. Space plants 4 to 6 inches apart. Plants tolerate exposed sites and dry, infertile soils. They thrive in coastal regions. Remove spent flowers to prevent self-seeding or they may become weedy.

Cucumis
(KEW-kew-mis)
CUCUMIS

Cucumis melo

Plant type: *annual*

Height: *6 feet*

Interest: *fruit*

Soil: *moist, fertile*

Light: *full sun*

This annual vine grows to 6 feet, producing rounded, arrow-shaped leaves and bright yellow flowers followed by small oval fruit no larger than an orange, with flattened ends. As the fruit matures it develops a sweet fragrance.

Selected species and varieties: *C. melo*, Dudaim Group (pomegranate melon, Queen Anne's pocket melon) is a relatively small member of this genus of generally coarse vines that includes numerous gourds and melons. When the fruit is young, it is green, but as it matures yellow stripes or marbling becomes evident and the background turns brown. Queen Anne supposedly carried one of these to fend off the less pleasant odors she was likely to encounter in her castle.

Growing conditions and maintenance: Start seed indoors in peat pots 4 weeks prior to the last frost, planting three seeds to a pot. Transplant outside after all danger of frost has passed, discarding the weaker two seedlings. Or sow directly in the garden when soil has warmed. To avoid mildew, do not wet the foliage late in the day.

Cucurbita
(kew-KUR-bi-ta)
GOURD

Cucurbita pepo var. ovifera

Plant type: *annual or tender perennial*

Height: *5 to 12 feet*

Interest: *fruit, foliage*

Soil: *well-drained, sandy*

Light: *full sun*

Plant these tropical squash and pumpkin vines on a trellis, a fence, or an arbor, and watch how quickly they will cover it with their lush foliage. Their brightly colored ornamental fruit can be harvested for fall decorations.

Selected species and varieties: *C. ficifolia* (Malabar gourd, fig-leaf gourd) is a perennial in Zones 9 to 11 and is grown as an annual elsewhere. It climbs to 12 feet, producing smooth, rounded, white-striped green fruit up to 12 inches long. *C. maxima* (Hubbard squash) is an 8-foot annual vine bearing edible rounded or oblong furrowed fruit; the variety 'Turbaniformis' (Turk's-cap squash, Turban squash) produces 6- to 7-inch orange, white, and green fruit that looks as if it is made of two separate parts. Annual *C. pepo* var. *ovifera* (pumpkin gourd) grows 5 to 12 feet and produces small fruit in a wide range of shapes and colors.

Growing conditions and maintenance: Sow seed directly in the garden after the last frost, allowing 9 to 12 inches between plants. Or start indoors in individual peat pots 4 weeks before the last frost. Plants thrive in warm weather and grow best when given some support for climbing.

Cuphea
(KYOO-fee-a)
CIGAR PLANT

Cuphea ignea

Plant type: *tender perennial*

Height: *8 to 18 inches*

Interest: *flowers, foliage*

Soil: *well-drained*

Light: *full sun to light shade*

These brightly flowered plants with their rounded, shrubby appearance are perfect candidates for an edging, a planter, or a rock garden. Grown as perennials from Zone 9 south, where they may reach 3 feet, they are treated as annuals elsewhere, where they bloom from midsummer to fall and rarely top 18 inches.

Selected species and varieties: *C. ignea* (Mexican cigar pant, firecracker plant), grows to 12 inches with an equal spread and narrow dark green leaves. Its scarlet tubular flowers are 1 inch long with a black-and-white tip. *C. llavea* 'Bunny Ears Mixed' grows to 18 inches with a neat, uniform habit and bright red flowers with two protruding stamens bearded with violet hairs. *C.* x *purpurea* grows to 18 inches with hairy 3-inch leaves and bright rose red flowers tinged with purple and borne in terminal clusters.

Growing conditions and maintenance: Start seed indoors in midwinter and transplant seedlings to the garden after soil has warmed. Plants can also be started from cuttings. Allow 12 to 18 inches between plants. They adapt to any well-drained soil and thrive in warm weather.

Cynara
(SIN-ah-ra)
CYNARA

Cynara cardunculus

Plant type: *tender perennial*

Height: *4 to 6 feet*

Interest: *flowers, foliage*

Soil: *moist, well-drained, fertile*

Light: *full sun*

Related to the edible artichoke, this species forms clumps of thick stems lined with spiny, lacy silver-gray leaves with woolly undersides that provide a bold accent in a border or form a fast-growing summer hedge. Fuzzy thistle-like flower globes tip each stem from summer through fall. Both leaves and flowers are prized by floral designers for fresh and dried arrangements. It is native to southern Europe.

Selected species and varieties: *C. cardunculus* (cardoon) will grow 6 feet tall in warm climates, though it often reaches only 4 feet in cooler regions. Leaves grow to 3 feet long. Both the leafstalks and the roots are edible. Flower heads are purplish, up to 3 inches across, and are surrounded by spiny bracts.

Growing conditions and maintenance: Start seed indoors in late winter, transplanting to successively larger pots as needed before moving to the garden in midspring. Allow 3 feet between plants. Cardoon can be grown as a perennial from Zone 8 south.

Cynoglossum
(sin-o-GLOSS-um)
HOUND'S-TONGUE

Cynoglossum amabile

Plant type: *biennial*

Height: *18 inches to 2 feet*

Interest: *flowers*

Soil: *moist to dry, well-drained*

Light: *full sun to light shade*

This Asian biennial produces tiny clear blue flowers throughout summer and into fall. It puts on a fine show in borders or beds and is excellent for massing and fresh flower arrangements.

Selected species and varieties: *C. amabile* (Chinese forget-me-not) has an irregular to rounded habit with a clump of erect stems with somewhat coarse leaves. Each stem is topped with an arching cluster of brilliant blue blossoms. Individual flowers are ¼ inch across and have five petals. Pink- and white-flowered forms are also available.

Growing conditions and maintenance: Though biennial, this species usually flowers the first year from seed. Start seed indoors 6 to 8 weeks before the last frost, or sow directly outside as soon as the soil can be worked in spring. Allow 9 to 12 inches between plants. It thrives in a wide range of soils and will often self-seed. When cutting for arrangements, submerge the stems three-quarters of their length in water immediately to prevent flowers from collapsing.

Dahlia
(DAH-lee-a)
DAHLIA

Dahlia 'Mickey'

Plant type: *tender perennial*

Height: *12 inches to 8 feet*

Interest: *flowers*

Soil: *moist, well-drained, fertile*

Light: *full sun*

Dahlias brighten the border over a long season with diverse blooms whose sizes range from a few inches across to the diameter of a dinner plate. Their tightly packed disk flowers are surrounded by one or more rows of petal-like ray flowers that may be doubled, curved, twisted, cupped, or rolled into tiny tubes. Colors range widely; some are bicolored or variegated. The more than 20,000 cultivars available today descend from a few wild species cultivated by Aztec botanists. Dwarf dahlias are cultivated in beds or borders as low-growing bushy edgings; standard dahlias are grown as medium to tall fillers in beds and borders or as specimens. All make long-lasting cut flowers.

Selected species and varieties: *Anemone-flowered dahlias*—a central disk obscured by a fluffy ball of short, tubular petals and rimmed by one or more rows of longer, flat petals. *Ball dahlias*—cupped, doubled petals crowding spirally into round domes or slightly flattened globes. *Cactus dahlias*—straight or twisted petals rolled like quills or straws over half their length to a pointed tip. *Chrysanthemum-type dahlias*—double rows of petals curving inward and hiding

the central disk. *Collarette dahlias*—central disks surrounded by a collar of short petals backed by a second collar of broader, flat petals; 'Mickey' bears neat yellow-centered blooms with red and yellow ruffles surrounded by red outer petals. *Formal decorative dahlias*—double rows of flat, evenly spaced petals covering the central disk; 'Audacity' produces lavender-pink petals that fade to white at the base. *Informal decora-*

Dahlia 'Audacity'

tive dahlias—double rows of randomly spaced flat petals hiding the central disk. *Peony-flowered dahlias*—two or three overlapping layers of ray petals surrounding a central disk. *Pompom dahlias*—small, round balls of tightly rolled petals less than 2 inches in diameter. *Semi-cactus dahlias*—flat petals curling over less than half their length into tubes at their tips. *Single dahlias*—one or two row of flat petals surrounding a flat central disk. *Star dahlias*—two or three rows of short petals curving inward. *Waterlily-flowered dahlias*—short petals tightly clasped over the central disk like a waterlily bud, surrounded by several rows of broad, flat petals. Dahlias are further categorized by flower size.

Growing conditions and maintenance: Start seed indoors in very early spring, or plant tubers directly in the garden in spring, spacing them 1 to 4 feet apart, depending on their type. Provide abundant water and mulch. Remove faded blooms to extend bloom period. Taller types require staking. Dahlias are perennial in Zones 9 to 11; elsewhere tubers may be dug up in fall and stored in a dry, cool location until planting time the next spring.

Datura
(da-TOOR-a)
ANGEL'S-TRUMPET

Datura inoxia

Plant type: *annual or tender perennial*

Height: *2 to 5 feet*

Interest: *flowers*

Soil: *moist, well-drained*

Light: *full sun to light shade*

Datura's large flower trumpets bloom above coarse, oval leaves on shrubby plants that are useful as fillers or as backdrops in a border. Each summer-blooming flower opens at sunset and lasts only a day. Though flowers are sometimes fragrant, the leaves are unpleasantly scented, and most plant parts are extremely poisonous. Plant them only in places where they are completely out of the reach of children and pets.

Selected species and varieties: *D. inoxia* (angel's-trumpet, thorn apple) grows to 3 feet with 10-inch leaves and pendant pink, white, or lavender flowers 8 inches long and 5 inches wide. *D. metel* (Hindu datura) grows 3 to 5 feet tall with 8-inch leaves and 7-inch white or yellow- or purple-tinged flowers. *D. stramonium* (jimson weed) grows to 5 feet with 8-inch leaves and white or purple 2- to 5-inch flowers; it is extremely poisonous.

Growing conditions and maintenance: Start seed indoors 6 to 8 weeks prior to moving outdoors to warmed soil. Space plants 1½ to 2 feet apart. Provide shelter from wind. *D. inoxia* may survive as a short-lived perennial in Zones 9 and 10.

Daucus
(DAW-kus)
DAUCUS

Daucus carota var. carota

Plant type: *biennial*

Height: *3 to 4 feet*

Interest: *flowers*

Soil: *average to poor, well-drained*

Light: *full sun*

This native of Eurasia has naturalized in the United States along roadsides and in abandoned fields. It is very closely related to the garden carrot but is grown for its dainty 4-inch flower heads, called umbels, which appear in late spring to midsummer. The flat-topped umbels consist of tiny white flowers with, often, a single dark red flower at the center. Its lacy appearance serves as a nice filler in a sunny border, and it naturalizes easily in wildflower meadows, attracting butterflies and bees. Flowers are valued for both fresh and dried arrangements.

Selected species and varieties: *D. carota* var. *carota* (Queen Anne's lace, Queen's lace, wild carrot) produces a prominent rosette of fernlike leaves in early spring, from which grows a 3- to 4-foot branched flowering stem. Each branch is topped by a 3- to 4-inch umbel.

Growing conditions and maintenance: Sow seed outdoors in late spring for flowers the following year. Once established, plant will vigorously self-seed. To prevent unwanted plants, remove flowers before seeds mature. Plants are easy to grow and thrive in nearly any well-drained soil.

Dianthus
(dy-AN-thus)
PINK

Dianthus chinensis 'Telestar Picotee'

Plant type: *annual, biennial, or tender perennial*

Height: *4 to 30 inches*

Interest: *flowers, foliage*

Soil: *moist, well-drained, slightly alkaline*

Light: *full sun to partial shade*

Pinks form mats of grassy foliage with white, pink, red, and bicolored flowers with fringed petals. Low-growing types make delightful edgings or rock-garden or container specimens, while taller selections are useful in the foreground or middle of a border, and as cut flowers.

Selected species and varieties: *D. barbatus* (sweet William) is a biennial that self-seeds freely; dwarf varieties grow 4 to 10 inches tall, while tall varieties may reach 2 feet. Flowers are borne in dense, flat-topped clusters from late spring to early summer. *D. chinensis* (China pink, rainbow pink) is an annual, biennial, or short-lived perennial that grows 6 to 30 inches tall with a dense, mounded habit; 1- to 2-inch flowers, often fragrant, are borne singly or in loose clusters from early summer to fall; 'Telestar Picotee' has a compact habit with deep pink flowers fringed with white.

Growing conditions and maintenance: Sow sweet William seed outdoors in late spring for flowers the following year. Start seed of China pinks indoors 6 to 8 weeks prior to the last frost for transplanting to the garden in midspring. Space plants 8 to 18 inches apart.

Diascia
(dy-ASS-ee-a)
TWINSPUR

Diascia barberae 'Ruby Fields'

Plant type: *annual*

Height: *8 to 12 inches*

Interest: *flowers*

Soil: *light, well-drained*

Light: *full sun*

A native of South Africa, twinspur is a slender plant with glossy dark green leaves and five-petaled pink flowers with a pair of spurs at the back. It adds a touch of elegance to the front of beds or borders or to a rock garden. It also makes a charming container plant, suitable for window boxes and hanging baskets.

Selected species and varieties: *D. barberae* has a mounding habit with slender stems bearing loose clusters of rosy pink flowers from early summer to early fall; 'Pink Queen' grows to 12 inches and bears pink flowers with yellow throats in 6-inch clusters; 'Ruby Fields' produces deep rose pink flowers over an exceptionally long period.

Growing conditions and maintenance: Start seed indoors 6 to 8 weeks prior to the last frost. Transplant to the garden after the soil has warmed, spacing plants 8 inches apart. Plants can also be seeded directly in the garden in early spring. Flowering begins about 14 weeks after seeding. Pinch young plants to encourage bushiness, and after flowering cut flower stems back to the base of the plant to stimulate production of more flowers.

Digitalis
(di-ji-TAL-us)
FOXGLOVE

Digitalis purpurea 'Excelsior'

Plant type: *biennial*

Height: *2 to 6 feet*

Interest: *flowers, foliage*

Soil: *moist, well-drained, acid*

Light: *partial shade*

Foxglove's striking summer-blooming flower trumpets line the tips of stiff stalks above clumps of coarse, hairy leaves. Most are native to Europe and North Africa but have been grown in the Americas since Colonial times. They add an old-fashioned look and a vertical accent to borders. They also fit well into naturalized plantings such as a woodland garden, and bees love their flowers. Though most bloom their second season, some varieties flower the first year from seed. Because foxglove self-seeds easily, new plants appear each year, giving it a perennial quality. Leaves contain digitalis and are poisonous if eaten.

Selected species and varieties: *D. ferruginea* (rusty foxglove) produces a basal clump of narrow, deeply veined dark green leaves, each up to 9 inches long. A leafy 5- to 6-foot flower stalk rises from the clump, bearing dense clusters of small yellowish blooms that open from mid- to late summer. Each flower is ½ to 1¼ inches long, yellow-brown, and netted with a rusty red. Tiny hairs fringe the flower lip. *D. purpurea* (common foxglove) produces a broad clump of large rough-textured woolly leaves from

which an erect flower stem with smaller leaves emerges in early summer. The flower stalk ranges in size from 2 to 5 feet. The 2- to 3-inch pendulous flowers are borne in a one-sided cluster up to 2 feet long. Their colors include purple, pink, white, rust, or yellow, and their throats are often spotted; 'Alba' grows to 4 feet with white flowers; 'Apricot' grows to 3½ feet with flowers ranging from pale

Digitalis purpurea 'Foxy'

pink to bold apricot; 'Excelsior' grows to 5 feet with blooms borne all around the stem rather than on one side, in colors of purple, pink, white, cream, and yellow; 'Foxy' grows 2½ to 3 feet with flowers in pastel shades from rose pink to white appearing the first year from seed; 'Giant Shirley' grows 5 feet or more, producing strong stems with large mottled blooms in shades of pink.

Growing conditions and maintenance: Start seed outdoors in spring or summer, thinning to stand 6 inches apart. Transplant seedlings to their flowering location in fall or early spring. Types that bloom their first year from seed should be started indoors about 10 weeks, and transplanted to the garden 2 weeks, before the last frost. Space plants 18 to 24 inches apart. Foxgloves thrive in a rich, loose soil and benefit from the addition of compost. Provide water during dry periods and mulch after the ground freezes in fall.

Dimorphotheca
(dy-mor-foe-THEE-ka)
CAPE MARIGOLD

Dimorphotheca sinuata

Plant type: *annual*

Height: *12 to 16 inches*

Interest: *flowers*

Soil: *well-drained to dry*

Light: *full sun*

These South African daisies come in a wide range of bright colors and appear over a very long season, from late spring until fall. Given the right growing conditions, they add a festive touch to the front of beds or borders and are a good choice for rock gardens. The flowers close at night.

Selected species and varieties: *D. pluvialis* (rain Cape marigold) grows to 16 inches with showy 2½-inch flower heads with yellow centers, often marked with violet, surrounded by white petal-like ray flowers with a purple to violet reverse. *D. sinuata* (winter Cape marigold) grows 12 to 15 inches with a compact, mounded habit, producing 1½-inch flower heads composed of white, yellow, pink, or orange rays surrounding golden centers.

Growing conditions and maintenance: Start seed indoors 4 to 6 weeks prior to the last frost or sow directly in the garden after all danger of frost has passed. Space plants 6 to 9 inches apart. Plants thrive in light, dry soils and tolerate heat and drought.

Dolichos
(DO-li-kos)
HYACINTH BEAN

Dolichos lablab

Plant type: *tender perennial*

Height: *10 to 20 feet*

Interest: *flowers, foliage, fruit*

Soil: *loose, well-drained*

Light: *full sun*

This lush, tropical twining vine produces purplish stems and purple-veined compound leaves. Attractive clusters of pink, purple, or white pea-like flowers appear in summer and are followed by showy red-purple seedpods. The seeds are edible and are an important food source in many parts of the world. As an ornamental, plants provide a colorful screen or covering for a fence, an arbor, or a trellis.

Selected species and varieties: *D. lablab* climbs to 20 feet in one season by twining stems. Leaves are composed of three heart-shaped leaflets, each 3 to 6 inches long. The loosely clustered flowers stand out against the deeply colored leaves. Pods are 1 to 3 inches long.

Growing conditions and maintenance: Start seed indoors in peat pots 4 to 6 weeks prior to the last frost, or sow directly in the garden after the soil has warmed. Space plants 12 to 24 inches apart and provide support for climbing. Hyacinth bean thrives in warm weather and is perennial in Zones 10 and 11.

Dyssodia
(dis-OH-dee-ah)
DAHLBERG DAISY

Dyssodia tenuiloba

Plant type: *annual or tender perennial*

Height: *4 to 8 inches*

Interest: *flowers, foliage*

Soil: *well-drained to dry*

Light: *full sun*

Their dainty blooms lavishly sprinkled on a dense carpet of finely divided foliage, Dahlberg daisies (also called golden-fleece) constantly flower throughout the summer. They are perfect for bedding and edging, in rock gardens, and in hanging baskets. They can be planted between steppingstones to add color to a sunny garden path.

Selected species and varieties: *D. tenuiloba* grows to 8 inches tall but spreads up to 18 inches wide. Its slender stems produce threadlike, bristle-tipped leaves that are aromatic. Flower heads are ½ to 1 inch across with orange-yellow ray flowers surrounding a yellow center.

Growing conditions and maintenance: Start seed indoors 6 to 8 weeks prior to the last frost to transplant to the garden after all danger of frost has passed. In warm areas they can be planted directly in the garden and will self-seed. Allow 6 to 12 inches between plants. Water sparingly and do not fertilize. Plants thrive in sunny, dry locations and tolerate heat, drought, and coastal conditions.

Echium
(EK-ee-um)
VIPER'S BUGLOSS

Echium candicans

Plant type: *biennial*

Height: *1 to 10 feet*

Interest: *flowers, foliage*

Soil: *dry, poor*

Light: *full sun*

These tropical natives provide a striking accent to borders and rock gardens with their brightly colored and closely packed tubular flowers, which appear from early to late summer. Plants often flower their first year from seed. They are especially useful in sunny, dry locations where the soil is poor.

Selected species and varieties: *E. candicans* (pride-of-Madeira) grows 3 to 6 feet tall with narrow gray-green leaves covered with silvery hairs and an erect 20-inch cluster of white or purple ½-inch flowers held well above the leaves. *E. lycopsis* (viper's bugloss) grows 1 to 3 feet tall with a bushy habit; flowers are blue, lavender, purple, pink, or white and appear on dense 10-inch spikes. *E. wildpretii* (tower-of-jewels) grows to a show-stopping 10 feet, with pale red blooms.

Growing conditions and maintenance: Start seed indoors 6 to 8 weeks before the last frost or outdoors as soon as soil can be worked in spring. In Zones 9 and south, seed can be sown in fall for earlier bloom. Space plants 12 to 18 inches apart. They thrive in poor soils and will produce few flowers on a fertile site. Water sparingly.

Emilia
(ee-MILL-ee-a)
TASSEL FLOWER

Emilia javanica

Plant type: *annual*

Height: *18 inches to 2 feet*

Interest: *flowers*

Soil: *dry, well-drained*

Light: *full sun*

Tassel flower (also called Emilia's paintbrush) is native to the tropics of both the Eastern and the Western Hemisphere. Throughout summer, it produces small, brilliantly colored flowers on wiry stalks that rise well above a cluster of gray-green leaves. Plant it among other annuals in a border. Flowers can be cut for both fresh and dried arrangements.

Selected species and varieties: *E. javanica* [also known as *E. coccinea* and *Cacalia coccinea*] develops a clump of oblong leaves 6 inches high. Erect stems up to 2 feet tall are topped with 1-inch clusters of flowers in shades of red, orange, and yellow.

Growing conditions and maintenance: Start seeds indoors 6 to 8 weeks prior to the last frost for earliest bloom, or sow directly in the garden after the soil has warmed. Space plants 6 to 9 inches apart. They thrive in coastal conditions and tolerate hot, dry locations.

Erysimum
(e-RISS-i-mum)
WALLFLOWER

Erysimum perofskianum

Plant type: *biennial*

Height: *9 to 24 inches*

Interest: *flowers*

Soil: *well-drained, slightly alkaline*

Light: *full sun*

This native of the mountains of Afghanistan and Pakistan is closely related to *Cheiranthus* species, with which it is sometimes confused. From spring to early summer, yellow and orange spicy-scented flowers appear in dense spikes. It is a good choice for rock gardens, beds, or window boxes.

Selected species and varieties: *E. perofskianum* [also listed as *Cheiranthus allionii*] (fairy wallflower) produces a rosette of narrow 3-inch leaves and erect 9- to 24-inch flower stems crowded with yellow, orange, or red-orange blossoms. Each flower is ½ inch long and is composed of four petals and four sepals.

Growing conditions and maintenance: In areas with mild winters, sow seed outdoors in fall; elsewhere, sow in early spring as soon as soil can be worked. Seed can also be started indoors, 6 weeks prior to the last frost. Space plants 6 inches apart.

Eschscholzia
(es-SHOL-zee-a)
CALIFORNIA POPPY

Eschscholzia californica

Plant type: *annual or tender perennial*

Height: *4 to 24 inches*

Interest: *flowers*

Soil: *dry*

Light: *full sun*

This genus includes both annuals and tender perennials native to the grasslands of California and the Southwest. Flowers open during the day and close at night and in cloudy weather. They are effective for massing in beds and borders and compete well in wildflower meadows.

Selected species and varieties: *E. caespitosa* (tufted California poppy, pastel poppy) is an annual with pale yellow flowers on 4- to 12-inch stalks above finely cut basal foliage. *E. californica* is a 1- to 2-foot tender perennial from Zone 8 south but is grown as an annual elsewhere, with 1- to 3-inch yellow or orange flowers from spring to fall and feathery blue-green foliage; 'Aurantiaca' is an old variety with rich orange single blooms; 'Monarch Mixed' bears single and semi-double flowers in yellow, orange, red, and pink; 'Orange King' bears translucent orange flowers.

Growing conditions and maintenance: Plant seed outdoors in early spring; seedlings do not transplant well. Once established, plants self-seed freely. Space them 6 inches apart. Though they tolerate most soils, they prefer a poor, sandy one.

Euphorbia
(yew-FOR-bee-a)
EUPHORBIA

Euphorbia marginata

Plant type: *annual*

Height: *18 inches to 2 feet*

Interest: *flowers, foliage*

Soil: *dry to wet*

Light: *full sun*

This hardy annual is native to many parts of the United States and is grown as much for its neatly variegated leaves as for its tiny green flowers surrounded by white bracts. It is an effective accent for annual beds, especially planted in groups of three or five among plants with dark leaves or brightly colored flowers. The sap may cause skin irritation.

Selected species and varieties: *E. marginata* (snow-on-the-mountain, ghostweed) produces erect, stout, branched stems bearing gray-green oval leaves attractively striped and margined with white. Though the late-summer flowers are small, they are surrounded by showy white leaflike bracts.

Growing conditions and maintenance: Sow seed directly in the garden in late fall or early spring. Allow 10 to 12 inches between plants. Moisture is needed for seed to germinate and for the plants to become established, but they become very drought tolerant as they mature. They self-seed easily and may become invasive. Use gloves when handling stems to avoid contact with the sap.

Eustoma
(yew-STO-ma)
TULIP GENTIAN

Eustoma grandiflorum 'Lion Mixed'

Plant type: *biennial*

Height: *2 to 3 feet*

Interest: *flowers*

Soil: *moist, well-drained*

Light: *full sun to partial shade*

This native American wildflower produces waxy blue-green leaves on a thick stem with upturned flowers that resemble small roses. Though exacting in their requirements, they are well worth the effort. When grown well, they are exquisite border or container plants and make superb cut flowers, lasting up to 2 weeks.

Selected species and varieties: *E. grandiflorum* [also known as *Lisianthus russellianus*] (prairie gentian) has an erect habit with sturdy stems and 3-inch oblong leaves. Flowers may be single or double, are 2 inches wide and are usually purple, although pink, blue, and white varieties are available; 'Lion Mixed' is a double-flowered strain with colors from white to deep purple.

Growing conditions and maintenance: Start seed indoors about 3 months prior to the last frost, barely covering them with soil. Move them to the garden after the soil warms, handling seedlings with care. Space plants 6 to 10 inches apart. Keep the soil evenly moist but not too wet. They are slow growers and need a long growing season to perform well. Once they have developed their taproot, plants tolerate drought and heat.

Exacum
(EKS-a-kum)
GERMAN VIOLET

Exacum affine

Plant type: *biennial*

Height: *8 to 24 inches*

Interest: *flowers*

Soil: *moist, well-drained*

Light: *partial to full shade*

The German violet hails from the island of Socotra in the South Indian Ocean. It has an attractive bushy habit and produces abundant sweet-smelling flowers that cover the plant from summer to early fall. It is an excellent choice for edging a shady border or walkway and is often used as a container plant.

Selected species and varieties: *E. affine* (Persian violet) has a compact, rounded habit with neat, glossy, oval leaves. Each ½-inch lavender-blue flower is star shaped with five pointed petals surrounding prominent yellow anthers. Varieties are available with white, purple, or blue flowers.

Growing conditions and maintenance: Start seed indoors 8 weeks prior to the last frost. Do not cover the seed; it needs light to germinate. Transplant to the garden after all danger of frost has passed, spacing plants 8 to 16 inches apart. Keep soil evenly moist. Plants thrive in warm weather but need some shade.

Foeniculum
(fee-NIK-you-lum)
FENNEL

Foeniculum vulgare 'Purpureum'

Plant type: *tender perennial*

Height: *3 to 5 feet*

Interest: *flowers, foliage*

Soil: *light, well-drained*

Light: *full sun*

The fine-textured, threadlike leaves of fennel are attractive from summer to frost and provide an attractive background for the flat clusters of small yellow flowers. Fennel combines well with bold-textured plants in the middle or back of a mixed border. Leaves, stems, and seed have an anise flavor and are used in cooking.

Selected species and varieties: *F. vulgare* produces multiply compound leaves and numerous yellow-green flowers in disklike umbels 3 to 4 inches across; 'Purpureum' (bronze fennel) is somewhat smaller in size and produces attractive bronze-red foliage that is particularly appealing combined with plants with gray or silver foliage.

Growing conditions and maintenance: Sow seed directly in the garden in late fall or early spring. Thin seedlings to stand 1 to 2 feet apart. Fennel is not particular about soil and tolerates drought. Though perennial in many areas, it is generally treated as an annual because it is so fast and is easy to grow from seed.

Gaillardia
(gay-LAR-dee-a)
BLANKET-FLOWER

Gaillardia pulchella

Plant type: *annual*

Height: *1 to 2 feet*

Interest: *flowers*

Soil: *well-drained, sandy*

Light: *full sun*

Gaillardias are native to the southern and western United States. They are easy to grow, producing their brightly colored flowers freely from midsummer to frost, and are most effective when planted in groups of five or more in beds, borders, or along walkways. Their lively colors are attractive in fresh flower arrangements.

Selected species and varieties: *G. pulchella* (Indian blanket) grows to 2 feet with woolly oblong leaves and daisylike flowers 2 to 3 inches wide. The petal-like rays may be dark red with yellow tips, yellow with red tips, or solid red or yellow, surrounding a reddish purple disk. Dwarf and double-flowered varieties are available.

Growing conditions and maintenance: Start seed indoors 6 weeks before the last frost, or outdoors in early spring. Space plants 6 to 12 inches apart. Plants will tolerate most soils as long as they are well drained, but thrive in sandy, open sites. They withstand heat, wind, and drought.

Gazania
(ga-ZAY-nee-a)
GAZANIA

Gazania rigens 'Fiesta Red'

Plant type: *tender perennial*

Height: *6 to 16 inches*

Interest: *flowers*

Soil: *well-drained to dry*

Light: *full sun*

This tender perennial from South Africa produces daisylike flowers from midsummer to frost. Blossoms open when the sun is out, and close at night and on overcast days. They provide a colorful show in beds or containers.

Selected species and varieties: *G. linearis* grows to 16 inches with narrow leaves and 2¾-inch flower heads with golden rays and orange-brown disks. *G. rigens* (treasure flower) grows 6 to 12 inches tall with 3-inch flower heads, borne on long stalks, that may be yellow, orange, pink, or red; 'Chansonette' grows to 10 inches with a compact habit and flowers in a wide range of colors; 'Fiesta Red' bears deep burnt orange flowers with a dark ring surrounding a yellow disk; 'Harlequin Hybrids' bear flowers in many shades with a brown zone around the central disk; 'Sunshine' grows to 8 inches with 4-inch multicolored flowers.

Growing conditions and maintenance: Sow seeds indoors in early spring to transplant to the garden after all danger of frost has passed. Space plants 12 inches apart. Do not overwater. They thrive in sunny, dry locations, and tolerate wind and coastal conditions.

Gomphrena
(gom-FREE-na)
GLOBE AMARANTH

Gomphrena globosa

Plant type: *annual*

Height: *8 to 24 inches*

Interest: *flowers*

Soil: *well-drained*

Light: *full sun*

Colorful cloverlike flower heads of gomphrena top upright stems from summer to frost. A native of India, this half-hardy annual is easy to grow and imparts a cheerful, informal appearance to beds and borders. Plants perform well in patio planters and window boxes. Flowers, which have a papery texture even when fresh, are excellent for both fresh and dried arrangements.

Selected species and varieties: *G. globosa* produces erect, branched stems and somewhat coarse, hairy leaves. The globular flower heads are 1 inch long and may be pink, white, magenta, orange, or red.

Growing conditions and maintenance: Start seed indoors 8 to 10 weeks before the last frost and transplant outdoors after all danger of frost has passed. Seed can be sown directly outside in late spring. Allow 8 to 15 inches between plants. Though slow to start, plants are easy to grow once established, and they thrive in warm weather. To use in dried arrangements, cut before the flowers are fully open and hang them upside down in an airy room until dry.

Gypsophila
(jip-SOFF-il-a)
BABY'S-BREATH

Gypsophila elegans

Plant type: *annual*

Height: *8 to 24 inches*

Interest: *flowers*

Soil: *well-drained, alkaline*

Light: *full sun*

This hardy annual from Europe and northern Asia produces a cloud of delicate, tiny flowers on sprawling, branched stems from midspring to early fall. It is beautiful as a filler between more brightly colored and boldly textured plants in flower borders or rock gardens and in indoor arrangements both fresh and dried.

Selected species and varieties: *G. elegans* has a mounded habit with thin, multibranched stems bearing pairs of narrow gray-green leaves and airy clusters of white, pink, red, or purple flowers. Each flower is ¼ to ¾ inch across.

Growing conditions and maintenance: Sow seed directly in the garden in midspring. Supplement acid soils with limestone. Plants are short-lived, so make successive sowings every 2 to 3 weeks for continuous bloom. Thin plants to stand 9 to 12 inches apart. Taller varieties may need staking. In Zone 9 and south, provide afternoon shade.

Helianthus
(hee-lee-AN-thus)
SUNFLOWER

Helianthus annuus 'Inca Jewels'

Plant type: *annual*

Height: *2 to 10 feet*

Interest: *flowers*

Soil: *moist, well-drained*

Light: *full sun*

The sunflower's daisylike blooms in yellow, cream, mahogany, crimson, and assorted blends appear from midsummer to frost on erect stalks. The flowers make a bold statement in mixed borders, and a row them of makes a delightful temporary screen. Flowers are great for cutting. The seeds are a favorite food of many wild birds.

Selected species and varieties: *H. annuus* (common sunflower) has an erect habit and a coarse texture, producing sturdy stems with broad, bristly leaves and flowers composed of petal-like, often yellow rays surrounding brown or purple disk flowers; 'Inca Jewels' has a multibranched habit with yellow-tipped orange rays; 'Italian White' grows to 4 feet with multibranched stems and 4-inch cream-colored flowers with a brown center; 'Sunbeam' grows 5 feet tall with 5-inch pollenless flowers ideal for cutting; 'Teddy Bear' produces single and double yellow flowers on 2-foot plants.

Growing conditions and maintenance: Sow seed directly outdoors after the last frost. Thin seedlings to allow 1 to 2 feet between plants. Plants thrive in hot, dry weather conditions.

Helichrysum
(bel-i-KRY-sum)
EVERLASTING

Helichrysum bracteatum

Plant type: *tender perennial*

Height: *1 to 3 feet*

Interest: *flowers*

Soil: *light, well-drained*

Light: *full sun*

This Australian native, also known as immortelle, produces papery-textured flowers in shades of white, yellow, orange, salmon, red, and pink. What appear to be the flower's petals are actually colorful bracts; the true flowers are at the center of the flower head. Use dwarf types for adding color to a rock garden or the edge of a border. Taller varieties are highly valued for cutting, especially for winter arrangements. Flowers retain their colors very well when dried.

Selected species and varieties: *H. bracteatum* (strawflower) produces narrow, coarsely toothed leaves on wiry, branching stems. Flower heads appear from midsummer to early fall and are 1 to 2½ inches across.

Growing conditions and maintenance: Start seed indoors 6 to 8 weeks prior to the last frost. In warm climates, seed can be sown directly in the garden. Allow 12 inches between plants. Once established, plants thrive in dry soil and often self-seed. They do not perform well in areas with very high humidity. For winter arrangements, cut flowers when they are about half open and hang them upside down in an airy room to dry.

Heliotropium
(bee-lee-oh-TRO-pee-um)
HELIOTROPE

Heliotropium arborescens 'Marine'

Plant type: *tender perennial*

Height: *1 to 3 feet*

Interest: *flowers*

Soil: *well-drained, fertile*

Light: *full sun to partial shade*

Heliotrope is a tender perennial from Peru grown as an annual in temperate zones. Large clusters of summer flowers range from deep purple to white and bear a lovely vanilla fragrance. Site plants in the foreground of a mixed border; they are especially effective in groups located where their fragrance will be appreciated. They are ideal container plants, and flowers can be cut for fresh arrangements.

Selected species and varieties: *H. arborescens* (cherry pie) grows 1 to 3 feet in the garden, though plants grown in a greenhouse or in their native range may reach 6 feet. Foliage is dark green and wrinkled. Five-petaled flowers are ¼ inch across, occurring in clusters as large as a foot across; 'Marine', a compact variety reaching 2 feet, has large deep purple flowers and is excellent for bedding, although it lacks intense fragrance.

Growing conditions and maintenance: Start seed indoors 10 to 12 weeks prior to the last frost, or buy young plants in spring. Plants can also be started from cuttings. Do not transplant to the garden until soil has warmed, as plants are very frost sensitive. Allow 12 inches between plants and keep them well watered.

Hibiscus
(hy-BIS-kus)
MALLOW, ROSE MALLOW

Hibiscus acetosella

Plant type: *tender perennial*

Height: *18 inches to 8 feet*

Interest: *flowers, foliage*

Soil: *moist, well-drained*

Light: *full sun to light shade*

These shrubby tender perennials are attractively grown as annuals in many temperate gardens. Some are grown for their ornamental foliage, while others produce large funnel-shaped five-petaled flowers with prominent stamens that add a tropical flavor to a border. You will find many uses for these bold-textured plants. Plant them individually as specimens or in groups as a fast-growing summer hedge. Tall types are effective as a background for mixed borders or as the centerpiece of an island bed. Shorter ones are useful for fronting shrub borders or planting in the foreground of annual beds. Both large and small types are excellent choices for patio containers.

Selected species and varieties: *H. acetosella* hails from Africa and is grown primarily for its attractive foliage. Purple flowers form so late in the season in most areas that they fail to open before frost. The plant grows to 5 feet tall, with glossy red leaves and stems. Leaves may be smooth in outline or deeply lobed. This plant makes a bold accent mixed with other annuals, or a stunning summer hedge; the variety 'Red Shield' produces burgundy leaves with a metallic sheen that resemble maple leaves in shape. *H. moscheutos* (common rose mallow, swamp rose mallow, wild cotton) grows 3 to 8 feet tall with a shrubby habit. It is native to marshlands of the eastern United States and can be grown as a perennial in Zones 7 and south, but is often grown as a half-hardy annual. The large gray-green leaves provide a

Hibiscus trionum

soft foil for the huge white, pink, rose, or red summer flowers that are often 8 inches across; 'Southern Belle' grows 4 to 6 feet tall with red, pink, or white flowers with a distinct red eye, up to 10 inches across. *H. trionum* (flower-of-an-hour) grows 18 to 36 inches with a bushy habit and dark green three- or five-lobed leaves. Flowers are 2 inches across and are creamy yellow with a deep maroon throat. Though flowers are short-lived, they appear in abundance from midsummer to late fall.

Growing conditions and maintenance: Start seed of *H. acetosella* and *H. moscheutos* indoors about 8 weeks prior to the last frost and transplant outdoors after all danger of frost has passed. Space *H. acetosella* 12 to 14 inches apart, *H. moscheutos* 3 feet apart. Because *H. trionum* is difficult to transplant, seed should be sown directly in the garden after all danger of frost has passed, allowing 12 inches between plants. Plants tolerate heat as long as abundant moisture is supplied.

Humulus
(HEW-mew-lus)
HOPS

Humulus japonicus

Plant type:	*tender perennial*
Height:	*10 to 20 feet*
Interest:	*foliage*
Soil:	*moist, fertile*
Light:	*full sun*

This fast-growing vine from Asia produces large deeply cut and coarsely toothed leaves. It is very useful for providing a quick screen over fences, arbors, trellises, or any unsightly object.

Selected species and varieties: *H. japonicus* (Japanese hopvine) climbs by twining its stems around its support. Leaves are broad, up to 8 inches across with five to seven deep lobes. Flowers are small and green and are often obscured by the foliage. Varieties with golden and variegated foliage are available.

Growing conditions and maintenance: Start seeds indoors 6 weeks prior to the last frost, or sow seed directly in the garden in midspring. Space plants 12 to 18 inches apart. Once established, they often self-seed, and may become invasive. Provide sturdy support for twining stems. Plants thrive in warm weather.

Iberis
(eye-BEER-is)
CANDYTUFT

Iberis umbellata

Plant type:	*annual*
Height:	*6 to 18 inches*
Interest:	*flowers*
Soil:	*well-drained*
Light:	*full sun*

These European wildflowers are easy to grow and free flowering. Like the perennial species *[I. sempervirens]*, annual candytufts produce clusters of tiny four-petaled flowers above dark green leaves. They flower throughout the summer and are effective in rock gardens and borders, or as an edging or in a planter, where their sweet fragrance will be noticed.

Selected species and varieties: *I. amara* (rocket candytuft) grows 12 to 18 inches tall with fragrant white flowers in cone-shaped spikes that can be cut for fresh arrangements. *I. odorata* (fragrant candytuft) grows 6 to 12 inches with flat clusters of white flowers. *I. umbellata* (globe candytuft) grows 8 to 16 inches with clusters of pink, red, lilac, or violet flowers that are not fragrant.

Growing conditions and maintenance: Sow seed in the garden in fall or as soon as soil can be worked in the spring, thinning to allow 6 to 9 inches between seedlings. Make successive sowings to extend the flowering season. Cut back lightly after bloom to stimulate growth. Plants thrive in city conditions.

Impatiens
(im-PAY-shens)
BALSAM, JEWELWEED

Impatiens wallerana 'Super Elfin Twilight'

Plant type: *annual*

Height: *6 inches to 8 feet*

Interest: *flowers, foliage*

Soil: *moist, well-drained*

Light: *full sun to full shade*

Massed as edgings or ground covers, impatiens brighten a shady garden with flowers in jeweled hues from summer through frost. Low-growing types are ideal for planters and hanging baskets.

Selected species and varieties: *I. balsamina* (garden balsam, rose balsam) grows to 3 feet, producing 1- to 2-inch flowers in mixed colors. *I. glandulifera* (Himalayan jewelweed) grows to 8 feet with 2-inch purple, pink, or white flowers in mid- to late summer. *I.* x *New Guinea* (New Guinea impatiens) grows to 2 feet with showy, often variegated leaves with flowers up to 3 inches across. *I. wallerana* (busy Lizzie) grows 6 to 18 inches tall with a compact, mounded habit and 1- to 2-inch flat-faced flowers available in many colors; 'Super Elfin Twilight' bears deep pink flowers on spreading plants.

Growing conditions and maintenance: Plant *I. glandulifera* seed outdoors in fall. Start impatiens indoors 3 to 4 months prior to the last frost, or purchase bedding plants to transplant to the garden after all danger of frost has passed. Space *I. glandulifera* 2 feet apart, others 12 to 18 inches apart. Most species prefer some shade and abundant water.

Ipomoea
(eye-po-MEE-a)
MORNING GLORY

Ipomoea purpurea

Plant type: *annual or tender perennial*

Height: *6 to 20 feet*

Interest: *flowers, foliage*

Soil: *well-drained*

Light: *full sun*

Twining over trellises and fences or cascading over walls and banks, morning glories produce a new crop of trumpet-shaped blossoms each day from summer until frost. They are native to the American tropics and are generally easy to grow. They can be used to provide a screen or temporary ground cover, and are charming ramblers on a fence or porch.

Selected species and varieties: *I. alba* (moonflower) is a tender perennial that climbs as much as 20 feet. Its large heart-shaped leaves provide a lush foil for the white blooms that appear from midsummer to frost. Spiraled flower buds are 4 inches long and open before your eyes to reveal 5- to 6-inch beautiful, fragrant flowers. Buds open at night, scenting the evening air and attracting night pollinators, then close by midmorning the following day. *I. coccinea* (starflower) is an annual that grows to 10 feet with 6-inch heart-shaped leaves and 1½-inch scarlet flowers with yellow throats that appear throughout summer. Annual *I.* x *multifida* (cardinal climber, hearts-and-honey vine) grows 6 to 10 feet, producing feathery leaves and bright red 2-inch flowers with white throats. *I. nil* (morning glory)

grows to 10 feet with 6-inch shallowly divided leaves and 4-inch blooms that may be fluted or fringed. Flower colors include purple, pink, red, white, and blue; 'Chocolate' bears flowers that are pale chocolate brown; 'Scarlett O'Hara' produces 6-inch cherry red flowers. *I. purpurea* (common morning glory) is an annual native to Mexico that has naturalized in many parts of the United States. It grows 8 to 10 feet with 5-inch leaves. The 2- to 4-inch single or double flowers are trumpet shaped and come in shades of blue, purple, pink, and white. *I. quamo-*

Ipomoea x multifida

clit (cypress vine, star-glory), also an annual, grows 10 to 20 feet with 2½- to 4-inch leaves that are finely divided into threadlike sections; its 1½-inch flowers are orange or scarlet.

Growing conditions and maintenance: Start seed indoors in individual peat pots 4 to 6 weeks prior to the last frost, or sow directly in the garden after all danger of frost has passed. To hasten germination, nick the hard seed coat and soak the seed overnight. Space plants 8 to 18 inches apart and provide support for climbing. Plants thrive in hot weather. Provide abundant water during dry periods. Do not overfertilize.

Kochia
(KOE-kee-a)
BURNING BUSH

Kochia scoparia f. trichophylla

Plant type: *annual*

Height: *2 to 4 feet*

Interest: *foliage*

Soil: *moist, well-drained*

Light: *full sun*

This Eurasian annual has naturalized in some parts of the United States. Its fine-textured foliage and neat, symmetrical form make it an attractive summer hedge, screen, or background for a flower border.

Selected species and varieties: *K. scoparia f. trichophylla* (summer cypress, firebush) has an erect, uniform habit with dense, feathery foliage that is light green in summer, turning bright red in fall, while flowers are insignificant; 'Acapulco Silver' produces variegated silver-tipped leaves.

Growing conditions and maintenance: Start seed indoors in individual peat pots 6 to 8 weeks prior to the last frost or plant directly in the garden after all danger of frost has passed. Do not cover the seed; it needs light for germination. Plants often self-seed and may become invasive. Allow 1½ to 2 feet between plants. Plants can be sheared to maintain their shape or size, and they tolerate heat. Avoid overwatering. In windy locations, plants may require staking.

Lagenaria
(la-jen-AIR-ee-a)
CALABASH GOURD

Lagenaria siceraria

Plant type: *annual*

Height: *10 to 30 feet*

Interest: *fruit*

Soil: *well-drained, fertile*

Light: *full sun*

These annual vines require a great deal of space to accommodate their lush growth. They are grown for their fruit, which comes in a variety of sizes and shapes. Depending on the shape, the gourds can be used for containers, bird feeders, and autumn decoration.

Selected species and varieties: *L. siceraria* produces a hairy stem with branched tendrils and broad 6- to 12-inch leaves. The 5-inch white flowers open in the evening or on overcast days, and are sweetly fragrant. The fruit ranges from 3 to 36 inches in length and may be rounded or flattened, coiled, bottle shaped, or dumbbell shaped.

Growing conditions and maintenance: Start seed indoors in peat pots 6 to 8 weeks prior to the last frost. In areas with long growing seasons, seed can be planted directly in the garden after the last frost. Space plants 24 inches apart, and provide a sturdy support for climbing. Plants require a long season for fruit to mature, so allow gourds to remain on the vine as long as possible. Harvest before the first hard frost, and dry in an airy room.

Lagurus
(lag-YOU-rus)
RABBIT-GRASS

Lagurus ovatus

Plant type: *annual*

Height: *12 to 18 inches*

Interest: *foliage, seed heads*

Soil: *light, well-drained*

Light: *full sun*

This annual ornamental grass is native to the Mediterranean region but has naturalized in parts of the western United States. Its furry seed heads add interest and soft texture to a border or beside a walkway. Plants are effective in drifts or massed beds. Seed heads are attractive for both fresh and dried arrangements.

Selected species and varieties: *L. ovatus* (hare's-tail grass) produces narrow, hairy leaves and distinctive seed heads that are fuzzy and light green, turning creamy white as they mature. At 1½ to 2½ inches long, they resemble a rabbit's tail, hence the common name; 'Nanus' is a dwarf variety that grows to 6 inches.

Growing conditions and maintenance: Start seed indoors 8 weeks prior to the last frost or sow directly outdoors as soon as the soil can be worked. Allow 6 to 12 inches between plants. This grass tolerates heat very well.

Lathyrus
(LATH-er-us)
LATHYRUS

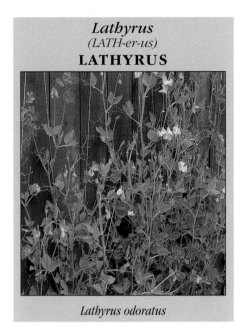

Lathyrus odoratus

Plant type: *annual*

Height: *6 inches to 6 feet*

Interest: *flowers*

Soil: *moist, well-drained*

Light: *full sun to partial shade*

The sweet pea is a hardy annual from southern Europe that bears puffy flowers on branching flowering stalks. It can be used as a trailing ground cover, a climbing vine for a screen or backdrop, or a bushy accent among bulbs.

Selected species and varieties: *L. odoratus* (sweet pea) produces fragrant spring or summer flowers up to 2 inches wide on compact 6-inch- to 2½-foot-tall annual bushes, or on a twining vine 5 to 6 feet long. Flower colors include deep rose, blue, purple, scarlet, white, cream, salmon, pink, and bicolors; 'Bijou Mixed' is a bush type that grows to 12 inches with a full range of colors; 'Royal Family' is a vining type that comes in a wide range of colors, grows to 6 feet, and is heat resistant.

Growing conditions and maintenance: Sow seed 2 inches deep in well-prepared soil in late fall or early spring. Provide climbing types with support. Mulch to keep soil cool, and provide abundant water. Remove faded blooms to prolong flowering.

Lavatera
(lav-a-TEER-a)
TREE MALLOW

Lavatera trimestris

Plant type: *annual*

Height: *2 to 6 feet*

Interest: *flowers*

Soil: *well-drained*

Light: *full sun*

Native to the Mediterranean region, lavatera is a hardy annual with a bushy habit and cup-shaped summer flowers that resemble hollyhocks. Their long blooming season makes these plants a good choice for the mixed border. They are also useful as a summer hedge, and flowers can be cut for fresh arrangements.

Selected species and varieties: *L. trimestris* produces pale green rounded leaves on branched stems that may reach 6 feet, although most varieties are between 2 and 3 feet; both leaves and stems are hairy. Solitary 2½- to 4-inch flowers, each with five wide petals, are borne in great numbers throughout the summer. Colors include shades of pink, red, and white; 'Mont Blanc' grows only 2 feet tall and bears pure white flowers; 'Silver Cup' also grows to 2 feet, bearing salmon pink flowers with darker veins.

Growing conditions and maintenance: Sow seed outdoors in midspring, thinning to allow plants to stand 1½ to 2 feet apart. Young plants require abundant water and should be mulched. Once established, plants are drought resistant. Deadhead to prolong flowering.

Layia
(LAY-ee-ah)
TIDYTIPS

Layia platyglossa

Plant type: *annual*

Height: *1 to 2 feet*

Interest: *flowers*

Soil: *well-drained*

Light: *full sun*

Layia is a member of the sunflower family and is native to California, where it grows as a wildflower. Its common name refers to the showy white-tipped ray petals that surround a golden disk. It is a good choice for beds, borders, rock gardens, and sunny banks. Flowers are excellent for fresh arrangements.

Selected species and varieties: *L. platyglossa* has a neat habit and coarsely toothed gray-green leaves covered with dense hairs. Flowers appear from spring to early summer; they are bright yellow, single, 2 inches across, and daisylike. This species is often included in wildflower mixes.

Growing conditions and maintenance: Start seed indoors 6 to 8 weeks prior to the last frost, or sow outdoors in early spring. In Zone 9 and warmer, seed can be sown in fall. Space plants 9 to 12 inches apart, and provide abundant moisture to seedlings. Once plants are established, they are quite drought tolerant. Remove flowers as they fade to prolong blooming period.

Limonium
(ly-MO-nee-um)
STATICE

Limonium sinuatum

Plant type: *annual or biennial*

Height: *10 to 24 inches*

Interest: *flowers*

Soil: *well-drained, sandy, slightly alkaline*

Light: *full sun*

Statice, also called sea lavender, is native to the Mediterranean region and bears clusters of brightly colored flowers surrounded by a papery calyx that remains after the rest of the flower drops. This long-lasting display is useful both in beds and for cutting. Flowers dry easily and retain their color well so are often used in dried arrangements.

Selected species and varieties: *L. sinuatum* (notchleaf statice) grows 18 to 24 inches with a clump of 4- to 8-inch basal leaves and branched, winged flower stems. The papery-textured flowers are borne in short one-sided clusters; colors include pink, blue, lavender, yellow, and white. *L. suworowii* [also known as *Psylliostachys suworowii*] (Russian statice) grows 10 to 20 inches tall with large basal leaves and spikes of lavender and green flowers from summer to frost.

Growing conditions and maintenance: Start seed indoors in individual peat pots 8 weeks prior to the last frost, or sow directly outdoors in midspring in warm climates. Allow 9 to 18 inches between plants. They tolerate drought and seaside conditions but will rot in soil that remains wet.

Linaria
(ly-NAY-ree-a)
TOADFLAX

Linaria maroccana 'Fairy Bouquet'

Plant type: *annual*

Height: *10 to 18 inches*

Interest: *flowers*

Soil: *moist, well-drained*

Light: *full sun to partial shade*

This hardy annual from Morocco, also called spurred snapdragon, has become naturalized in much of the northeastern United States. Its dainty spikes of bicolored flowers resemble small snapdragons and are at home in mixed borders and rock gardens. Flowers can be cut for indoor arrangements.

Selected species and varieties: *L. maroccana* (Moroccan toadflax) has an erect, bushy habit with narrow light green leaves and slender spikes of ½-inch flowers in shades of pink, purple, yellow, and white, usually with a contrasting throat; 'Fairy Bouquet' grows to 10 inches and bears flowers in shades of pink, rose, coppery orange, purple, white, and pale yellow, all with a deeper yellow throat, and are suitable for an edging or a window box.

Growing conditions and maintenance: Sow seed directly in the garden in early spring, thinning seedlings to stand 6 inches apart. Although it prefers cool weather, linaria will grow well in warm areas if provided with abundant water.

Lobelia
(lo-BEE-lee-a)
LOBELIA

Lobelia erinus 'Sapphire'

Plant type: *annual or tender perennial*

Height: *4 to 8 inches*

Interest: *flowers*

Soil: *moist, well-drained*

Light: *full sun to partial shade*

Lobelia hails from South Africa and is grown for its profusion of dainty, brightly colored blooms, which appear from early summer to frost on airy plants. Both trailing and compact, erect forms are available. Trailing types are well suited to hanging baskets and window boxes or for use as a ground cover. Compact varieties fit well into the foreground of borders and make colorful edgings.

Selected species and varieties: *L. erinus* develops a rounded and compact or a trailing and spreading habit, with narrow to oblong serrated leaves. Flowers are ¾ inch long and are typically blue, although violet, pink, purple, and white varieties are available. Flowers generally display a yellow or white throat; 'Sapphire' bears deep blue flowers with white eyes.

Growing conditions and maintenance: Start seed indoors 10 to 12 weeks prior to the last frost for transplanting to the garden after the danger of frost has passed. New plants can also be started from cuttings. Allow 6 to 10 inches between plants. Lobelia thrives in cool regions; in areas with warm summers, grow in partial shade. Plants may be sheared to encourage compact growth.

Lobularia
(lob-yew-LAIR-ee-a)
SWEET ALYSSUM

Lobularia maritima

Plant type: *tender perennial*

Height: *4 to 12 inches*

Interest: *flowers*

Soil: *well-drained*

Light: *full sun to partial shade*

This Mediterranean native spreads to nearly twice its height, producing tiny fragrant flowers from late spring to frost. It makes a good choice for an edging, for a rock garden, along dry walls, or for window boxes. In the front of a mixed border, it neatly covers the dying foliage of spring-flowering bulbs.

Selected species and varieties: *L. maritima* is a fine-textured plant with alternate narrow leaves 1 to 2 inches long. It has a low-branching and spreading habit. Four-petaled flowers are borne in clusters and bear a honeylike scent; colors include white, lilac, pink, and purple.

Growing conditions and maintenance: Start seed indoors 6 to 8 weeks prior to the last frost, or sow directly in the garden in early spring. Avoid overwatering seedlings. Space plants 6 inches apart; they tolerate crowding. In warm areas, they will self-seed. They thrive in cool weather; flowering may stop in hot temperatures. Cutting back plants will encourage further flowering.

Lonas
(LO-nas)
YELLOW AGERATUM

Lonas annua

Plant type: *annual*

Height: *10 to 18 inches*

Interest: *flowers*

Soil: *light, well-drained*

Light: *full sun*

This native of Italy and northwestern Africa produces showy yellow flower clusters all summer. It adds color to an informal border and is long-lasting when cut for fresh or dried flower arrangements.

Selected species and varieties: *L. annua* is a vigorous grower with an open, rounded habit. It develops finely divided leaves along erect, multibranched stems and tiny yellow flowers borne in dense clusters 1 to 2 inches across.

Growing conditions and maintenance: Start seed indoors 6 to 8 weeks prior to the last frost or sow directly in the garden when danger of frost has passed. Thin seedlings to 10 inches apart. Plants thrive in light, infertile soil and tolerate seaside conditions. To use for winter arrangements, cut flowers when they reach full color, tie in bunches, and hang upside down in an airy room until dry.

Lunaria
(loo-NAY-ree-a)
HONESTY, MONEY PLANT

Lunaria annua

Plant type: *biennial*

Height: *2 to 3 feet*

Interest: *fruit*

Soil: *well-drained*

Light: *full sun to partial shade*

This old-fashioned biennial is native to southern Europe. It is grown primarily for its fruit, a flat, oval, translucent seedpod. Plants are best suited to the cutting garden, an informal border, or a wildflower meadow. Their papery seedpods are highly valued for dried arrangements.

Selected species and varieties: *L. annua* (silver-dollar, bolbonac) has an erect habit with broad, coarsely toothed leaves and fragrant pink or purple flowers, each with four petals, borne in terminal clusters in late spring. Flowers are followed by the seedpods, which fall apart, revealing a thin, silvery white disk, 1 to 2 inches across, to which the seeds cling; 'Alba' produces white flowers well displayed when grown against a dark background.

Growing conditions and maintenance: Lunaria can be grown as an annual or a biennial. For flowers and seedpods the first year, sow seed outdoors in very early spring, or plant in midsummer to early fall for flowers and seedpods the following year. Once established they will reseed through Zone 4. Space plants 8 to 12 inches apart. They tolerate wet and dry conditions and are not fussy about soil quality, as long as it is well drained.

Matthiola
(ma-THY-o-la)
STOCK

Matthiola incana

Plant type: *annual or biennial*

Height: *12 to 30 inches*

Interest: *flowers*

Soil: *well-drained, fertile*

Light: *full sun to light shade*

The blossoms of stock perfume a garden throughout summer. Plant them in beds, window boxes, or patio containers where their fragrance can be appreciated. Flowers add a dainty appearance and sweet scent to fresh indoor arrangements.

Selected species and varieties: *M. bicornis* [also known as *M. longipetala* ssp. *bicornis*] (night-scented stock, evening stock, perfume plant) has a bushy habit and grows 12 to 18 inches tall. It bears single ¾-inch flowers in shades of lilac and pink that open at night from mid- to late summer and are extremely fragrant. *M. incana* (common stock, gillyflower) grows 12 to 30 inches with gray-green oblong leaves and terminal clusters of 1-inch-long flowers that may be single or double and bear a spicy fragrance; colors include pink, purple, white, and blue.

Growing conditions and maintenance: Start seed indoors 6 to 8 weeks prior to the last frost, or sow directly in the garden in early spring. Space plants to stand 6 to 12 inches apart; they tolerate crowding. Plants thrive in cool weather and may stop flowering when temperatures rise. *M. bicornis* will tolerate poorer soil and drier conditions than will *M. incana*.

Mentzelia
(ment-ZEE-lee-a)
MENTZELIA

Mentzelia lindleyi

Plant type: *annual or biennial*

Height: *1 to 4 feet*

Interest: *flowers*

Soil: *well-drained to dry*

Light: *full sun*

These natives of the western United States bear fragrant yellow or white flowers that brighten borders and beds from summer until frost.

Selected species and varieties: *M. decapetala* (petal mentzelia) is a biennial that grows 2 to 4 feet with 3- to 5-inch starburst-shaped flowers opening in the evening. *M. laevicaulis* (blazing star, evening star) is a biennial or short-lived perennial that grows to 3½ feet with narrow leaves and pale yellow 4-inch flowers, also opening at night. *M. lindleyi* [also known as *Bartonia aurea*] is an annual species that usually grows 1 to 2½ feet with fragrant bright yellow flowers displaying a colorful orange-red center with a buss of yellow stamens.

Growing conditions and maintenance: Sow seed of the biennial species in fall, or stratify the seed and sow it in spring, directly in the garden. Sow *M. lindleyi* outdoors in midspring. This genus does not transplant well. Thin to allow 6 to 10 inches between plants. Keep seedlings moist, but once established keep plants on the dry side. Plants tolerate heat, wind, poor soil, and drought.

Mimulus
(MIM-yew-lus)
MONKEY FLOWER

Mimulus x hybridus

Plant type: *tender perennial*

Height: *10 to 14 inches*

Interest: *flowers*

Soil: *moist, well-drained, fertile*

Light: *partial to full shade*

Blooming from midsummer to fall, this native of both North and South America provides bright color to shady beds and borders. It fits well alongside a garden pond or stream and also makes an attractive container plant. Funnel-shaped, two-lipped flowers are thought to resemble monkeys' faces.

Selected species and varieties: *M. x hybridus* has a mounded habit with glossy 2- to 2½-inch leaves and 2-inch tubular flowers in shades of red, yellow, orange, rose, and brown, usually with brown or maroon spotting or mottling.

Growing conditions and maintenance: Start seed indoors 10 to 12 weeks prior to the last frost for transplanting to the garden after all danger of frost has passed. Space plants 6 inches apart. Plants benefit from the addition of organic matter to the soil. They require some shade and ample moisture. In fall, plants can be dug and potted to continue flowering indoors over the winter.

Mina
(MEE-na)
CRIMSON STARGLORY

Mina lobata

Plant type: *tender perennial*

Height: *15 to 20 feet*

Interest: *flowers*

Soil: *moist, well-drained, fertile*

Light: *full sun to partial shade*

This vigorous, fast-growing vine is native to Mexico and climbs by twining its reddish stems around supports. Throughout the summer numerous red buds open to reveal tubular flowers that turn from orange to white as they mature. Plants provide an elegant light-textured screen or background for other flowers when grown on a trellis or fence. They can also be grown in containers.

Selected species and varieties: *M. lobata* produces attractive dark green three-lobed leaves along self-twining stems. The 1-inch flowers appear in showy long-stalked clusters, beginning as red boat-shaped buds that open orange, change to yellow, and eventually turn creamy white. All colors are present on a single cluster.

Growing conditions and maintenance: Start seed indoors in individual peat pots 6 weeks prior to the last frost or directly in the garden after danger of frost has passed. Keep plants well mulched and supplied with abundant water. Plants are hardy from Zone 8 south, but in warmer areas will benefit from midday shade.

Mirabilis
(mi-RAB-i-lis)
FOUR-O'CLOCK

Mirabilis jalapa

Plant type: *tender perennial*

Height: *18 to 36 inches*

Interest: *flowers*

Soil: *well-drained to dry, sandy*

Light: *full sun to partial shade*

This native of the American tropics produces a fresh crop of fragrant blossoms in a wide range of colors each evening throughout the summer and into fall. Plants fit well into beds and borders and provide a dense, shrubby edging for walkways and vegetable gardens.

Selected species and varieties: *M. jalapa* (marvel-of-Peru, beauty-of-the-night) has a bushy, shrublike habit with broad deep green leaves up to 6 inches long that provide a perfect foil for colorful 1- to 2-inch-long trumpet-shaped flowers; colors include white, red, yellow, pink, violet, and bicolors. The flowers open in late afternoon and remain open until the following morning.

Growing conditions and maintenance: For earliest blooms start seed indoors 6 to 8 weeks prior to the last frost or sow seed directly in the garden in spring. Allow 1 to 2 feet between plants. Once established, plants often self-seed. They grow equally well in sun or partial shade, and are tolerant of heat and pollution.

Moluccella
(mol-lew-SELL-a)
BELLS OF IRELAND

Moluccella laevis

Plant type: *annual*

Height: *2 to 3 feet*

Interest: *flowers*

Soil: *moist, well-drained*

Light: *full sun*

This native of the eastern Mediterranean region provides a lovely vertical accent to beds, borders, and indoor arrangements both fresh and dried. It is grown for its showy calyxes, which surround the bases of tiny flowers in late summer and fall.

Selected species and varieties: *M. laevis* has an erect habit and grows to 3 feet tall and 18 inches wide. Its rounded leaves are about an inch across with rounded teeth along each margin. Flowers are fragrant, pink or white, and rather inconspicuous but are surrounded by a 1- to 2-inch white-veined, light green calyx that resembles a bell. These are borne close to the stem, giving the plant a graceful, vertical form.

Growing conditions and maintenance: Start seed indoors 6 to 8 weeks prior to the last frost; do not cover seed with soil as it needs light to germinate. Seed can also be sown directly in the garden in early spring. Space plants 9 to 12 inches apart. In areas exposed to wind and rain they may require staking.

Myosotis
(my-oh-SO-tis)
FORGET-ME-NOT

Myosotis sylvatica 'Ultramarine'

Plant type: *annual or biennial*

Height: *6 to 10 inches*

Interest: *flowers, foliage*

Soil: *moist, well-drained*

Light: *full sun to partial shade*

Airy clusters of dainty flowers with prominent eyes open above the forget-me-not's low mounds of delicate foliage. Forget-me-nots provide a soft filler or a delicate border edging. They are particularly attractive in combination with spring-flowering bulbs such as tulips.

Selected species and varieties: *M. sylvatica* (woodland forget-me-not, garden forget-me-not) produces 8- to 10-inch stems in clumps almost as wide, lined with soft, elongated leaves and tipped with loose clusters of ¼-inch yellow-centered blue flowers from spring through early summer; 'Ultramarine' is very dwarf, growing to 6 inches, with dark blue flowers; 'Victoria Blue' grows 6 to 8 inches, forming neat mounds and producing early flowers of gentian blue.

Growing conditions and maintenance: Start seed outdoors in late summer to early fall for flowers the following spring. Once established, forget-me-nots self-seed readily, performing like a perennial. Enrich the soil with organic matter. Allow 6 to 12 inches between plants, and water during dry periods.

Nemesia
(ne-ME-see-a)
NEMESIA

Nemesia strumosa 'Carnival Mixed'

Plant type: *annual*

Height: *9 to 24 inches*

Interest: *flowers*

Soil: *moist, well-drained*

Light: *full sun to partial shade*

These brightly colored annuals from South Africa bear pouched, orchidlike flowers from early summer to fall, and are perfect for massing in beds and borders or for growing in containers in areas where summers are cool. They also make effective edgings and provide an attractive cover for the dying foliage of spring bulbs.

Selected species and varieties: *N. strumosa* has an attractive bushy, mounded habit with narrow bright green toothed leaves and spurred five-lobed flowers in clusters 4 inches long. Flower colors include yellow, white, red, purple, orange, pink, and bicolors; 'Carnival Mixed' is a dwarf variety that grows to 9 inches with brightly colored flowers.

Growing conditions and maintenance: Start seed indoors 4 to 6 weeks prior to the last frost and transplant to the garden after danger of frost has passed, or sow directly outdoors in late spring. Allow 6 inches between plants. Plants require a long, cool growing season to perform well. Pinch young plants to encourage bushiness, and provide water during dry periods.

Nemophila
(nem-OFF-i-la)
BABY-BLUE-EYES

Nemophila menziesii

Plant type: *annual*

Height: *6 to 10 inches*

Interest: *flowers*

Soil: *moist, well-drained*

Light: *full sun to partial shade*

Baby-blue-eyes hails from California and Oregon, where it grows as a wildflower. In the garden its low, mounded habit and dainty flowers make good edgings, rock-garden specimens, and companions for spring-flowering bulbs. They are also attractive when planted so that their trailing stems spill over the edge of a wall.

Selected species and varieties: *N. menziesii* produces trailing stems to form a mounding plant, usually about 6 inches tall and 12 inches across, with deeply cut light green leaves. Flowers are tubular, 1 to 1½ inches across, and sky blue in color with white centers; 'Pennie Black' has deep purple ¾-inch blooms edged with silvery white.

Growing conditions and maintenance: Sow seed directly in the garden in early spring, thinning the seedlings to stand 6 inches apart. Enrich the soil with organic matter and provide abundant moisture. Plants thrive in areas with cool summers and will self-seed under favorable conditions.

Nicotiana
(ni-ko-she-AN-a)
TOBACCO

Nicotiana sylvestris

Plant type: *annual*

Height: *1 to 6 feet*

Interest: *flowers, foliage*

Soil: *moist, well-drained*

Light: *full sun to partial shade*

Flowering tobacco produces clusters of fragrant, flat-faced flowers with elongated tubular throats growing at the tips of soft stems, and clumps of large leaves. Plants are useful as border fillers or specimens. Flowers of some varieties close in sunlight but open on cloudy days or in the evening. Leaf juices are poisonous.

Selected species and varieties: *N. alata* (jasmine tobacco) produces 1- to 2-foot-tall clumps with flowers that bloom from spring to fall; 'Domino Hybrids' have compact cushions of foliage to 15 inches and early-spring flowers in mixed colors; 'Nikki' grows to 18 inches tall with pink, red, white, yellow, or lime green flowers; 'Sensation Mixed' grows 2 to 2½ feet tall with red, pink, purple, white, and yellow blooms. *N. langsdorffii* produces nodding green flowers with turquoise anthers at the tips of 5-foot stems. *N. sylvestris* (woodland tobacco) produces drooping white flowers tinged pink or purple on branching plants 3 to 6 feet tall.

Growing conditions and maintenance: Start seed indoors 6 to 8 weeks prior to the last frost, or sow directly outdoors in late spring. Space plants about 12 inches apart. Deadhead spent blooms.

Nigella
(nye-JEL-a)
LOVE-IN-A-MIST

Nigella damascena

Plant type: *annual*

Height: *18 to 24 inches*

Interest: *flowers, seed heads*

Soil: *well-drained*

Light: *full sun*

Love-in-a-mist adds a delicate, fine texture to any border or flower arrangement in which it is used. Its fernlike leaves are light green, and solitary flowers are nestled in a mist of foliage at the ends of stems throughout the summer. Interesting seed capsules replace the flowers and are attractive in dried flower arrangements. This annual is native to southern Europe and North Africa.

Selected species and varieties: *N. damascena* has an erect multibranched habit with delicate leaves divided into threadlike segments. Flowers are 1 to 1½ inches across with blue, white, or pink notched petals. The papery 1-inch seed capsules are pale green with reddish brown markings.

Growing conditions and maintenance: Start seed directly outdoors in early spring, and make additional sowings every 2 or 3 weeks until early summer to extend the flowering season. Plants are not easily transplanted. Thin to allow 6 to 10 inches between plants. Water during dry periods. If pods are allowed to remain on plants, they will self-seed.

Ocimum
(OS-si-mum)
BASIL

Ocimum basilicum

Plant type: *annual*

Height: *1 to 2 feet*

Interest: *foliage*

Soil: *moist, well-drained*

Light: *full sun*

This annual native of Asia and Africa has been cultivated for centuries as a culinary and medicinal herb. Its lush, fragrant foliage and mounded form make it an exceptional edging for borders and beds. Basil can also be effectively combined with flowering plants in window boxes and patio containers. Plant enough to allow for snipping leaves for seasoning.

Selected species and varieties: *O. basilicum* (common basil, sweet basil) has a rounded growth habit and square stems typical of the mint family to which it belongs. Green or purple leaves are opposite, oval, and slightly crinkled. Flowers are tiny, white or purple, and borne in terminal clusters, but are often removed to promote leafy growth; 'Dark Opal' grows 1 to 1½ feet with dark purple leaves and lavender-pink flowers, and makes an outstanding accent plant in a bed or border.

Growing conditions and maintenance: Start seed indoors 8 weeks prior to the last frost to transplant outdoors after all danger of frost has passed. Allow 10 to 12 inches between plants. Pinch out flowers as they appear to promote leaf growth.

Oenothera
(ee-no-THEE-ra)
EVENING PRIMROSE

Oenothera biennis

Plant type: *biennial*

Height: *2 to 8 feet*

Interest: *flowers*

Soil: *well-drained to dry*

Light: *full sun to partial shade*

Among this genus of mostly perennial plants are a few hardy biennials that can be treated as annuals. Their pale yellow funnel-shaped blooms appear from early summer to midfall, opening in the evening atop tall, erect stems. They are suitable for massing at the rear of a border or for use in a wildflower garden.

Selected species and varieties: *O. biennis* produces a clump of coarse basal leaves from which a stout, erect flower stem rises. Stems may reach 6 feet and bear 1- to 2-inch flowers that open pale yellow and turn gold. *O. erythrosepala* [also called *O. glaziovinia*] grows 2 to 8 feet tall with yellow flowers that turn orange or red; 'Tina James' grows 3 to 4 feet with showy yellow flowers that burst open in 1 to 2 minutes and are pleasantly fragrant.

Growing conditions and maintenance: Start seed indoors 8 to 12 weeks prior to the last frost, or outdoors in early spring. Where winters are mild, seed can be sown outdoors in fall. Once established, plants will often self-seed, and may become invasive. Space plants 12 inches apart. They thrive in warm weather and tolerate poor soil.

Omphalodes
(om-fa-LO-dez)
NAVELWORT, NAVELSEED

Omphalodes linifolia

Plant type: *annual*

Height: *6 to 12 inches*

Interest: *flowers, foliage*

Soil: *moist, well-drained, acid*

Light: *full sun to partial shade*

This dainty little annual is native to Spain and Portugal. It produces loose one-sided spikes of white flowers set among silvery gray leaves. Appearing from summer to fall, the flowers are slightly fragrant and excellent for cutting. Plants are well suited to growing in a rock garden or along a stone wall.

Selected species and varieties: *O. linifolia* produces narrow gray-green lance-shaped leaves and sprays of ½-inch-wide five-petaled flowers. Each petal displays a prominent vein running from its tip to its base, giving it a starlike appearance. Seeds resemble navels.

Growing conditions and maintenance: Start seed indoors 4 to 6 weeks prior to the last frost, or sow directly outdoors in midspring. Allow 4 to 6 inches between plants. They prefer a somewhat acid soil and benefit from the addition of peat moss. Water plants during dry periods.

Onopordum
(o-no-POR-dum)
THISTLE

Onopordum acanthium

Plant type: *annual or biennial*

Height: *6 to 9 feet*

Interest: *flowers, foliage*

Soil: *well-drained to dry*

Light: *full sun*

Scotch thistle produces fuzzy, globular flower heads on tall, stiffly erect branching stems lined with spiny gray-green leaves. The unusual flowers and foliage add both color and texture as vertical accents in a border.

Selected species and varieties: *O. acanthium* (Scotch thistle, cotton thistle, silver thistle) produces stiff, downy leaves to 2 feet long, deeply lobed and scalloped into spiny segments on branching stems 6 to 9 feet tall. In late spring to summer, stems are tipped with purple or white round, prickly flowers that have flat, fuzzy tops up to 2 inches in diameter.

Growing conditions and maintenance: Start seed indoors 6 to 8 weeks prior to the last frost, or sow directly in the garden after all danger of frost has passed. Space plants 3 feet apart. Once established they will self-seed and may become invasive. To avoid self-seeding, remove faded flowers. Plants thrive in hot, dry locations.

Orthocarpus
(or-tho-KAR-pus)
OWL'S CLOVER

Orthocarpus purpurascens

Plant type: *annual*

Height: *12 to 15 inches*

Interest: *flowers*

Soil: *light, well-drained*

Light: *full sun*

Owl's clover is native to the southwestern United States, where it covers entire hillsides with rose-purple blooms set off by red-tinged bracts. Individual flowers resemble snapdragons and are tipped with yellow or white on their lower lip. These annuals are useful in wildflower meadows and informal borders, where they provide a long season of color. They are also effective for massing.

Selected species and varieties: *O. purpurascens* (escobita) grows to 15 inches with linear leaves often tinged with brown and either cut or smooth margins, and red-tipped bracts. The two-lipped rose-purple or crimson flowers are about 1 inch long and appear from early to midsummer.

Growing conditions and maintenance: Sow seed directly outdoors as soon as the soil can be worked in early spring. Thin plants to stand 6 to 8 inches apart. Plants thrive in warm weather. Water during dry periods.

Oxypetalum
(ox-y-PET-a-lum)
BLUE MILKWEED

Oxypetalum caeruleum

Plant type: *tender perennial*

Height: *15 to 36 inches*

Interest: *flowers*

Soil: *well-drained, fertile*

Light: *full sun*

This elegant tender perennial from South America produces its exquisite star-shaped flowers the first year from seed. Flowers are borne in graceful sprays of pink buds that open to reveal baby blue flowers, which mature to lilac-purple. Plant it where its long-lasting flowers can be viewed up close: at the edge of a border, or in a patio planter or hanging basket.

Selected species and varieties: *O. caeruleum* has a weakly twining habit, and though it becomes a 3-foot shrub in Zones 10 and 11, where it is perennial, it rarely exceeds 18 inches when grown elsewhere as an annual. Leaves are heart shaped and covered with downy hairs. The ½- to 1-inch flowers are borne in open clusters from summer to early fall.

Growing conditions and maintenance: Start seed indoors 6 to 8 weeks prior to the last frost, and transplant to the garden after all danger of frost has passed. Space plants 8 to 12 inches apart. Plants thrive in cool weather and tolerate dry soil. They can be dug and potted in the fall for growing indoors in winter.

Papaver
(pa-PAY-ver)
POPPY

Papaver nudicaule

Plant type: *annual or tender perennial*

Height: *1 to 4 feet*

Interest: *flowers*

Soil: *well-drained to dry*

Light: *full sun to light shade*

Poppy's showy spring flowers surround prominent centers above clumps of coarse, hairy, deeply lobed leaves. The brightly colored flower petals are extremely delicate in appearance, with a tissuelike texture. Flowers may be single, with four overlapping petals, or double, with many petals forming a rounded bloom. They are borne on solitary stems, and are suitable for mixed borders and good for cutting.

Selected species and varieties: *P. nudicaule* (Iceland poppy, Arctic poppy) produces a fernlike clump of 6-inch lobed gray-green leaves from which 12- to 18-inch leafless flower stems rise from spring to early summer. Flowers are fragrant, 2 to 4 inches across, and saucer shaped; colors include white, yellow, orange, salmon, pink, and scarlet. *P. rhoeas* (corn poppy, Flanders poppy, Shirley poppy, field poppy) grows to 3 feet with wiry, branching stems and pale green deeply lobed leaves. Flowers may be single or double, and are borne from late spring to early summer in colors of red, purple, pink, and white; 'Fairy Wings' produces flowers in soft shades of blue, lilac, dusty pink, and white with faint blue margins; 'Mother of Pearl' bears flowers in shades of blue, lavender, pink, gray, white, and peach, and the flowers may be solid or speckled. *P. somniferum* (opium poppy) grows 3 to 4 feet tall with large white, red, pink, or mauve flowers that appear throughout summer and are often double or fringed; 'Alba' bears white blooms; 'Pink Chiffon' produces double bright pink flowers; 'White Cloud' bears large double white blooms on sturdy stems.

Growing conditions and maintenance: *P. nudicaule* can be started indoors 10 weeks prior to the last frost for trans-

Papaver rhoeas

planting in late spring. Handle seedlings carefully because they are difficult to transplant. You can also sow directly in the garden in late fall or early spring. Other species are so difficult to transplant that they are best sown in place. Papaver seed is very small and can be mixed with sand for easier handling. Thin *P. nudicaule* to stand 8 to 10 inches apart, *P. rhoeas* about 12 inches apart, and *P. somniferum* 4 to 8 inches apart. Double-flowered varieties of *P. somniferum* often require staking. Poppies will often self-seed. Deadhead plants to prolong flowering season. For use in indoor arrangements, cut the flowers as the buds straighten on their nodding stems but before the flowers actually open.

Pelargonium
(pel-ar-GO-nee-um)
GERANIUM

Pelargonium x hortorum 'Freckles'

Plant type:	*annual or tender perennial*
Height:	*10 to 36 inches*
Interest:	*flowers, foliage*
Soil:	*moist, well-drained*
Light:	*full sun*

These tender perennials are primarily hybrids of South African natives, and since their introduction over 100 years ago they have become some of the most popular bedding plants grown. Geraniums have a shrubby habit with showy leaves and clusters of vividly colored flowers. They have many uses in the garden: Their reliable and long-lasting flowers are well suited to formal beds, they provide nonstop color for hanging baskets and window boxes, and trailing types can be used for ground covers.

Selected species and varieties: *P.* x *domesticum* (show geranium, regal geranium, Martha Washington geranium) has a shrubby habit and usually grows 1 to 1½ feet tall, although in Zone 9 and warmer it may reach 3 feet. Plants bear light green deeply lobed, serrated leaves and huge, dense clusters of red, white, or pink flowers that are often blotched or veined with a darker color. *P.* x *hortorum* (zonal geranium, house geranium, bedding geranium) typically grows 10 inches to 3 feet tall, with a rounded habit; in frost-free areas, it may grow considerably taller. Plants produce rounded, pale to medium green leaves

that have scalloped edges and are usually marked with a brown or maroon horseshoe-shaped zone. Flowers are single, semidouble, or double; appear in 5-inch dense, long-stemmed clusters; and include shades of red, pink, white, and salmon; 'Freckles' has a compact habit and pink flowers with a dark rose spot at the base of each petal. *P. peltatum* (ivy-

Pelargonium x domesticum

leaved geranium, hanging geranium) has a vinelike habit with gracefully trailing stems up to 3 feet long and medium green leathery leaves. Flowers are borne in loose clusters and range from single to very double; colors include pink, white, lavender, and cherry red. These are particularly attractive in hanging baskets or in planters where their stems are allowed to trail over the edge.

Growing conditions and maintenance: Start seed indoors 12 to 16 weeks prior to last frost. Geraniums can also be started indoors from cuttings taken from overwintered plants. Transplant after all danger of frost has passed. Space plants 8 to 15 inches apart. Geraniums, especially regal types, prefer cool climates and may die out during the heat of summer in southern zones. Water during dry periods. Remove faded flowers to encourage blooming. Geraniums may be dug and potted in the fall for growing indoors.

Pennisetum
(pen-i-SEE-tum)
FOUNTAIN GRASS

Pennisetum setaceum 'Rubrum'

Plant type: *tender perennial*

Height: *2 to 4 feet*

Interest: *flowers, foliage*

Soil: *moist, well-drained*

Light: *full sun*

Fountain grass produces narrow spikes of tiny, bristly summer flowers above dense mounds of arching leaves. Place plants individually or in small groups in the border. They can also be used as a background or specimen planting. The flowers last through fall and are effective in fresh flower arrangements, but they shatter too easily to be used for dried arrangements.

Selected species and varieties: *P. setaceum* (annual fountain grass) has an upright, arching habit. Nodding foot-long flower spikes in shades of pink to purple rise above a leafy clump that is 2 to 4 feet tall and equally wide; 'Rubrum' has burgundy leaves and deep purple flowers.

Growing conditions and maintenance: Start seed indoors 6 to 8 weeks before the last frost for transplanting to the garden after all danger of frost has passed. Space plants 18 to 36 inches apart. In Zones 9 and 10 they may be grown as perennials. Water during dry periods.

Perilla
(per-RILL-a)
BEEFSTEAK PLANT

Perilla frutescens 'Crispa'

Plant type: *annual*

Height: *2 to 3 feet*

Interest: *foliage*

Soil: *well-drained to dry*

Light: *full sun to partial shade*

This Asian native is grown for its attractive foliage, which resembles that of coleus or purple basil. Plants are useful as accents in borders, especially toward the back, where the dark leaves contrast well with brightly colored flowers. Leaves are used as a seasoning in oriental cooking.

Selected species and varieties: *P. frutescens* has an upright habit with the square stems and opposite leaves typical of the mint family. Leaves are up to 5 inches long, have a quilted texture, and are purple-bronze, green, or variegated in color; 'Crispa' develops bronze leaves with wrinkled margins; 'Atropurpurea' has very dark purple leaves.

Growing conditions and maintenance: Start seed indoors 6 weeks prior to the last frost, or sow directly in the garden after the soil has warmed. Space plants 15 to 18 inches apart. Once established, perilla will self-seed and may become invasive; to avoid this problem, remove flowers as they develop. Plants will tolerate poor soil.

Petunia
(pe-TOO-nya)
PETUNIA

Petunia x hybrida 'Fluffy Ruffles'

Plant type: *annual*

Height: *8 to 18 inches*

Interest: *flowers*

Soil: *well-drained*

Light: *full sun*

Open flower trumpets bloom in profusion from summer until frost along petunia's trailing or upright stems amid small, hairy, pointed leaves. Petunias are effective cascading over walls or banks or when massed as bedding plants. Their nonstop flower display is ideal for window boxes and hanging baskets.

Selected species and varieties: *P. x hybrida* (common garden petunia) produces white, yellow, pink, red, purple, blue-purple, or lavender blooms that may be speckled, splotched, veined, or striped in a contrasting color on compact, bushy, or trailing plants; 'Fantasy Pink Morn' bears small light pink flowers with a creamy white center on plants that reach 10 to 12 inches in height and spread up to 18 inches; 'Fluffy Ruffles' produces 5- to 6-inch flowers that are often tricolored with contrasting veins and throats; 'Heavenly Lavender' produces 2½- to 3-inch double lavender blooms on compact plants 8 to 12 inches tall.

Growing conditions and maintenance: Start seed indoors 10 to 12 weeks before the last frost date. Pinch to develop bushy plants; remove dead blooms to encourage further flowering.

Phacelia
(fa-SEEL-ee-a)
HAREBELL PHACELIA

Phacelia campanularia

Plant type: *annual*

Height: *6 to 20 inches*

Interest: *flowers*

Soil: *well-drained to dry, sandy*

Light: *full sun*

This annual, also called scorpion weed, is native to the southwestern United States, where it grows on dry, rocky slopes and in deserts. Bell-shaped flowers appear in clusters along one side of a curved stem in spring and midsummer. The plants are useful for massing and creating low borders, and are also well suited to rock gardens. Some people develop a skin rash from handling the leaves.

Selected species and varieties: *P. campanularia* (California bluebell) has a creeping habit with 1-inch hairy, round or heart-shaped leaves and ¾- to 1-inch bright blue bell-shaped flowers borne in loose clusters.

Growing conditions and maintenance: Sow seed directly in the garden in fall in Zones 9 and warmer; elsewhere sow in midspring. Plants are difficult to transplant. Thin young plants to stand 6 to 8 inches apart. They thrive in dry conditions and poor soil. Make successive sowings at 3- to 4-week intervals for extended flowering.

Phaseolus
(faz-ee-OH-lus)
BEAN

Phaseolus coccineus

Plant type: *tender perennial*

Height: *6 to 10 feet*

Interest: *flowers, foliage, fruit*

Soil: *moist, well-drained, fertile*

Light: *full sun*

This tender perennial twining vine from tropical America produces abundant dark green leaves that are a perfect foil for its brilliant scarlet flowers. The vine will grow quickly to cover a trellis or fence, or climb up a porch railing. It also forms a dense and dramatic backdrop for a flower border. The flowers attract hummingbirds.

Selected species and varieties: *P. coccineus* (scarlet runner bean) produces twining stems with 5-inch dark green leaves composed of three leaflets. Flowers are bright red and pea-like and appear in large clusters from early to midsummer, followed by flat 4- to 12-inch pods filled with black-and-red mottled seeds. Both flowers and beans are edible.

Growing conditions and maintenance: Plant seed outdoors in spring after danger of frost has passed. Thin to allow 2 to 4 inches between plants. Provide support for climbing, and water when dry.

Phlox
(flox)
PHLOX

Phlox drummondii 'Palona Rose with Eye'

Plant type: *annual*

Height: *6 to 20 inches*

Interest: *flowers*

Soil: *dry, sandy*

Light: *full sun to partial shade*

This Texas native provides a long season of colorful blooms on low, spreading plants that are useful as edgings, in rock gardens, massed in beds, and in containers. Flowers are also good for cutting. Their colors include white, pink, red, purple, yellow, and bicolors.

Selected species and varieties: *P. drummondii* (annual phlox, Drummond phlox) grows to 20 inches with a spreading, mounded habit, hairy leaves and stems, and five-lobed flowers that are 1 inch across; 'Palona Rose with Eye' is compact, 6 to 8 inches tall, with rose flowers with contrasting white eyes; 'Petticoat' series are compact 6-inch plants that come in a mix of colors with good drought and heat tolerance; 'Twinkle' series are 8 inches with small, early, star-shaped flowers in mixed colors.

Growing conditions and maintenance: Start seed indoors 8 weeks prior to the last frost. In Zone 8 and warmer, seed can also be sown in fall. Remove spent flowers to extend bloom, and provide water when dry. Flowering often declines in midsummer but will resume in fall.

Portulaca
(por-tew-LAK-a)
MOSS ROSE

Portulaca grandiflora 'Sundance'

Plant type: *annual*

Height: *6 to 8 inches*

Interest: *flowers, foliage*

Soil: *well-drained to dry*

Light: *full sun*

This spreading, low-growing annual is native to South America. Its succulent leaves cover the ground like a carpet and set off its brightly colored blooms. Flowers appear from early summer to frost, opening in the morning and closing late in the day. Portulaca is a fine choice for a rock garden, an edging, a ground cover, or containers, especially in hot, dry sites where few other flowers will thrive.

Selected species and varieties: *P. grandiflora* (sun plant, eleven-o'clock) produces sprawling succulent stems that bear fleshy, narrow leaves and showy bowl-shaped flowers. Blooms may be single, semidouble, or double, and may be red, pink, white, yellow, orange, magenta, or striped; 'Sundance' bears semidouble flowers in a mixture of red, orange, yellow, cream, and white; 'Sundial' blooms early with double flowers.

Growing conditions and maintenance: Start seed indoors about 6 weeks prior to the last frost for transplanting to the garden after the soil has warmed. Seed can also be sown directly in the garden after danger of frost is past. Space plants 6 to 8 inches apart. Moss rose often self-seeds. Do not fertilize; it likes poor, dry soils.

Proboscidea
(pro-bo-SID-ee-a)
DEVIL'S-CLAW

Proboscidea louisianica

Plant type: *annual*

Height: *1 to 2 feet*

Interest: *flowers, fruit*

Soil: *well-drained, sandy*

Light: *full sun*

This annual native of North America bears tubular flowers followed by very unusual fruit: a fleshy 4- to 6-inch pod that splits into two clawlike, curved ends as it dries. The green pods can be pickled and eaten, while the dried pods are outstanding for dried arrangements.

Selected species and varieties: *P. louisianica* (ram's horn, proboscis flower) grows to 2 feet with a bushy, spreading habit. The wavy-margined leaves are 7 to 10 inches across with long petioles and are covered with sticky hairs. Flowers have five lobes and are yellow, white, or pink with purple markings; they commonly appear right after a rain, and have an unpleasant odor. The unique fruits appear after the blooms have faded.

Growing conditions and maintenance: Start seed indoors 6 to 8 weeks before the last frost. In Zone 8 and warmer, seed can be sown directly in the garden in midspring. Plants may self-seed and become invasive in warm climates. Space them 6 to 12 inches apart and at least 5 feet away from other plants so that their odor does not overpower more delicate or appealing scents.

Reseda
(re-ZEE-da)
MIGNONETTE

Reseda odorata

Plant type: *annual*

Height: *6 to 18 inches*

Interest: *flowers*

Soil: *well-drained, fertile*

Light: *full sun to partial shade*

This native of northern Africa produces thick spikes of small, deliciously fragrant flowers from late summer through fall. Star-shaped flowers are creamy white to greenish yellow with bright orange stamens. Use plants at the edge of a border or in a patio planter or window box where their fragrance can be appreciated. Flowers are long-lasting and excellent for cutting.

Selected species and varieties: *R. odorata* develops thick stems and small oval leaves. Flowers are $\frac{1}{3}$ inch across with four to seven fringed petals. Although not extremely showy, the flowers are so fragrant as to be well worth growing.

Growing conditions and maintenance: Plants are difficult to transplant, so sow seed directly in the garden in early spring. Seeds require light to germinate; do not cover. A second planting a month later will extend the flowering season. In Zones 9 and 10 seed can be planted in fall for earlier flowers. Thin seedlings to stand 6 to 12 inches apart. Water and mulch to keep soil evenly moist and cool.

Rhodochiton
(ro-DOH-ki-ton)
RHODOCHITON

Rhodochiton atrosanguineum

Plant type: *tender perennial*

Height: *5 to 15 feet*

Interest: *flowers, foliage*

Soil: *well-drained, fertile*

Light: *full sun*

Native to Mexico, where it is a perennial, the purple bell vine is grown as an annual north of Zone 9. It climbs by twisting its long petioles around any nearby support. From summer to frost, tubular deep purple flowers hang from thin stalks and are surrounded by a four-pointed fuchsia calyx. Plants make an attractive cover for a fence or trellis, or can be allowed to cascade from a hanging basket.

Selected species and varieties: *R. atrosanguineum* [also called *R. volubile*] (purple bell vine) grows to 15 feet in its native habitat but usually reaches 5 to 8 feet in temperate zones. Its thick-textured, heart-shaped leaves are tipped with purple. Elongated bell-shaped flowers are about an inch in length.

Growing conditions and maintenance: Start seed indoors in individual peat pots 3 to 4 months prior to the last frost. Place several seeds in each pot because germination may be spotty. Cut out all but the strongest seedling. Transplant to the garden after soil has warmed, allowing 1 foot between plants. They thrive in warm weather. Fertilize and water regularly.

Ricinus
(RISS-i-nus)
CASTOR-OIL PLANT

Ricinus communis 'Carmencita'

Plant type: *tender perennial*

Height: *8 to 10 feet*

Interest: *foliage*

Soil: *well-drained*

Light: *full sun*

Ricinus's clumps of large, glossy leaves make an effective coarse-textured backdrop in sunny borders, and because the plants grow rapidly, they are also used as screens. Flowers, which are insignificant, are followed by prickly husks filled with tiny brown seeds. These are extremely poisonous—and a particular danger to children, who find them attractive. Care must be taken to locate ricinus plants appropriately.

Selected species and varieties: *R. communis* (castor bean) produces leaves until frost on plants that grow up to 10 feet tall and 3 to 4 feet wide; leaves emerge tinged with red and turn glossy green and are broad, up to 3 feet across, with narrow, pointed segments; 'Carmencita' produces early-blooming bright red flowers and deep brown leaves.

Growing conditions and maintenance: Plant seed indoors 6 to 8 weeks prior to the last frost. Plants grow best in hot, humid climates. Provide ample water and fertilizer; they may survive as perennials in warm climates.

Rudbeckia
(rood-BEK-ee-a)
CONEFLOWER

Rudbeckia hirta 'Double Gold'

Plant type: *annual, biennial, or tender perennial*

Height: *1 to 3 feet*

Interest: *flowers*

Soil: *moist to dry, well-drained*

Light: *full sun to partial shade*

Rudbeckias have prominent dark centers fringed with petal-like ray flowers. The yellow summer flowers bloom on stems lined with large, hairy leaves. They are useful as a filler or backdrop in a border or sunny meadow garden.

Selected species and varieties: *R. hirta* (black-eyed Susan) may be an annual, a biennial, or a short-lived perennial with single or double 2- to 3-inch flower heads whose drooping yellow rays surround dark centers; 'Double Gold' produces spectacular double yellow blooms; 'Gloriosa Daisy' bears flowers in shades of yellow with mahogany centers, and other bicolors; 'Goldilocks' grows to 15 inches with 3- to 4-inch double flowers; 'Green Eyes' (also called 'Irish Eyes') grows to 30 inches and bears 5-inch flowers with golden rays around a green eye.

Growing conditions and maintenance: Start seed indoors 8 to 10 weeks prior to the last frost, or sow directly outdoors in fall or early spring. Allow 9 to 24 inches between plants. Once established they may self-seed. They tolerate a wide range of soils and drought.

Salpiglossis
(sal-pi-GLOSS-is)
PAINTED TONGUE

Salpiglossis sinuata 'Bolero'

Plant type: *annual*

Height: *2 to 3 feet*

Interest: *flowers*

Soil: *well-drained, fertile*

Light: *full sun*

The flowers of salpiglossis come in an incredible range of colors, including red, pink, purple, blue, white, yellow, and brown. Blooms are typically veined or spotted with a contrasting color. Plants add a cheerful accent to beds and borders, and are excellent for cutting.

Selected species and varieties: *S. sinuata* has an erect, bushy habit with narrow 4-inch leaves. Both leaves and stems are slightly hairy and sticky. Flowers resemble petunias, are 2 to 2½ inches wide, have a velvety texture, and appear in terminal clusters; 'Bolero' is 18 to 24 inches tall with flower colors that include gold, rose, red, and blue.

Growing conditions and maintenance: Start seed indoors 6 to 8 weeks prior to the last frost for transplanting to the garden after all danger of frost has passed, or plant directly outdoors in late spring. Space plants 10 to 12 inches apart. Prepare soil deeply to provide excellent drainage. Taller varieties may need staking. Plants thrive in cool weather and die in high heat and humidity.

Salvia
(SAL-vee-a)
SAGE

Salvia coccinea 'Lady in Red'

Plant type: *annual or tender perennial*

Height: *8 inches to 4 feet*

Interest: *flowers, foliage*

Soil: *sandy, dry to well-drained*

Light: *full sun to partial shade*

Whorled spikes of tiny hooded summer- to fall-blooming flowers line the tips of salvia's erect stems above soft, sometimes downy leaves. Salvias are particularly effective in masses that multiply the impact of their flowers. Tender perennial salvias that cannot withstand frost are grown as annuals in Zone 8 and colder.

Selected species and varieties: *S. argentea* (silver sage) produces branching clusters of white flowers tinged yellow or pink on 3-foot stems above rosettes of woolly gray-green 6- to 8-inch leaves. *S. coccinea* (Texas sage) produces heart-shaped leaves on 1- to 2-foot branching stems; 'Lady in Red' has slender clusters of bright red flowers. *S. farinacea* (mealycup sage) grows 2 to 3 feet tall with gray-green leaves and spikes of small blue flowers; 'Silver White' grows 18 to 20 inches tall with silvery white flowers; 'Strata' reaches 16 to 24 inches with 6- to 10-inch spikes of bicolored flowers in blue and white that are useful in both fresh and dried arrangements; 'Victoria' grows to 18 inches with a uniform habit and a 14-inch spread with violet-blue flowers. *S. greggii* (autumn sage) grows 2 to 4 feet tall with an erect, shrub-

by habit, medium green leaves, and red, pink, yellow, or white flowers that bloom from midsummer through fall and attract hummingbirds. *S. leucantha* (Mexican bush sage) grows 2 to 4 feet with gracefully arching stems, gray-green leaves, and arching spikes of purple and white flowers in summer and fall. *S. officinalis* (common sage, garden sage, culinary sage) bears whorls of tiny white, blue, or

Salvia farinacea 'Victoria'

purple flowers above hairy, aromatic gray-green leaves used for cooking; 'Icterina' grows 18 inches tall with variegated leaves of golden yellow and green; 'Tricolor' grows to 18 inches and produces leaves that are white and purple with pink margins. *S. splendens* (scarlet sage) grows 8 to 30 inches with bright green 2- to 4-inch leaves and terminal clusters of red, pink, purple, lavender, or white flowers up to 1½ inches long; 'Blaze of Fire' grows 12 to 14 inches with bright red blooms; 'Laser Purple' bears deep purple flowers that resist fading; 'Rodeo' grows to 10 inches with early red flowers. *S. viridis* (clary sage, painted sage) grows to 18 inches with white and blue flowers with showy pink to purple bracts throughout summer and fall, and is superb for fresh and dried arrangements.

Growing conditions and maintenance: Start seed indoors 6 to 8 weeks prior to the last frost. Space smaller types 12 to 18 inches apart, larger types 2 to 3 feet apart. Salvias are generally drought tolerant. Remove faded flowers to extend bloom.

Sanvitalia
(san-vi-TAY-lee-a)
CREEPING ZINNIA

Sanvitalia procumbens

Plant type: *annual*

Height: *5 to 6 inches*

Interest: *flowers*

Soil: *well-drained to dry*

Light: *full sun*

This low-growing annual from Mexico produces a nonstop display of flowers from early summer to frost. Flowers resemble zinnias, but each head is only ¾ inch across. Sanvitalia makes a superb edging or ground cover, and it is well suited to a sunny rock garden.

Selected species and varieties: *S. procumbens* (trailing sanvitalia) grows to a height of 6 inches, although its trailing stems spread to 18 inches, with pointed, oval leaves that are ½ to 1 inch long. Flowers are composed of yellow or orange rays surrounding a dark purple center and may be single, semidouble, or double; 'Gold Braid' produces double yellow blooms; 'Mandarin Orange' bears semidouble orange flowers.

Growing conditions and maintenance: Start seed indoors 4 to 6 weeks prior to the last frost, or sow directly outdoors in late spring. Allow 6 to 12 inches between plants. Sanvitalia thrives in hot, humid weather and is drought tolerant.

Scabiosa
(skab-ee-O-sa)
SCABIOUS

Scabiosa atropurpurea

Plant type: *annual*

Height: *18 inches to 3 feet*

Interest: *flowers*

Soil: *well-drained, fertile*

Light: *full sun*

Scabiosa is easy to grow and produces long-lasting flowers that are well suited to borders, massing, and both fresh and dried arrangements. Flower heads are 1 to 2 inches across with prominent stamens that resemble pins stuck in a pincushion; colors include lavender, pink, purple, maroon, red, and white.

Selected species and varieties: *S. atropurpurea* grows 2 to 3 feet tall with an erect habit and showy, domed flower heads on long stems. *S. stellata* (paper moon) grows 1½ to 2½ feet with pale blue flowers that become papery when dry and are highly valued for dry arrangements; 'Drumstick' bears faded blue flowers that quickly mature to bronze; 'Ping-Pong' bears white flowers on heads the size of a ping-pong ball.

Growing conditions and maintenance: Start seed indoors 4 to 6 weeks prior to the last frost and transplant to the garden after danger of frost has passed, or sow directly outdoors in late spring. Space plants 8 to 12 inches apart. Water during dry periods.

Schizanthus
(ski-ZAN-thus)
BUTTERFLY FLOWER

Schizanthus pinnatus

Plant type: *annual*

Height: *1 to 4 feet*

Interest: *flowers*

Soil: *moist, well-drained, fertile*

Light: *full sun to partial shade*

Schizanthus is a native of Chile that produces exotic flowers resembling orchids. Borne in loose clusters, the two-tone flowers, which come in many colors, are pleasantly displayed against fernlike foliage. They are useful in beds or containers and are excellent for cutting.

Selected species and varieties: *S. pinnatus* grows to 4 feet with light green finely cut leaves and 1½-inch flowers produced in open clusters from early summer to early fall. Flowers have a tropical appearance, and colors include pink, rose, salmon, vivid red, lavender, violet, and cream. Each displays contrasting markings on the throat.

Growing conditions and maintenance: Start seed indoors 8 weeks before the last frost, or plant directly outdoors in midspring. Make successive plantings to extend the blooming season. Space plants 12 inches apart. Provide abundant moisture in a soil with excellent drainage. Grow in light shade where summers are hot. Tall varieties require staking; shorter types are better for borders.

Senecio
(sen-EE-see-o)
GROUNDSEL, RAGWORT

![Senecio cineraria photo]

Senecio cineraria

Plant type: *tender perennial*

Height: *6 to 30 inches*

Interest: *foliage*

Soil: *well-drained*

Light: *full sun to light shade*

Woolly white to silvery gray leaves combine well with brightly colored flowers in borders and beds. Native to the Mediterranean region, the species commonly known as dusty-miller is perennial from Zone 9 south but is grown as an annual elsewhere. It makes an attractive edging, rock-garden specimen, or container plant.

Selected species and varieties: *S. cineraria* (dusty-miller, silver groundsel) has a rounded, branched habit. Leaves are thick, up to 8 inches long, and deeply cut into rounded lobes; they are covered with dense woolly hairs, giving the foliage a feltlike texture. Flowers are yellow or cream, appearing in small terminal clusters in late summer, but are best removed to encourage foliage growth.

Growing conditions and maintenance: Start seed indoors 8 to 10 weeks prior to the last frost. Do not cover the seed; light is necessary for germination. Transplant outdoors when all danger of frost has passed, spacing plants 10 inches apart. Avoid soils that are too fertile, and do not overwater as this will result in weak growth and susceptibility to disease. Plants tolerate drought.

Setaria
(see-TAIR-ee-a)
BRISTLE GRASS

![Setaria italica photo]

Setaria italica

Plant type: *annual*

Height: *2 to 5 feet*

Interest: *flowers, foliage, seed heads*

Soil: *well-drained*

Light: *full sun*

Setaria is an ornamental grass from Asia with narrow, linear leaves that have a pungent odor when crushed. Cylindrical seed heads appear in late summer to fall and are up to 12 inches long; they often bow down to the ground under the weight of the seed. Plants can be used as a background or summer hedge and are often cut for dried indoor arrangements.

Selected species and varieties: *S. italica* (foxtail millet) produces rough-textured leaves, each with a hairy basal sheath, and long-stemmed, dense flower spikes with green, purple, or brown bristles.

Growing conditions and maintenance: Setaria is easy to grow. Start seed indoors in individual peat pots, 4 to 6 weeks prior to the last frost, or sow directly outdoors in early spring. Allow 12 to 36 inches between plants. Once established, plants often self-seed and may become weedy.

Silene
(sy-LEE-ne)
CAMPION, CATCHFLY

Silene coeli-rosa

Plant type: *annual or biennial*

Height: *6 to 24 inches*

Interest: *flowers*

Soil: *well-drained*

Light: *full sun to light shade*

Silene is robust and easy to grow and provides an abundance of summer flowers for borders and beds. Low-growing types are well suited to rock gardens or for use as edgings, and taller types are attractive when cut for fresh arrangements.

Selected species and varieties: *S. armeria* (sweet William catchfly) grows 12 to 18 inches tall with blue-gray leaves and 3-inch clusters of pink or red flowers. It is often included in wildflower mixes and is suitable for naturalizing. *S. coeli-rosa* [also known as *Lychnis coeli-rosa* and *Viscaria coeli-rosa*] usually grows to about 12 inches with narrow, pointed leaves and blue, lavender, pink, or white flowers that often sport a contrasting eye; each single, saucer-shaped flower is 1 inch across. *S. pendula* (drooping catchfly) grows 6 to 16 inches tall with a compact habit, hairy medium green leaves, and loose clusters of pale pink flowers.

Growing conditions and maintenance: Sow seed directly outdoors in early spring as soon as the soil can be worked. Established plants often self-seed. Allow 8 inches between plants. They perform best in well-drained, sunny locations but will tolerate light shade.

Silybum
(sil-LY-bum)
BLESSED THISTLE

Silybum marianum

Plant type: *annual or biennial*

Height: *to 4 feet*

Interest: *flowers, foliage*

Soil: *well-drained*

Light: *full sun*

Silybum is grown primarily for its spiny, glossy foliage, which is dark green with silvery white spots. The 12- to 14-inch deeply lobed basal leaves form an attractive wide-spreading rosette from which 2-inch thistlelike flowers rise in late summer. It is useful as a ground cover in dry, sunny sites. The roots, leaves, and flower heads can be eaten as a vegetable.

Selected species and varieties: *S. marianum* grows to 4 feet with coarse, prominently veined and spotted leaves and solitary nodding flower heads ranging in color from rose to purple. Flowers are surrounded by curved, spiny bracts.

Growing conditions and maintenance: Sow seed directly outdoors in early spring. Once established, plants often self-seed and may become weedy. Space plants 2 feet apart. They tolerate poor soil and dry conditions.

Tagetes
(ta-JEE-tez)
MARIGOLD

Tagetes erecta 'Primrose Lady'

Plant type: *annual or tender perennial*

Height: *6 inches to 3 feet*

Interest: *flowers, foliage*

Soil: *well-drained*

Light: *full sun*

Marigolds are among the most popular bedding plants in the United States. They are easy to grow, provide a reliable display, and are available in a wide range of heights. Their flowers typically range from pale yellow to bright orange and burgundy and are produced nonstop from early summer to frost in many varieties. Some species are grown for their fernlike foliage, which is often quite aromatic. Marigolds are suited to many uses, depending on their size: They can be placed in the background of a border, used as an edging, or massed in a bed. They are suitable for cutting for fresh arrangements and can be effectively grown in patio planters and window boxes. Despite some of their common names, marigolds are native to Mexico and Central and South America.

Selected species and varieties: *T. erecta* (American marigold, African marigold, Aztec marigold) has an erect to rounded habit and a wide range of heights, categorized as dwarf—10 to 14 inches, medium—15 to 20 inches, or tall—to 36 inches; flower heads are solitary, single to double, and 2 to 5 inches across; 'Primrose Lady' is 15 to 18 inches with a

compact habit and double yellow carnationlike flowers. *T. filifolia* (Irish lace) is grown primarily for its finely divided fernlike foliage; it grows 6 to 12 inches tall and wide and produces small white blooms in late summer. *T. lucida* (Mexican tarragon, sweet-scented marigold) grows 2 to 2½ feet tall with dark green tarragon-scented leaves and small, single yellow flowers in clusters; it may be perennial in warm climates. *T. patula* (French marigold, sweet mace) grows 6 to 18 inches tall with a neat, rounded

Tagetes tenuifolia

habit and deeply serrated bright green leaves; flower heads are solitary, up to 2½ inches across, and may be single or double; double flowers often display a crest of raised petals at their center; colors include yellow, orange, maroon, and bicolors. *T. tenuifolia* (dwarf marigold, signet marigold) grows 6 to 12 inches tall with compact mounds of fernlike foliage and single yellow or orange 1-inch flowers that are so profuse they almost completely cover the leaves; excellent for edgings and window boxes.

Growing conditions and maintenance: Start seed indoors 6 to 8 weeks prior to the last frost, or sow directly outdoors 2 weeks before that date. Space plants 6 to 18 inches apart, depending on the variety, and pinch the seedlings to promote bushiness. Marigolds thrive in a moist, well-drained soil but tolerate dry conditions. Remove dead blossoms to encourage continuous flowering. Avoid overwatering.

Thunbergia
(thun-BER-jee-a)
CLOCK VINE

Thunbergia alata

Plant type: *tender perennial*

Height: *3 to 6 feet*

Interest: *flowers*

Soil: *moist, well-drained, fertile*

Light: *full sun to partial shade*

Thunbergia, native to South Africa, is a small climbing or trailing vine that produces a mass of neat, triangular leaves and trumpet-shaped flowers in shades of yellow, orange, and cream, usually with a very dark center, throughout the summer. Plants are attractive in window boxes and hanging baskets, and are excellent as a fast-growing screen on a trellis or fence.

Selected species and varieties: *T. alata* (black-eyed Susan vine) develops twining stems with 3-inch leaves with toothed margins and winged petioles. The solitary flowers are 1 to 2 inches across with 5 distinct, rounded petal segments, usually surrounding a black or dark purple center.

Growing conditions and maintenance: Start seed indoors 6 to 8 weeks prior to the last frost, or sow directly outdoors after danger of frost is past. Space plants 12 inches apart and provide support if you wish them to climb. Plants thrive where summer temperatures remain somewhat cool. Water during dry periods.

Tithonia
(ti-THO-nee-a)
MEXICAN SUNFLOWER

Tithonia rotundifolia

Plant type: *annual*

Height: *2 to 6 feet*

Interest: *flowers*

Soil: *well-drained*

Light: *full sun*

This native of Mexico and Central America is exceptional in its ability to withstand heat and dry conditions. Its daisylike flowers range in color from yellow to red and are borne atop erect stems with coarse-textured leaves. Plants are suitable for the background of borders and for cutting; they can also be used as a fast-growing summer screen.

Selected species and varieties: *T. rotundifolia* has a vigorous, erect habit with broadly oval, velvety, serrated leaves that may reach 10 inches in length. Flower heads consist of orange, yellow, or scarlet raylike petals surrounding an orange-yellow disk; 'Goldfinger' grows 2 to 3 feet with 3-inch orange-scarlet blooms.

Growing conditions and maintenance: Start seed indoors 6 to 8 weeks prior to the last frost, or sow directly outdoors after all danger of frost has passed. Do not cover seed. Space plants 24 to 30 inches apart. Plants tolerate poor soil, heat, and drought. When cutting flowers for indoor arrangements, cut in the bud stage and sear the stem.

Torenia
(to-REE-nee-a)
WISHBONE FLOWER

Torenia fournieri

Plant type: *annual*

Height: *6 to 12 inches*

Interest: *flowers*

Soil: *moist, well-drained*

Light: *partial to full shade*

The blossoms of wishbone flower, also called blued torenia, have upper and lower lobed lips and are borne above a mound of foliage from midsummer to early fall. Because they thrive in shady locations, they are the perfect choice for a woodland bed or shady border. They are also well suited to hanging baskets and patio planters.

Selected species and varieties: *T. fournieri* (bluewings) has a rounded, compact habit with neat, oval leaves 1½ to 2 inches long. The 1-inch flowers appear in stalked clusters; each bloom displays a pale violet tube with a yellow blotch and flaring lower petal edges marked with deep purple-blue. A pair of fused yellow stamens resemble a poultry wishbone, hence the common name.

Growing conditions and maintenance: Start seeds indoors 10 to 12 weeks prior to the last frost; in Zone 9 and warmer, seed can be sown directly outdoors in early spring. Space seedlings 6 to 8 inches apart. Plants thrive in humid areas, and they tolerate full sun only in cool climates.

Tropaeolum
(tro-PEE-o-lum)
NASTURTIUM

Tropaeolum majus

Plant type: *annual*

Height: *6 inches to 8 feet*

Interest: *flowers, foliage*

Soil: *poor, well-drained to dry*

Light: *full sun*

Nasturtiums' bright flowers and attractive shieldlike leaves make them excellent fast-growing screens or bedding plants. Blooms appear from summer through frost. Young leaves and flowers are edible, and flowers are ideal for cutting.

Selected species and varieties: *T. majus* (common nasturtium) may be bushy, about 1 foot tall and twice as wide, or climbing, reaching 6 to 8 feet; leaves are round, 2 to 7 inches across, with long stems, and the showy 2- to 3-inch flowers are red, yellow, white, or orange and may be spotted or streaked. *T. minus* (dwarf nasturtium) reaches 6 to 12 inches in height, with a bushy habit suitable for edgings or massing; 'Alaska Mixed' grows 8 to 15 inches with variegated leaves and a wide range of flower colors. *T. peregrinum* (canary creeper, canarybird vine) is a climbing vine up to 8 feet long with pale yellow fringed flowers and deeply lobed leaves that resemble those of a fig.

Growing conditions and maintenance: Sow seed directly outdoors after danger of frost has passed. Nasturtiums do not transplant well. Space dwarf types 12 inches apart, vines 2 to 3 feet apart. Do not fertilize.

Verbascum
(ver-BAS-cum)
MULLEIN

Verbascum bombyciferum

Plant type: *biennial*

Height: *2 to 8 feet*

Interest: *flowers, foliage*

Soil: *well-drained*

Light: *full sun*

Mulleins develop a rosette of coarse leaves and tall, sturdy spikes of long-lasting summer flowers followed by attractive dried seedpods. Plant them in the rear of a border or in a wildflower garden.

Selected species and varieties: *V. blattaria* (moth mullein) grows 2 to 6 feet with dark green glossy leaves and slender spikes of pale yellow flowers with a lavender throat. *V. bombyciferum* (silver mullein) produces rosettes of oval leaves covered with silvery, silky hairs and 4- to 6-foot spikes of sulfur yellow flowers; 'Arctic Summer' is a heavy-flowering form with powdery white stems and leaves; 'Silver Candelabra' grows to 8 feet, with silver leaves and pale yellow blooms; 'Silver Lining' produces cool yellow flowers and metallic silver leaves and stems. *V. thapsus* (flannel mullein) bears felt-textured leaves and 3-foot spikes of yellow flowers, and may be found growing wild along the roadside.

Growing conditions and maintenance: Sow seed directly outdoors in spring to bloom the following year. Established plants will self-seed. Space 1 to 2 feet apart. Plants tolerate dry conditions.

Verbena
(ver-BEE-na)
VERVAIN

Verbena bonariensis

Plant type: *annual or tender perennial*

Height: *6 inches to 4 feet*

Interest: *flowers*

Soil: *moist, well-drained*

Light: *full sun*

From summer through frost, small, vividly colored flowers bloom in clusters on wiry stems with soft green foliage. Verbenas are useful as ground covers or as fillers in a border; smaller types are a good choice for containers, while taller types are excellent for cutting.

Selected species and varieties: *V. bonariensis* (Brazilian verbena) grows to 4 feet tall with slender, multibranched stems; wrinkled, toothed leaves grow primarily on the lowest 12 inches of the stem so that the fragrant rosy violet flower clusters seem nearly to float in the air. *V. x hybrida* (garden verbena) grows 6 to 12 inches tall and spreads to 2 feet, with wrinkled leaves and small flowers in loose, rounded heads to 2 inches across in shades of pink, red, blue, purple, and white; 'Peaches and Cream' bears flowers in shades of apricot, orange, yellow, and cream; flowers of 'Silver Ann' open bright pink and fade to blended pink and white.

Growing conditions and maintenance: Start seed indoors 12 weeks prior to the last frost and transplant outdoors after all danger of frost has passed. Allow 12 inches between plants of common verbena and 2 feet between Brazilian verbenas.

Viola
(vy-O-la)
PANSY

Viola tricolor

Plant type: *annual*

Height: *3 to 12 inches*

Interest: *flowers*

Soil: *moist, well-drained, fertile*

Light: *full sun to partial shade*

Although many pansies are technically short-lived perennials, they are considered annuals because they bloom their first year from seed and their flowers decline in quality afterward, regardless of region. They may also be treated as biennials, sown in late summer for bloom early the following spring. Their vividly colored and interestingly marked flowers are borne over a long season, often beginning with the first signs of spring and lasting until the summer heat causes them to fade, although a bit of shade and water may encourage the blossoms to continue throughout most of the summer. The rounded flower petals overlap, and their patterns often resemble a face. Pansies are a good choice for planting with bulbs, combining well with the flower forms and providing cover for fading foliage. They are attractive when massed in beds and useful as edgings or combined with other annuals in patio planters or window boxes.

Selected species and varieties: *V. rafinesquii* (field pansy) is a true annual that is native to much of the United States and grows 3 to 12 inches tall. Its ½-inch flowers are pale blue to cream, often

with purple veins and a yellow throat. *V. tricolor* (Johnny-jump-up, miniature pansy) is a European native that has naturalized in much of the United States. It typically grows to 8 inches with a low, mounded habit and small, colorful flowers that have been favorites in the garden since Elizabethan times. The 1-inch flowers are fragrant, and colors include deep violet, blue, lavender, mauve, yellow, cream, white, and bicolors; flowers are

Viola 'Melody Purple and White'

edible and are often used as a garnish; 'Bowles' Black' bears blue-black flowers. *V.* x *wittrockiana* (common pansy) grows 4 to 8 inches tall and spreads to 12 inches. The 1- to 2-inch flowers are usually three-tone in shades of purple, blue, dark red, rose, pink, brown, yellow, and white. Many varieties are available; 'Melody Purple and White' bears flowers with white and purple petals marked with deep violet-blue.

Growing conditions and maintenance: Sow seed outdoors in late summer for earliest spring blooms or purchase transplants. Pansies started in late summer should be protected over the winter in a cold frame or by covering plants after the first hard frost with a light mulch or branches. They can also be started indoors in midwinter to transplant to the garden in midspring. Germination can be enhanced by moistening and chilling the seed (between 40° and 45° F) for 1 week prior to planting. Space plants about 4 inches apart. Pansies prefer a cool soil. Remove faded blooms and keep plants well watered to extend flowering.

Xeranthemum
(zer-RAN-the-mum)
EVERLASTING

Xeranthemum annuum

Plant type: *annual*

Height: *18 inches to 3 feet*

Interest: *flowers*

Soil: *moist, well-drained to average*

Light: *full sun*

Xeranthemum's fluffy flower heads in purple, pink, and white are displayed on long stems from summer to early fall. This Mediterranean native is a good choice for the midground of a mixed border and is exceptional for cutting, for both fresh and dried arrangements.

Selected species and varieties: *X. annuum* has an erect habit and gray-green leaves that are concentrated toward the bottom of the wiry stems. The 1½-inch flowers may be single or double, and they are surrounded by papery bracts that are the same color as the true flowers at the center of the head.

Growing conditions and maintenance: In colder zones, start seed indoors in individual peat pots 6 to 8 weeks prior to the last frost, but handle carefully because they are difficult to transplant. In warmer climates, sow seed directly in the garden in spring after all danger of frost has passed. Allow 6 to 9 inches between plants. They adapt to most soils. For use in winter arrangements, cut flowers when they are fully open and hang them upside down in a well-ventilated room until dry.

Zea
(ZEE-a)
CORN

Zea mays

Plant type: *annual*

Height: *2 to 15 feet*

Interest: *seed heads*

Soil: *moist, well-drained, fertile*

Light: *full sun*

Corn is native to the American tropics and is one of the most important cereal crops in the world. Several varieties are grown for their ornamental appeal; they provide a vertical accent in the garden and kernels that can be enjoyed in the garden or harvested for fall decoration.

Selected species and varieties: *Z. mays* grows to 15 feet with an erect habit and broad, grasslike blades to 3 feet long and 4 inches wide. Male flowers (tassels) form in spreading terminal panicles, while the female flowers (silks) are found in the leaf axils where the ear forms; 'Indian Corn' produces multicolored kernels that can be harvested for fall decoration as the husks begin to dry; var. *japonica* grows 5 to 6 feet with leaves attractively striped green, white, pink, and yellow; var. *rugosa* bears 1½-inch rounded ears with red kernels that are useful for both decoration and popcorn.

Growing conditions and maintenance: Sow seed directly in the garden after soil warms in spring. Incorporate organic matter and fertilizer into soil prior to planting. For proper pollination, plant in blocks with rows 18 to 30 inches apart; allow 8 to 12 inches between plants.

Zinnia
(ZIN-ee-a)
ZINNIA

Zinnia elegans

Plant type: *annual*

Height: *8 to 36 inches*

Interest: *flowers*

Soil: *well-drained*

Light: *full sun*

Zinnias brighten the border with pom-pom or daisylike blooms whose petal-like rays may be flat and rounded, rolled into fringes, or crowded around yellow or green centers that are actually the true flowers. Hues range from riotous yellows, oranges, and reds to subdued pinks, roses, salmons, and creams, and maroon and purple. Flowers bloom from summer through frost and are best massed for effect as edgings or in the border. Low, spreading types are at home in window boxes and patio planters, while taller forms are excellent for fresh summer arrangements.

Selected species and varieties: *Z. angustifolia* (narrowleaf zinnia) has a compact, spreading habit, grows 8 to 16 inches in height with narrow, pointed leaves and 1-inch wide single orange flowers, and is excellent as an edging or ground cover; 'White Star' bears abundant 2-inch flowers consisting of white rays surrounding orange-yellow centers. *Z. elegans* (common zinnia) grows 1 to 3 feet with an erect habit, rough-textured, clasping leaves up to 4 inches long, and showy flowers in many colors up to 6 inches across; 'Big Red' bears blood red 5- to 6-

inch blooms on vigorous plants that reach 3 feet in height; 'Cut and Come Again' is a mildew-resistant variety that grows 2 feet tall and bears abundant 2½-inch flowers in a wide range of colors on long, sturdy stems that are suitable for cutting; 'Peter Pan' is an early bloomer with a uniform habit reaching 10 to 12 inches tall and 3- to 4-inch flowers in a wide range of colors. *Z. haageana* (Mexican zinnia) grows 1 to 2 feet tall with

Zinnia angustifolia 'White Star'

narrow leaves and 1½- to 2½-inch single or double flowers in colors that include red, mahogany, yellow, orange, and bicolors; 'Persian Carpet' has a bushy habit and 2-inch, mostly bicolored flowers with pointed petals and crested centers in shades from maroon through chocolate to gold and cream.

Growing conditions and maintenance: Zinnias are among the easiest annuals to grow. Start seed indoors 6 weeks prior to the last frost, or sow directly outdoors after all danger of frost has passed. Space seedlings 6 to 12 inches apart and pinch young plants to encourage bushiness. Remove spent blooms to keep plants attractive and to encourage flowering. Zinnias thrive in hot weather but benefit from regular watering. *Z. angustifolia* tolerates dry conditions.

Acknowledgments and Picture Credits

The editors wish to thank the following for their valuable assistance in the preparation of this volume:

Hank Doon, Beltsville, Maryland; Sandra H. and James R. Ely, Tacoma, Washington; Trudy W. and Robert W. Pearson, Alexandria, Virginia; Joe Seals, Warminster, Pennsylvania; Richard T. Wagner, Portland, Oregon.

Bibliography

BOOKS:

Annuals. Mt. Vernon, Va.: American Horticultural Society, 1982.

Annuals: 1001 Gardening Questions Answered (Garden Way Publishing). Pownal, Vt.: Storey Communications, 1989.

Annuals and Perennials. Menlo Park, Calif.: Sunset Publishing, 1993.

Art, Henry Warren. *The Wildflower Gardener's Guide* (Garden Way Publishing). Pownal, Vt.: Storey Communications, 1989.

Bales, Suzanne Frutig. *Annuals* (Burpee American Gardening series). New York: Prentice Hall Press, 1991.

Binetti, Marianne. *Tips for Carefree Landscapes* (Garden Way Publishing). Pownal, Vt.: Storey Communications, 1993.

Bodin, Svante. *Weather and Climate in Colour.* Poole, Dorset, U.K.: Blandford Press, 1978.

Chaplin, Lois Trigg. *The Southern Gardener's Book of Lists.* Dallas: Taylor Publishing, 1994.

Clarke, Graham, and Alan Toogood. *The Complete Book of Plant Progagation.* London: Ward Lock, 1993.

Cochran, Doris M. *Living Amphibians of the World* (The World of Nature series). Garden City, N.Y.: Doubleday, 1967.

Colborn, Nigel. *Annuals and Bedding Plants.* North Pomfret, Vt.: Trafalgar Square Publishing, 1995.

Color with Annuals. San Ramon, Calif.: Ortho Books, 1993.

Creasy, Rosalind. *The Complete Book of Edible Landscaping.* San Francisco: Sierra Club, 1982.

David, Chet. *Cutting Gardens* (Burpee American Gardening series). New York: Prentice Hall Gardening, 1994.

Ellis, Barbara W., and Fern Marshall Bradley (Eds.). *The Organic Gardener's Handbook of Natural Insect and Disease Control.* Emmaus, Pa.: Rodale Press, 1992.

Fell, Derek:
Annuals. Tucson, Ariz.: HPBooks, 1983.
The Essential Gardener. New York: Arch Cape Press, 1990.

Genders, Roy. *Perfume in the Garden.* London: Museum Press, 1955.

Glattstein, Judy. *Garden Design with Foliage* (Garden Way Publishing). Pownal, Vt.: Storey Communications, 1991.

Hill, Lewis. *Cold-Climate Gardening* (Garden Way Publishing). Pownal, Vt.: Storey Communications, 1981.

Lacey, Stephen. *The Startling Jungle.* New York: Viking, 1986.

Lacy, Allen. *Gardening with Groundcovers and Vines.* New York: HarperCollins, 1993.

Landscaping with Wildflowers and Native Plants. San Francisco: Ortho Books, 1984.

Loewer, Peter:
The Annual Garden. Emmaus, Pa.: Rodale Press, 1988.
Annuals. (Better Homes and Gardens® Step-by-Step Successful Gardening series). Des Moines: Meredith® Books, 1994.
The Evening Garden. New York: Macmillan, 1993.
Rodale's Annual Garden. New York: Wings Books, 1992.

Lovejoy, Ann. *The American Mixed Border.* New York: Macmillan, 1993.

Marston, Ted (Ed.). *Annuals* (Hearst Garden Guides). New York: Hearst Books, 1993.

Martin, Laura C. *The Wildflower Meadow Book.* Charlotte, N.C.: Fast & McMillan, 1986.

Missouri Botanical Garden, with Ruth Rogers Clausen. *Annual Gardening* (The American Garden Guides). New York: Pantheon Books, 1995.

Mulligan, William C. *The Adventurous Gardener's Sourcebook of Rare and Unusual Plants.* New York: Simon & Schuster, 1992.

Ohrbach, Barbara Milo. *The Scented Room.* New York: Clarkson Potter, 1986.

Ortho's Complete Guide to Successful Gardening. San Francisco: Ortho Books, 1983.

Ortloff, Henry Stuart. *A Garden Bluebook of Annuals and Biennials.* New York: Doubleday, Doran, 1931.

Proctor, Rob. *Annuals.* New York: HarperCollins, 1991.

Reader's Digest Illustrated Guide to Gardening. Pleasantville, N.Y.: Reader's Digest Association, 1978.

Rockwell, F. F., and Esther C. Grayson. *The Complete Book of Annuals.* Garden City, N.Y.: American Garden Guild and Doubleday, 1955.

Schenk, George. *The Complete Shade Gardener.* Boston: Houghton Mifflin, 1984.

Seidenberg, Charlotte. *The New Orleans Garden.* New Orleans: Silkmont & Count, 1990.

Snyder, Leon C. *Gardening in the Upper Midwest.* Minneapolis: University of Minnesota Press, 1978.

Springer, Lauren. *The Undaunted Garden.* Golden, Colo.: Fulcrum Publishing, 1994.

Step-by-Step Successful Gardening (Better Homes and Gardens®). Des Moines: Meredith, 1987.

Strahler, Arthur N. *Physical Geography.* New York: John Wiley, 1960.

Taylor, Jane:
Climbing Plants (Kew Gardening Guides). Portland, Ore.: Timber Press, 1987.
Fragrant Gardens. Topsfield, Mass.: Salem House, 1987.
The Shady Garden (The Wayside Gardens Collection). New York: Sterling Publishing, 1994.

Taylor, Norman. *Fragrance in the Garden.* New York: D. Van Nostrand, 1953.

Taylor's Guide to Annuals. Boston: Houghton Mifflin, 1986.

Taylor's Master Guide to Gardening. Boston: Houghton Mifflin, 1994.

Verner, Margaret (Ed.). *Annuals, Perennials, Biennials.* New York: Galahad Books, 1981.

Wasowski, Sally, with Andy Wasowski. *Native Gardens for Dry Climates.* New York: Clarkson Potter, 1995.

Weather-Wise Gardening. San Francisco: Ortho Books, 1974.

Williams, Robin, Robin Templar Williams, and Mary-Jane Hopes. *The Complete Book of Patio and Container Gardening.* London: Ward Lock, 1992.

Wilson, Jim. *Landscaping with Wildflowers.* Boston: Houghton Mifflin, 1992.

Winterrowd, Wayne. *Annuals for Connoisseurs.* New York: Prentice Hall, 1992.

Woodward, Lucia. *Poisonous Plants.* New York: Hippocrene Books, 1985.

Zeman, Anne. *Growing Annuals* (NK Lawn and Garden Step-by-Step Visual Guide). Corte Madera, Calif.: BMR, 1992.

PERIODICALS:

The American Cottage Gardener, July 1995.

"Annuals: A Gardener's Guide." *Plants and Gardens, Brooklyn Botanic Garden Record,* 1992.

Ashmun, Barbara. "Gray Leaves Make Gardens Glow." *Pacific Horticulture,* Winter 1993.

Bridgelal, Parbatie Maharaj. "Adventures with Annuals." *Fine Gardening,* March/April 1994.

Bubel, Nancy. "Hordes of Gourds." *Horticulture,* November 1993.

Cox, Jeff. "These Are a Few of *My* Favorite Vines." *Organic Gardening,* November 1992.

Eskilson, Melissa Dodd. "Dahlias." *Horticulture,* October 1995.

"Gardening for Fragrance." *Plants and Gardens, Brooklyn Botanic Garden Record,* 1989.

Gates, Galen. "Cold-Weather Annuals." *Fine Gardening,* September/October 1995.

Lovejoy, Ann:
"Fine Vines." *Horticulture,* August/September 1991.
"Inspired by Verbascums." *Horticulture,* August/September 1995.

McDonald, Nancy. "Biennials." *American Cottage Gardener,* July 1994.

"Ornamental Grasses." *Plants and Gardens, Brooklyn Botanic Garden Record,* 1988.

Pleasant, Barbara. "Poppies Make the World Go 'Round." *Organic Gardening,* May/June 1995.

Proctor, Rob. "In Praise of Biennials." *Country Living Gardener,* Summer 1995.

Roach, Margaret. "Filling the Gaps." *Martha Stewart Living,* June 1995.

Ruttle, Jack. "Soil for Seeds." *National Gardening,* November/December 1995.

Taylor, Patricia A.:
"Biennials." *Flower and Garden,* August/September 1992.

"Eight Sure-Fire Annuals." *Flower and Garden,* February/March 1993.

Wintz, Robert P. "Annuals in the Shade." In "Gardening in the Shade." *Plants and Gardens, Brooklyn Botanic Garden Record,* 1990.

OTHER SOURCES:

Kirkland, A. H. "Usefulness of the American Toad." U.S. Department of Agriculture Farmers' Bulletin no. 196. Washington, D.C.: Government Printing Office, 1904.

Index

Other Publications:
VOICES OF THE CIVIL WAR
THE NEW HOME REPAIR AND IMPROVEMENT
JOURNEY THROUGH THE MIND AND BODY
WEIGHT WATCHERS® SMART CHOICE RECIPE COLLECTION
TRUE CRIME
THE AMERICAN INDIANS
THE ART OF WOODWORKING
LOST CIVILIZATIONS
ECHOES OF GLORY
THE NEW FACE OF WAR
HOW THINGS WORK
WINGS OF WAR
CREATIVE EVERYDAY COOKING
COLLECTOR'S LIBRARY OF THE UNKNOWN
CLASSICS OF WORLD WAR II
TIME-LIFE LIBRARY OF CURIOUS AND UNUSUAL FACTS
AMERICAN COUNTRY
VOYAGE THROUGH THE UNIVERSE
THE THIRD REICH
MYSTERIES OF THE UNKNOWN
TIME FRAME
FIX IT YOURSELF
FITNESS, HEALTH & NUTRITION
SUCCESSFUL PARENTING
HEALTHY HOME COOKING
UNDERSTANDING COMPUTERS
LIBRARY OF NATIONS
THE ENCHANTED WORLD
THE KODAK LIBRARY OF CREATIVE PHOTOGRAPHY
GREAT MEALS IN MINUTES
THE CIVIL WAR
PLANET EARTH
COLLECTOR'S LIBRARY OF THE CIVIL WAR
THE EPIC OF FLIGHT
THE GOOD COOK
WORLD WAR II
THE OLD WEST

For information on and a full description of any
of the Time-Life Books series listed above, please call
1-800-621-7026 or write:
Reader Information
Time-Life Customer Service
P.O. Box C-32068
Richmond, Virginia 23261-2068